UNDERSTANDING CHILDREN

UNDERSTANDING CHILDREN

Volume 1:
State, Education and Economy

Edited by Anne Cleary,
Máire Nic Ghiolla Phádraig and Suzanne Quin

Oak Tree Press
19 Rutland Street,
Cork, Ireland.
www.oaktreepress.com

Volume 1: State, Education and Economy
ISBN 1 86076 228-X

Volume 2: Changing Experiences and Family Forms
ISBN 1 86076 229-8

A catalogue record of this book is
available from the British Library.

Printed in Ireland by ColourBooks Ltd.

Contents

About the Contributors .... *ix*

Preface .... *xi*

Introduction .... *xvii*

PART 1: CHILDREN AND THE STATE

1. "Cherishing all the Children of the Nation Equally": State
   Provision and Responsibility for Children in Ireland 3
   Nóirín Hayes

2 Legal and Constitutional Rights of Children in Ireland 21
   Valerie Richardson

3. "Mercy unto Thousands": Constructing the Institutional
   Child 45
   Eoin O'Sullivan

4. Children Out-of-Home in Ireland 79
   Frank Houghton, Patricia Kelleher & Carmel Kelleher

5. Children and Political Violence: The Northern Ireland
   Conflict 99
   Ed Cairns and Frances McLernon

PART 2: CHILDREN IN EDUCATION

6. Some Aspects of Quality in Early Childhood Education .. 119
   Mary Horgan and Francis Douglas

7. Locating the Child's Voice in Irish Primary Education 145
   Dympna Devine

8. Gender Identity in the Primary School Playground.......... 175
   Anne Lodge and Marie Flynn

9. "Bluebells, cockle shells": Irish Children's Skipping
   Games and Rhymes 197
   Geraldine Lynch

10. "In the Land of Youth" — Irish Children and Literature ... 225
    Pat Donlon

PART 3: CHILDREN AND THE ECONOMY

11. Child Poverty in Ireland 245
    Brian Nolan

12. Children as Workers: A Case Study of Child
    Employment in Belfast 261
    Madeleine Leonard

UNDERSTANDING CHILDREN

*Volume 2: Changing Experiences
and Family Forms*
(ISBN 1-86076-229-9)

PART 1: NEW FAMILY FORMS

1. The Changing Role of Fathers
   Gabriel Kiely

2. Single Mothers and Parenting Outcomes
   Niamh Flanagan

3. Parental Separation — Children's Responses
   Gemma O'Donohoe

4. "Family Fostering": Children's Experiences of Care by Relatives.
   Valerie O'Brien

5. Children's Experiences in After-School Care
   Eilis Hennessy

PART 2: CHALLENGES FOR CHILDREN AND FAMILIES

6. Children's Exposure to Drug-Use: Concerns of Drug-using and Non-drug- using Parents
   Diane Hogan & Louise Higgins

7. The Child, the Family and Disability
   Anne Cleary

8. Children Who Survive Cancer
    Suzanne Quin

9. Resisting Daughters: Father-Daughter Child Sexual
    Abuse Disclosure
    Imelda McCarthy and Nollaig Byrne

PART 3: CHILDREN OF CULTURAL MINORITIES

10. "Out of the mouths of Babes and Innocents . . ." —
    Children's Attitudes towards Travellers
    Brendan O'Keefe and Pat O'Connor

11. Traveller Childhood in Ireland
    Máirín Kenny

12. A Foreshortened Childhood: Refugee and Asylum-
    seeking Children in Ireland
    Geraldine Nolan

13. "Tá Gaeilge agam, ach ní ag mo chara" — Irish-speaking
    Children
    Máire Nic Ghiolla Phádraig

About the Contributors

Ed Cairns is a professor of Psychology in the School of Psychology and Communication Sciences at the University of Ulster in Coleraine. Much of his work has been conducted through the Centre for the study of Conflict at the University of Ulster and more recently through INCORE, the joint United Nations University/University of Ulster programme on conflict resolution and ethnicity. He has written some 80 books, chapters in books and articles in this area. His most recent book, *Children and Political Violence*, was published by Blackwell in 1996.

Dympna Devine is a lecturer in the sociology of education at the Education Department, University College, Dublin. She has carried out and published research into children's perspectives on schooling, school effectiveness in primary schools and professional development needs of primary and post-primary teachers. She is currently researching the experience of ethnic diversity in primary and second level schools.

Pat Donlon was Director of the National Library of Ireland from 1989-1998. Her academic appointments include that of Senior Visiting Research Fellow in the Institute of Irish Studies, Queen's University Belfast; Sandars Reader in Bibliography at the University of Cambridge; Research Fellow in the Faculty of Applied Arts, Dublin Institute of Technology. She lectured on Children's Literature at University College Dublin from 1979-1989 and in 1997 was the recipient of the Children's Books Ireland Award for distinguished services to Irish Children's Literature. She has served as Chair of the Irish Children's Museum Advisory Board.

Francis Douglas is a statutory lecturer in the Education Department, University College Cork where he is Director of the BA Degree in Early Childhood Studies and currently Head of the Education Department. His main interest is in early years education and care having published at national and international levels in the area. As patron of the IPPA, he has a particular affinity with the playgroup movement. He co-directed the externally funded UCC Early Years Curriculum Project (Project EYE) and co-directs the Early Years Postgraduate Studies Programme.

Marie Flynn is Assistant Director of St. Helen's Education Office, the official agency of the Christian Brothers' Trustees. Its primary objectives are the promotion of good practice in leadership, management, and school development. Her research interests include equality issues in schools, curriculum development and assessment, teaching and learning theory, and school restructuring. She has recently completed a doctoral thesis examining equality in the classroom with particular reference to issues of access, participation, outcome and respect.

Nóirín Hayes is a developmental psychologist and Head of the School of Social Science and Legal Studies at the Dublin Institute of Technology. She is a founder member and vice-chair of the Children's Right's Alliance. She has written a number of books and articles on both Early Childhood Care and Education and on Children's Rights.

Mary Horgan is a lecturer in Education Department, University College Cork and Deputy Director of the BA Degree in Early Childhood Studies. With her Masters and Doctoral research in Early Years Education and Care, she has published both nationally and internationally in the area. She co-directed Project EYE — an externally funded early years curriculum project — and is currently co-director of the UCC Early Year's Postgraduate Studies Programme.

Frank Houghton is a health geographer formerly employed as Research Manager in Focus Ireland. He has worked in the areas of health, equality and cross-community research in both Northern Ireland (Centre for the Study of Conflict, UUC; Centre for Research on Women, UUC) and the Republic of Ireland (National Council On Ageing & Older People; Department of Public Health, MWHB).

Patricia Kelleher and **Carmel Kelleher** are founders of Kelleher Associates. The firm, established in 1987 specialises in the areas of evaluation research and community consultation and has undertaken assignments on women's issues, disadvantaged youth and homelessness. It has extensive experience working jointly with the voluntary and statutory sector in developing inter-agency policies and strategies.

Madeleine Leonard is a Senior Lecturer in the School of Sociology and Social Policy at Queen's University Belfast. Her main research interests are the sociology of childhood and in particular links between childhood and gender. She has researched and published work on children's involvement in paid and unpaid work including children's involvement in term-time jobs, children's participation in housework and children as carers.

Anne Lodge is a member of the Education Department, NUI Maynooth, where she teaches sociology of education and research methods. She previously worked as a Research Officer in the Equality Studies Centre. Her research interests include the sociology of childhood, with a particular focus on issues of identity and schooling, and the self and imagination; equality and education; classroom climate and interaction patterns.

Geraldine Lynch obtained her MA at University College Dublin for her thesis on Riddles from County Wicklow in 1979 and qualified as a primary school teacher in the following year. Her publications include articles on children's folklore. She received her PhD from the National University of Ireland in 1995 for a study of skipping games in Ireland. Currently she is principal teacher of Gaelscoil Chill Mhaintáin in her native Wicklow.

Frances McLernon is a Research Officer in the School of Psychology and Communication Sciences at the University of Ulster in Coleraine. She is currently working on a three-year research project investigating the role of intergroup contact in the processes of forgiveness and reconciliation in Northern Ireland. Her PhD research was based on Northern Irish children's attitudes to war and peace before and after the paramilitary ceasefires, and was published in the International Journal of Behavioural Development, 1997.

Brian Nolan is a Research Professor at the Economic and Social Research Institute. He has published widely on income inequality, poverty, public economics, social policy, and health inequalities. His publications include *Resources, Deprivation and the Measurement of Poverty*, with C.T. Whelan, Clarendon Press, 1996. He is currently working with colleagues on a programme of research on poverty and related issues using the European Community Household Panel Survey.

Eoin O'Sullivan is a lecturer in Social Policy in the Department of Social Studies, Trinity College, Dublin. His recent publications include *Suffer the Little Children: The Inside Story of Ireland's Industrial Schools* (1999, Dublin: New Island Books, with Mary Raftery) and *Crime Control in Ireland: The Politics of Intolerance* (2001, Cork: Cork University Press with Ian O'Donnell).

Valerie Richardson is a senior lecturer in the Department of Social Policy and Social Work in University College Dublin. She has published widely in the area of childcare policy and practice and in the area of lone parenthood, in particular teenage parenting. Other interests centre on family policy, particularly the integration of work and family roles and she is currently writing on social work practice and the law.

Preface

We have many nostalgic accounts of childhood in Ireland in the first six decades of the twentieth century, notably Alice Taylor's *To School through the Fields*. Books such as these give a somewhat rosy picture of childhood given what we now know of child sexual abuse and bullying. More recent publications have emphasised the darker side of Irish childhood, Frank McCourt's *Angela's Ashes* being the most successful of the genre. Corporal punishment was legal in schools and a daily experience for many children at the hands of parents, teachers and older siblings. Relative poverty was not as marked as in recent times, but absolute poverty was probably more acute and there were fewer social welfare safety-nets. In the 1960s, emigration was still rife (many fathers went to England to support their families), Dublin tenements still housed up to six per room and over half of rural dwellings still lacked indoor sanitation and running water. If the "normal" family circumstances were not in place, through birth out of wedlock, marital separation/desertion or the illness or death of a parent, a child could well end up in an orphanage. Many of the legislative and regulatory changes introduced since the 1970s have removed or reduced some of the graver sources of suffering for children and improved their rights and quality of life. The main thrust of such changes has been to support the upbringing of children with their biological parent(s).

While acknowledging what is good about these changes for the quality of life for children, we need to look also at the negative aspects of the changes and to see if there are ways of improving matters for children today. Within living memory, the context of childhood in Ireland has been transformed from a matrifocal neighbourhood within which to range freely, to a looser network of carers and activities, often scattered over several localities, to which the children are driven or bussed. It is important to examine the implications of such changes for the experience of childhood today.

In setting out to produce this book we set a goal of focusing on children in the context of a changing Ireland. Despite the changing nature of childhood and children's lives over the past 30 years, no book has charted these changes specifically for children. Existing work on Irish children tends to focus specifically on child welfare and child abuse and therefore on negative aspects of childhood. Insofar as such matters will be dealt with in these volumes, the emphasis is not on "social problems affecting children" but on how do children cope with, resist, or accommodate to adversity of various kinds.

Scholarly interest in children in Ireland initially surfaced in the context of social problems. Concerns around children and childhood began to be voiced in the 1980s in relation to revelations about child sexual abuse. This gave rise to a series of commissions, fora etc. The discourse of these reports and the terms of reference of the bodies producing them both illustrate what the norms of childhood in Ireland are and how these are perceived to be threatened or inadequately served. Children were also constituted as a "residual" problem in the process of a more comprehensive incorporation of women within the labour force. This is very much the emphasis within the Expert Working Group on Child Care Report. Children are identified as a barrier to women's continued participation and promotion in the labour force. Children emerged as a "muted group" in marital separation cases and very little evidence pertaining to them was uncovered in analysis of legal documents (Fahey and Lyons, 1995). Ireland ratified the UN Convention on the Rights of the Child in 1989 and this has acted to set standards and provide greater moral weight to the work of child advocacy groups such as Barnardos and the Children's Rights Alliance. It has also helped to heighten awareness of children as persons with rights and to stimulate research questions around the situation of children generally.

The aim of this book is to present a more comprehensive and positive profile of childhood and children in Ireland by bringing together recent research and analysis of the lives of Irish children. The focus is on contemporary aspects of children's lives and on the challenges facing children in adjusting to the changing context of childhood. The contributors are drawn from a range of disciplinary backgrounds in the social sciences, but share a similar approach to the study of childhood in their questioning of common assumptions of childhood as a passive, residual category of "becoming adults" who may be simply described as being in the process of being socialised. In this the book is allied with the contemporary approach to the study of childhood and its concerns:

> Most of the new sociological thinking about childhood is *structural* rather than individual; it is *relational*, first of all with respect to an intergenerational perspective; and it seems to be far more interested in typical, normal and common conditions for the majority of children, i.e. the focus is no longer merely on children in particular critical situations (Qvortrup, 1995, p. 10).

Childhood cannot be taken as a biological given but is socially constructed, deconstructed and reconstructed in changing times. The social construction of Irish childhood is contributed to by the State, families, the churches, the legal and administrative system and the media among others, but also, to some extent, by children themselves. While children are among the least powerful categories of people in society, they are more than objects of socialisation, concern, abuse, neglect, parental ambition etc. Children may also be viewed as social actors in their own right who contribute to the culture and social groups in which they participate. The degree of social competency and agency of children is likely to vary not only by age but also by context. While it is important to examine the contexts and social forces influencing childhood and children's lives, a more important focus is that of the experience of childhood in different contexts. How do children react to and engage in different situations, changing conditions, new cultural trends, etc.? In accordance with international convention, the upper age-limit of childhood is taken to be the minimum school-leaving age (i.e. 15 years).

Accordingly, contributors were requested to draw on primary research with children themselves, where possible. Many were able to do so, using a variety of techniques — questionnaires, interviews, focus groups, ethnography, observation — with sometimes unpredictable findings. The range of research methods employed in the study of children and childhood is as extensive as that used in the study of adults. While there are limits of lack of literacy and articulation in the methods used with younger children, the choice of method is fully comprehensive from the age of about 8 or 9 years (Hill, 1998, p. 15). Very young children can only be studied by observational methods or indirectly by interviews with carers, whereas older children can co-operate with written questionnaires, interviews, focus groups, etc. "Visual sociology" methods utilising photography or video are highly suited to recording children's group interactions (see *Visual Sociology*, 1999, Vol. 14). Particular ethical issues arise in relation to research on children. It is usually necessary to negotiate access and consent from parents and guardians. To the extent that the child population of study is constituted through institutional arrangements such as schools or day care facilities, such access and consent must first be negotiated with the management; the consent of children themselves is less frequently prioritised. This may not be very realistic if children are very young, but the option to refuse should be available as soon as children are capable of understanding they are being sought to co-operate in research (Hill, 1998, p. 15).

The project of producing this book was originally inspired by our former colleague and mentor, Emeritus Professor Helen Burke. It was conceived as offering a vehicle for co-operation between members of the Department of Social Policy and Social Work and the Department of Sociology. We are pleased that papers were produced by contributors from a broad range of social science disciplines.

In inviting contributions, we sought to provide an analysis of as broad as possible a cross-section of children in Ireland (a term not co-terminus with "Irish children"). Another goal was to examine the impact of social and cultural processes in varied institutional settings. Sadly, there are gaps which we did not succeed in filling. In particular, the impact of the media on the lives of children in Ireland is not represented here. Neither is that most negative element of peer culture, namely bullying. And try as we might we were unable to discover a researcher who had studied the situation of being children of a religious minority in Ireland.

Despite these gaps, we are confident that *Understanding Children* will introduce readers to many facets of the lives of children in Ireland not previously published. It is our hope that the gaps in our knowledge and understanding of childhood in Ireland that remain will soon begin to be filled by further re-search — indeed, the National Children's Strategy planned Longitudinal Study of Children promises to do so.

The quantity of papers resulting from our invitations was so large that, at our publishers' recommendation, we have divided it into two volumes. *Volume 1: State, Education and Economy* deals with the macro-structures which define children's lives and the way in which children themselves respond to them. *Volume 2: Changing Experiences and Family Forms* looks at micro-level aspects and cultural variations in the experience of childhood in contemporary Ireland. The Table of Contents of the companion volume is listed after the Table of Contents for this volume.

References

Expert Working Group on Childcare (1999), *National Childcare Strategy*, Dublin: Stationery Office.

Fahey, Tony and Lyons, Maureen (1995), Marital *Breakdown and Family Law in Ireland: A Sociological Study*, Dublin: Oak Tree Press and ESRI.

Hill, Malcolm (1998), "Ethical Issues in Qualitative Methodology with Children", in Hogan, Diane and Gilligan, Robbie (eds.) *Researching*

Children's Experiences: Qualitative Approaches, Proceedings of conference, The Children's Research Centre, Trinity College Dublin.

National Children's Strategy (2000), *Our Children — Their Lives*, Dublin: Stationery Office.

Qvortrup, Jens (1995), "Childhood in Europe: a New Field of Social Research" in Chisholm, L. et al. (eds) *Growing Up in Europe: Contemporary Horizons in Childhood and Youth Studies*, Berlin: Walter de Gruyter and Co.

Visual Sociology (1999), Vol. 14.

Introduction

This volume deals with the macro-structures which frame the context of childhood and analyses some of the ways in which children react to and engage with such structures. While we tend to associate young children, in particular, with the family, from birth they are linked to broader societal structures, some of which — in particular, the education system — have been elaborated specifically to incorporate children as new citizens of Ireland. The State acts to define the relationship between children, their parents, and their carers, and also has a key role in distributing resources to them, and in monitoring child-related services. While children have been defined as economic dependants and consumers of resources, we will find that older children, especially, are frequently economically active.

PART 1: CHILDREN AND THE STATE

The State plays a major role in the social construction of childhood and this begins from the moment of birth. All births are required to be registered, and public health nurses visit infants in their homes on a regular basis. The State regulates which biological parents may retain custody of their children and, through the adoption laws, may appoint others as parents of children not born to them. Parents have a duty of care and also of education of their children. While parents have a constitutional right to choose the type of education their children receive, in practice there is a legal requirement to send children to school.

Four Government departments have major responsibilities in the lives of children. The Department of Health and Children plays the main role on behalf of the State in the lives of pre-school children. Developmental testing, immunisation programmes, school health check-ups, etc. are organised, funded and overseen by health boards on behalf of the Department. A Minister of State with special responsibility for children is attached to the Department. The Department of Education and Science is the major state influence in the lives of children at primary and second level education. The Department sets the curriculum and examinations and, especially because of the competitive entry to third level education, has a major role in the reproduction of the labour force. The state examinations also provide a major tool in the control of the teenage population. The Department of Justice, Equality and Law Reform is responsible for legal matters, including criminal law. This Department has a major impact on the lives of children, e.g. through legal proceedings concerning custody, child care, adoption orders and the detention/supervision of young offenders. A broad range of legal age limits to childhood are administered by this Department. Children are legally prohibited from purchasing alcohol (under 15 years), drinking alcohol in a pub (under 18 years), driving a car (under 17 years) or having a job (under 15 years). The Department of Social, Community and Family Affairs is of great significance in the lives of the more impoverished sections of the child population. Income support is offered to them as dependants of adults (parents or guardians) who have qualified for benefits or assistance on a variety of grounds such as unemployment, illness, disability, or lone parenthood. The amount payable varies depending on the scheme under which they qualify and on their place in the family. A universal monthly payment — Child Benefit — is available in respect of every child, regardless of means. The degree of fragmentation of responsibility for children between different Departments has been seen as an obstacle in the delivery of appropriate services to them. The recently established National Children's Office is expected to provide a coherence between the work of various Departments and agencies in relation to children.

In Chapter One, "Legal and Constitutional Rights of Children in Ireland", Richardson provides a comprehensive overview of the current legislative situation regarding children. Richardson utilises the UN Convention on the Rights of the Child to review the extent to which Irish legislation meets the needs of children. The aspects of children's lives that come within legislative ambit are manifold: age as a criterion of childhood and the extent to which this varies; protection from discrimination on the basis of marital status of parents or of ethnic background, child care and protection rights, child abuse, homeless children, adoption, children in conflict with the law and child abduction. Although the UN Convention on the Rights of the Child cannot be enforced as such, its value in setting standards has been of immense importance in the lives of children in Ireland. This can be seen in the attempts by the Irish Government to address some of the criticisms of Ireland's failure to achieve the standards of the Convention through such measures as the National Children's Strategy (2000) and the drafting of legislation for the appointment of an independent Ombudsman for children.

Hayes' paper, "'Cherishing all the Children of the Nation Equally': State Provision and Responsibility for Children", also refers to the UN Convention on the Rights of the Child (1989). The approach taken is to analyse the discourse and ideology of protectionism, and of the conceptualising of children as dependants, which underpins various child-related policies, and to look at the scope for making them more responsive to children's needs and views. However, she cautions that the move from protectionism to enabling participation has "still a distance to travel". The paper also traces the development of child-related policies since the adoption of the Convention and the extent to which administrative structures and Departmental titles and briefs have altered to accommodate these transitions.

While the State may be depicted in some analyses as overwhelmingly the chief architect of childhood, there are important examples of its "subsidiarity" to other interests, notably those of the Catholic Church. O'Sullivan argues that the "institutional child", once a numerous category, was largely the construction of the Roman Catholic Church in the nineteenth century. Although an alternative model of care for orphaned, abandoned, destitute or "wayward" children existed in the form of "boarding out", the institutional system dominated until its decline in the 1970s. This dominance was largely to serve the purpose of religious congregations and local bishops, rather than that of the children themselves. State financial support for industrial schools, but not for other childcare institutions, led to the flourishing of this category. Efforts by the State to curb the growth of industrial schools largely failed. Given the volume of allegations that some such institutions were sites of child abuse, it would appear that the avowed aim that they should provide a morally superior and protective context for children also partly failed.

Alternative care for children has moved from the large institutional settings described by O'Sullivan in his chapter to seeking to replicate as closely as possible the family setting by the provision of foster care and small residential units (see also Richardson's and Hayes's chapters, this volume). This trend is reflected in care provision in other countries also. A recent study of residential childcare facilities in Finland, Ireland, Scotland and Spain shows that, in spite of the very different starting points in these countries, in recent years there has been convergence in the nature and type of residential childcare being provided (Craig, 1998, p. vi). The report further notes that there are an increasing number of younger children entering care.

Home and school are the appropriate contexts for children defined within State legislation and policies. Where these are lacking, the alternative care provided by the State offers a poor preparation for independent living to the young people involved. One of the key factors predisposing to youth homelessness is the experience of having been in care — of either the institutional or foster variety. Houghton, Kelleher and Kelleher's paper, "Children Out-of-Home in Ireland", draws on a follow-up study of young people leaving care. The paper provides evidence of lack of preparation to leave and lack of aftercare support, leading to a majority experiencing criminal detention or homelessness within six months of leaving care. Most children placed in special schools for young offenders come from impoverished homes with multiple family problems. School attendance and achievement are very poor for almost all such children. Children placed in care are almost equally disadvantaged. The picture which emerges is that the newer, smaller residential units and foster care arrangements, which replaced the large industrial schools of O'Sullivan's account, are less than successful in preparation for life. The failure of the State to protect and support the most vulnerable of the child population is inexcusable in these affluent times.

Given the importance of the State in defining and contextualising childhood, what happens when the State itself is contested, and conflict affects every member of society, regardless of age? The situation in Northern Ireland, as outlined in McLernon and Cairns' paper, "Children and Political Violence", is a legacy of hundreds of years of inter-community conflict, which, from the late 1960s until 1996, featured armed resistance. Gloomy predictions were made about the effects of the conflict on the "normal" process of socialisation, the encouragement of violence and the long-term effects of trauma on children's psychological well-being. The paper examines the evidence regarding the possible impact of the "Troubles" on children. Although NI children were more aware of conflict and the artefacts of guerrilla war than children in other areas of Britain, their mental health indicators, educational participation and attainments, juvenile crime levels and moral reasoning were all in advance of children in other similar, but "untroubled" societies. When linked to the findings of the previous chapter, it appears that the State *in loco parentis* has failed to fill the gap left by family failure/inadequacy, but, when the State itself is contested as a failed political entity, that children cope and adapt very well with family support.

PART 2: CHILDREN IN EDUCATION

Ariès (1973) has equated the development of schooling with the rise of the modern concept of "childhood" in that schools became institutions to provide life training for children. Children spend a great deal of time within these socialising institutions and this makes the educational setting a key environment in children's lives. Yet, from a child-centred point of view, how appropriate are these institutions? According to Lynch (1998), who has written extensively about Irish education, there are a number of difficulties in the Irish system. One problem is the unitary view of children which underpins the system. Another difficulty is the minimalist approach to education adopted by the Irish State, which has resulted, she says, in an uneven system that is firmly rooted in adultist philosophy. Underpinning this minimalist approach, Lynch says, are deeply held traditional values about the subordinate status of children and these attitudes are embedded in our Constitution. The empowerment of children fits uneasily within this framework, which is based essentially on disempowerment. There is, as yet, in her view, little recognition of emerging child-centred perspectives for children in the contemporary Irish educational system. This theme of disempowerment emerges in a number of the papers presented in this section. Another feature of the Irish educational system, cited by Lynch, is inequality. Despite the increased participation by all social groups in education over the last 30 years (over 80 per cent of the age cohort complete second-level education, with approximately 40 per cent transferring to higher education) there are still major differences in both access to and participation in education, based on socioeconomic background (Clancy and Wall, 2000).

The first paper in this section looks at initial experiences of children in the formal education system. According to Horgan and Douglas, although early childhood education is, and should be, culturally sensitive, research demonstrates quite significant agreement in relation to indicators of quality. The long-term benefits of early education, Horgan and Douglas state, stem not from what children are specifically taught but from the effects on their attitudes to learning, task orientation and self-esteem. Early education is thus crucial in the child's general development and producing models of best practice should be an important aim of educators. The optimum early educational approach, according to Horgan and Douglas, appears to be a holistic, flexible and dynamic model which is child-centred. Despite the importance of this educational process, however, there is, as the authors show, little consistency in terms of policy or practice in Ireland. Experiences of early education vary by type of school and also by teacher. Their paper demonstrates the importance of the individual teacher, in that some teachers have the ability to overcome curriculum difficulties and poor facilities in highly creative ways. Their contribution synthesises the findings of a number of observational studies of the main forms of early childhood education on offer, preschool playgroups, Naíonraí, Montessori and junior infants in national schools and in Gaelscoileanna. Their conclusion is that situations which allowed some degree of agency to children in progressing their own learning, within a structured programme, have the most positive outcomes. While class-based inequalities in some aspects of early childhood education facilities are apparent, their findings indicate that, although quality varies, there are some valuable experiences for children in all educational settings.

The issues of agency and empowerment for children emerge also in Devine's paper. Children are central actors within schools, she points out, yet it is frequently presumed that they do not have the capacity to reflect critically and constructively on their experience. Children in school are constituted as a collectivity in a less powerful situation than teachers, yet children do not necessarily accept this, as Devine's paper demonstrates. Children, especially in the senior classes in primary schools, query the adult-dictated order and find it alienating. They themselves may also exercise power in the form of bullying, teasing or, indeed, admiration of others in relation to their prowess at schoolwork. Devine's Foucauldian analysis dwells on academic and disciplinary aspects of schooling and discovers that children are perceptive and critical of their experiences. Her study suggests that, as children's experience of the school system grows, so too does their level of alienation and disenchantment. This has obvious implications for the educational inclusion of children generally, and some groupings of children in particular. Devine concludes her paper with some suggestions on how to make the system more democratic. A more democratic, child-centred structure will, she says, help to develop within children a capacity to be reflective, autonomous learners, able to articulate their voices in a clear and articulate manner, respectful of the perspectives of others. Such children will incorporate concepts of equality, difference and respect into their world view and this, she says, has implications for their childhood as well as future adult lives.

Power is a theme in Lodge and Flynn's gender analysis of playground relationships. Gender, as they demonstrate, is a fundamental part of each person's identity and is incorporated early into one's sense of self. It is a means of differentiating between people in terms of access to power and privilege. Lodge and Flynn show how children actively participate in the reproduction of gender inequality. In their study, they used observation and administered questionnaires to give a direct voice to children in describing their play. Many of the children tended to define themselves and their peers in ways which reflected traditional gendered expectations of behaviour, attitudes and characteristics. The children in the study tended to operate within, as Lodge and Flynn show, quite limited and stereotypical ranges of gendered behaviour. Gender dominance is indicated by boys annexing larger sections of playgrounds for their own use and "invading" girls' sections of the playground, if their own area is unusable. Boys are reported as sometimes breaking up girls' games, but the reverse rarely, if ever, happens. Issues of power, leadership and the presence of conflict were associated with the play of both boys and girls. Inclusion, conflict resolution and co-operative play were more a feature of girls' play.

Lodge and Flynn found that mixed play was infrequent amongst boys and girls, but that the most popular form of mixed play involved matters pertaining to the exploration of sexuality. Lynch's study of skipping rhymes and games indicates that similar themes run through this play form. Skipping involves organisation and physical energy, but is also intertwined with cultural products of the children themselves. "Skippers" accompany their physical activity by the recitation of a rich store of rhymes. This is part of the repertoire of children's lore, games and rhymes, which belongs to an oral tradition stretching back over centuries. Such cultural products have led to the argument that children should be regarded as having a separate culture or subculture. Drawing both on archival and contemporary data sources, Lynch's contention is that children use skipping rhymes to confront various developmental issues and as a form of cultural exchange among themselves.

The next contribution in the section takes us from traditional games to another established children's activity — reading. The explosion of media outlets has, according to Donlon, made available to children a vast array of entertainment options yet, perhaps surprisingly, reading still retains children's interest. In fact, Donlon's paper points to the phenomenal growth in the production of books for Irish children by Irish authors in less than 20 years. There is, as she says, a question as to whether the consumer demand for such books is parent-led and primarily middle class. Nevertheless, such books are an important input to children's cultural diet. Approximately one in six readers, in the study of senior classes of primary schools cited by Donlon, named Irish books as their favourite titles. However, the study also identifies almost one-fifth of senior primary schoolchildren as non-readers. This may be linked to Hennessy's finding (Chapter 5 of Volume 2) that approximately one in four children in after-school care do not have books available to them.

PART 3: CHILDREN AND THE ECONOMY

> Children will be provided with the financial supports neces-
> sary to eliminate child poverty (National Children's Strat-
> egy: *Our Children — Their Lives*, Objective G, p. 63).

Ireland has recently experienced a rapidly improved level of economic growth, yet this growth has not benefited all sections of the community equally. Signs of wealth have been contrasted with signs of growing levels of inequality and this applies to children also, large proportions of them remaining in impoverished situations. Irish levels of childhood poverty are well above those elsewhere in the European Union, at a time when our economic growth rates are also the highest in the EU. Indeed, there is a fundamental problem that the costs of child rearing are not reflected in earnings and are reflected inadequately in State income support.

As an economically dependent population, children, unlike older people, do not have the safeguard of a basic standard of living guaranteed by the State (Makrinioti, 1994). As a result, Makrinioti points out, children's economic welfare depends entirely on their parents' economic status: "they share their parents' affluence or poverty" (p. 278). Even the existence of universal Child Benefit does not guarantee that the money will be used to the benefit of the child or children in a family equally. Makrinioti makes the point that parents are given the responsibility for allocating welfare provision within the family:

> The interests of both parties are conceived as being identical and inseparable, and the possibility that children vary in the amount of tangible and intangible goods they receive from parents is not considered (p. 275).

Neither does the state make adequate provision for the real costs of dependent children in the welfare system (Carney et al., 1994).

It is evident in relation to income support that the State has played a role of subsidiarity vis-à-vis the family, based on assumptions of adequacy and equity. As such, it has reinforced the dependent status of children as part of a larger unit, the family, rather than being regarded as citizens whose physical, psychological and emotional vulnerability should be safeguarded. Moreover, Nolan's chapter demonstrates the extent to which child poverty remains an important social issue in Ireland today.

During the 1980s and early 1990s, there was a trend of widening inequalities in living standards and increasing poverty for children by comparison with the adult population. Nolan's paper demonstrates that incomes in the top income decile grew by at least five times as much as those in the bottom decile and the proportion of children living below the EU poverty line increased from 1 in 10 to 1 in 3. While the economic position of children from small families improved somewhat over the period 1987 to 1994, and the gaps narrowed significantly between 1994-1997, overall children are still more at risk of poverty than adults. When the definition of poverty is extended to look at broader material goods associated with "normal" lifestyles (e.g. "having two pairs of strong shoes"), the extent of poverty among children relative to adults is seen to be higher than when income alone is the criterion.

The National Children's Strategy refers to child poverty as:

> a significant barrier, limiting children's potential and participation . . . (which) impacts on all aspects of children's lives and therefore curtails their progress. . . . Poor children tend to do less well in school, suffer more ill health and are more likely to be homeless or become involved in criminal behaviour (2000, p. 63).

The evidence put forward in the chapter by Houghton, Kelleher and Kelleher in this volume indicates that this is a considerable understatement of the long-term corrosive effects of childhood poverty. Specific targets, of increasing Child Benefit over the next three years and a variety of other measures under the National Anti-Poverty Strategy, have been set to attempt to improve the situation.

Children and Economic Activity

The importance of children as a consumer group is evidenced by the degree of marketing focused both directly and indirectly on them. Apart from greater disposable income from pocket money or allowance provided by parents, older children in increasing numbers are entering the workforce on a part-time basis. As such this represents a return to an earlier era where children's contribution to production was central to survival. Now it is not always a matter of survival per se but the importance placed on an independent source of income for the purchase of consumer goods and entertainment. Whether or not this is a desirable trend depends on a number of factors such as the hours worked, the pay and conditions and, most importantly, the impact of work on other aspects of the child's life. Children are not impervious to macro-cultural trends in their society; in many ways they may act as its barometer. The increased emphasis on work in the formation of identity for women may well have contributed to the increased involvement of children, from all classes in society, in part-time and holiday employment. It is seen as an assertion of independence and as an opportunity to be treated as an adult. "Work" may also act as a form of "babysitter" for parents who would like to know where their teenagers are, and what they are doing, during the long summer vacation. The alternative is to enrol them in costly activities, which may be rejected by them as childish. A summer or weekend job may be construed, by parents, as useful work experience and as a way of broadening their horizons. James, Jenks and Prout argue that "children's work is not inherently invisible but is rendered so" by such interpretations (1998, p. 115). Lavalette claims that child labour has been "deproblematised" (1994, p. 226). Certain sectors of service and retail industries rely very heavily on the availability of this cheap, seasonal labour-force. The existence of legislation and regulations to protect children by banning their employment, under certain ages, and in certain settings and hours, is frequently ignored and goes unchallenged. Indeed, in some cases such protective legislation renders child employees more vulnerable by restricting them to the informal sector. This makes them an attractively cheap source of labour. There are, therefore, a very complex set of forces drawing children into paid employment.

Leonard's paper provides data from her research of a large sample of 15-year-old school goers in Belfast about their involvement in paid employment. She found that "children are a permanent feature of the adult labour market rather than being solely involved in jobs typically defined as children's work". The reasons soon emerged in the low levels of remuneration achieved by them. There was also a penalty to be paid, in relation to feeling tired at school, by a significant number of them. The world of the worker-scholar is gendered — girls worked longer hours for lower pay than boys. Almost half of the sample had some experience of paid employment (excluding babysitting), with more than a quarter starting work at 13 or younger. It is interesting that social aspects of employment and the experience of being treated like an adult emerge as more important motives for working, in the children's responses, than that of earning. Children may be seen as renegotiating the boundaries and social construction of childhood by combining the roles of scholar and worker.

CONCLUSION

In all three sections of this volume, we see that complex frameworks have been established, in which childhood is perceived as being encompassed. The State, the education system and the economy each play an important role in setting parameters within which childhood is constructed and within which the lived experience of childhood takes place. However, in each sector, there is evidence that children, to some extent, exercise agency and respond creatively to the structures which confront them.

References

Ariès, P. (1962), *Centuries of Childhood*, London: Jonathon Cape

Carney, C., Fitzgerald, E., Kiely, G. & Quinn, P. (1994), *The Cost of a Child*, Combat Poverty Agency/Family Studies Centre, UCD.

Clancy, P. and Wall, J. (2000), *Social Background of Higher Education Entrants*, Dublin: Higher Education Authority.

Craig, S. (1998), *Learn to Listen: The Irish Report of a European Study on Residential Child Care*, Dublin: DIT, Centre for Social and Educational Research

James, A., Jenks, C. and Prout, A. (1998), *Theorising Childhood*, London: Polity

Lavalette, M. (1994), *Child Employment in the Capitalist Labour Market*, Aldershot: Avebury

Lynch, K. (1998), "The Status of Children and Young Persons: Educational and Related issues" in Healy, S. and Reynolds, B. (eds), *Social Policy in Ireland: Principles, Practice and Problems*, Dublin, Oak Tree Press, pp. 321-353.

Makrinioti, D. (1994), "Conceptualization of Childhood in a Welfare State: A Critical Reappraisal" in Qvortrup, J., Bardy, M., Sgritta, G. & Wintersberger, H. (eds), *Childhood Matters, Social Theory, Practice and Policy*, European Centre Vienna, Aldershot: Avebury.

National Children's Strategy (2000), *Our Children — Their Lives*, Dublin: Stationery Office.

Part 1:
Children and the State

Chapter 1

"Cherishing all the Children of the Nation Equally": State Provision and Responsibility for Children in Ireland

Noírín Hayes

INTRODUCTION

The UN Convention on the Rights of the Child (1989) is a comprehensive agreement on the rights of children, which has been ratified by almost every country in the world. As is the case with other international treaties and conventions, there is an obligation on those parties who have ratified the Convention to implement it as fully and effectively as possible. To this end a monitoring process has been established to evaluate the progress of countries in fulfilling their obligations arising from ratification. Ireland ratified the Convention, without reservation, in September 1992 and the Convention came into force in October 1992.

The realisation that children's rights require special attention emerged from the wider discourse on human rights. Debate and discussion acknowledged that children are different to adults and that this difference deserved recognition in the shape of specific rights. The UN Convention on the Rights of the Child is an international convention, which frames in international law many of the aspects of children's rights being advocated over the last number of years. It is an interesting convention in that it included the non-governmental organisations (NGOs) as active participants from the drafting phase through to the implementation and monitoring process. Boyden (1997) notes that, at the outset, not all child interest groups were supportive of the Convention. For instance, "UNICEF . . . initially reluctant to endorse children's rights, has now thrown its weight behind the instrument" (p. 216). Interestingly, UNICEF in Ireland has been active in support of children's rights and is a founder member of the Children's Rights Alliance (CRA), an alliance formally established in 1995 to promote the implementation of the Convention in Ireland (CRA, 1997, 1998).

Ratification of the Convention affords a unique opportunity for professionals, policymakers and academics to review attitudes to children and childhood. Recent research, in both sociology and psychology, has seen a move away from the traditional approach to considering children in isolation from the complex contexts in which they develop towards understanding childhood and children in a wider socio-cultural context where children themselves are seen as active participants (Bronfenbrenner, 1979, 1993; Qvortrup et al, 1994; James and Prout, 1997; Corsaro, 1997). Woodhead (1997, p. 78) has noted that, in psychology in particular:

> The Universalist theories are gradually being eclipsed. . . . In
> their place a more fully "cultural psychology" is emerging.

Researchers are urged to study children and childhood within the cultural contexts that they experience.

As children are increasingly recognised as interactive agents in their own development they can no longer be regarded simply as the passive recipients of adult-designed laws and institutions. With this shift in focus there has been increased attention given to the issue of specific rights for children. Verhellen (1992) suggests that there are a number of different motives for this increased interest. He identifies one of the most powerful factors influencing the debate on children's rights as the discovery that instead of loving and protecting children many adults actually cause children harm. The realisation that adults, either directly or indirectly, are neglecting their responsibilities to children has forced adults to look at the way they dominate children and out of this attention has emerged an interest in the rights of children. He argues, however that adults can abuse the children's rights' perspective to dominate children through child protection laws, which he sees as a form of social control, and through education laws, which he characterises as socialisation instruments. In Ireland, Fahey (1992) has argued that compulsory education can be conceptualised as a form of state control as much as a response to an entitlement to children to education. Such laws were introduced as a response to the image of children as passive "adults-in-waiting" at the turn of the twentieth century, and have led to the separation of children from mainstream society into institutions designed for them by adults. This trend towards the creation of separate worlds has, to a degree, made children more vulnerable to adult control and exploitation. The Convention provides a valuable framework within which to redress the balance.

THE UN CONVENTION ON THE RIGHTS OF THE CHILD

The Convention is made up of a series of Articles, which cover children's *civil rights*, for example in relation to their treatment under the law; their *social, economic and cultural rights*, for example to an adequate standard of living and their *rights to protection*. It does not address the issue of their political rights. Under the Convention the child is defined as a person under the age of 18 years and this definition has been incorporated into Irish legislation in, for instance, the Child Care Act, 1991. Franklin (1992) notes, however, that this definition of the child is not without its difficulties as it can represent a population that includes "members of the armed forces, taxi drivers, building workers, student nurses and young people with children of their own" (p. 105). Such diversity challenges policymakers to give careful attention in the framing of policies impacting on children.

There are four Articles regarded as "general principles" which are basic to the implementation of the Convention. These are:

*   Article 2, which states that all the rights guaranteed by the Convention must be available to all children without discrimination of any kind.

- Article 3, which states that the best interests of the child must be a paramount consideration in all actions concerning children.

- Article 6, which states that every child has the right to life, survival and development.

- Article 12, which states that the child's view must be considered and taken into account in all matters affecting them.

The Convention also identifies the primacy of the family in relation to children. Indeed, Article 5 recognises that children's rights must be promoted as well as protected and places responsibility for this, in most cases, on parents. However, parents — and guardians — can be the abusers of children, not only in the characteristic ways we have seen reported in the media but also by being over-ambitious and demanding of their children to a degree where they can damage and undermine their rights. While there may be times when parental rights will take precedence over those of the child, the Convention requires States Parties to ensure that the child's rights are well protected. Archard (1993) notes that it is reasonable to concede authority to parents so that they may bring up their own children in a way they consider appropriate. He notes, however, that parents do not own their children but "the fact that one's children are one's own needs to be properly acknowledged in any talk of rights and duties" (p. 12). Authors commenting on childhood in Ireland have noted that, in general, families are emphasised as the unit for the protection of children and are only assisted in this responsibility where there is evidence of serious disadvantage or where parents have manifestly failed to provide for their children (Gilligan, 1996; Greene, 1994). It has been argued that the Irish state has failed to adequately recognise its impact on families or to respond to the fact that the quality of family life is interdependent on society and the state (Fahey, 1998). The capacity of families to, for instance, access high quality childcare in contemporary Ireland is often dictated by factors over which they may have limited control such as availability (Hayes, 1995).

The Constitution of Ireland recognises the family "as the natural primary and fundamental unit group of Society" (Article 41.1.1) while recognising the "natural and imprescriptible rights of the child" (Article 42.5). This latter recognition does not refer explicitly to the rights of all children and has been interpreted as limited to situations where families have, somehow, failed in their duty towards their children. This limiting of stated rights for children has given rise to a number of calls for Constitutional review including the Task Force on Child Care Services (1981) and the Kilkenny Incest Investigation Team (1993). The latter report noted that the "high emphasis on the rights of the family in the Constitution may consciously or unconsciously be interpreted as giving higher value to the rights of parents than to the rights of children" (p. 56). The report went on to recommend an alteration to Articles 41 and 42 to include an explicit statement on the constitutional rights of children. In 1996 the Constitutional Review Group (CRG) recommended an amendment of the Constitutional definition of the family to recognise the diversity of family types now prevalent in Ireland, some of which are headed by parents who are, by definition, children themselves. The CRG also recommended that the Constitution should include an express obligation to treat the best interests of the child as a paramount consideration in any action relating to children. *Strengthening Families for Life: The Report from the Commission on the Family* (1998), a policy document relating to children and the family in Ireland, has endorsed the position of the Constitutional Review Group in its recommendation for a wider definition of family. It also recommends that public policy on family affairs should affirm most Irish people's commitment to marriage while recognising that children are individuals within the family with rights to adequate support, care and promotion of their well-being. While referring to the rights of children within the Report the language of the Commission continues in the tradition of portraying children as passive, identifying adults as protecting them and working on their behalf. This is contrary to the spirit of Article 12 of the Convention, which emphasises the need for adults to recognise and include children as active participants in relation to the promotion and protection of their rights.

Woodhead (1997) writes that the UN Convention, in promoting a "rights" perspective, is serving as a powerful antidote to the "needs" approach in many areas of policy making.

> Children's rights break through the web of paternalistic protectionist constructions that emphasise children as powerless dependents, separated off from adult society and effectively excluded from participation in shaping their own destiny. This is especially true in respect of rights that empower children to participate in the process of defining their "needs", treatment and destiny (p. 80-81).

Some authors have characterised the UN Convention as an idealistic document with a Western ethos dominating (Freeman, 1992; Boyden, 1996). However, careful analysis of the Convention shows that it is a complex but sensitive instrument that does allow for cultural diversity in its interpretation. Whatever its limitations the Convention is an impressive manifesto on behalf of children. It protects children while moving away from the paternalistic and passive approach to children as objects and moves to the protection of children's rights while giving children an active role as subjects.

As with any complex instrument there are possible tensions and conflicts internal to the Convention. Freeman (1992) has drawn attention to this, particularly with respect to Article 3 and Article 12. Article 3 states that "in all actions concerning children, whether undertaken by public or private social welfare institutions, courts of law, administrative authorities or legislative bodies, the best interests of the child shall be a primary consideration" and this, he argues, can be seen as a welfarist Article. Article 12, on the other hand, states that States Parties shall "assure to the child who is capable of forming his or her own views the right to express these views freely on all matters affecting the child, the views of the child being given due consideration in accordance with the age and maturity of the child". This Article can be characterised as giving a degree of autonomy to the child. Such tensions highlight the need for signatories to consider carefully what the Convention means in terms of its implementation and wider legislation and policy making. The quality of children's lives does not necessarily improve by giving them explicit rights. However, naming children's rights as worthy of consideration can act as a drive to improving the quality of life of children as it is an important step in placing them as a constituency on the political agenda.

Although presenting a radically new way of considering children and their rights, the UN Convention is not a hugely radical instrument in terms of structural or administrative impact. In framing children's rights it does not propose any substantial changes to the basic structure of existing institutions, rather, it proposes an extension of access to these institutions. Central to this aspect of the Convention is the principle of participation (Article 12). Franklin (1992) suggests that democratic and participatory structures should be introduced to all those institutions where children constitute the consumer body for the services they provide. So, for instance, "children should elect representatives to School and College councils to decide issues relating to disciplinary matters and curriculum"(p. 108). Given the centralised nature of the Irish education system, Irish children have little or no opportunity for direct input into curriculum development. While the Education Act, 1998, under Section 28, does provide for the establishment of school-based student councils, the provision is limited in that it applies only to second level schools. Recent developments, which have led to the establishment of a Union of Secondary Students (*Irish Times*, 2001), have the potential to provide a mechanism for giving voice to students on education matters impacting directly on them.

Freeman (1992) points to a weakness in the Convention noting that, while allowing for children to participate in proceedings impacting on them and to make their views known, there is no explicit reference to a right for separate representation where necessary. This issue has been addressed by the Council of Europe in their wide-ranging response to the UN Convention on the Rights of the Child. *The European Convention on the Exercise of Children's Rights* (1997) is the result of the deliberations of a Committee of Experts on Family Law established by the Council of Europe. The European Convention notes in Article 1, para. 2 that:

> The object of the [present] convention is, in the best inter-
> ests of children, to promote their rights, to grant them pro-
> cedural rights and to facilitate the exercise of these rights
> by ensuring that children are, themselves or through per-
> sons or bodies, informed and allowed to participate in pro-
> ceedings affecting them before a judicial authority (p. 6).

Critical to the appropriate implementation of this Article is a
real commitment to the true participation of children themselves. In Ireland the Guardianship of Infants Act, 1964 recognised that the wishes of a child may be taken into account by a
Court and, in order to ascertain these wishes, the Court may
interview the child. The Child Care Act, 1991 ensures, as a primary principle, that the wishes of the child are respected where
legal proceedings are taken under the terms of the Act and allows for the appointment of a guardian *ad litem* (GAL) at the
discretion of the courts. However, concerns have been expressed that the appointment of a GAL is at the discretion of the
courts, only applies in certain circumstances and that no effort
has been made by statutory bodies in Ireland to ensure best
practice in relation to the service (CRA, 1997).

CHILDREN'S RIGHTS IN IRELAND

It is often said that the childhood years are the "best years of
our lives". Franklin (1992) disagrees with this dominant view of
childhood. He attempts to explode what he considers a myth by
suggesting that a cursory examination of the wider circumstances in which children live tells a different story. What is it
like to be a child in Ireland at the end of the 20th century? Although there is little empirical research on childhood in Ireland
a review of what is available indicates that children in contemporary Ireland experience different childhoods depending on
their circumstances, and there are certain childhoods which are
very uncomfortable and even damaging for Irish children
(O'Connor, 1992; Greene, 1994). Cousins (1996), reviewing the
status of Irish children, found that, although accurate statistics
were difficult to find, a significant number live in situations of
considerable disadvantage. These include children living in
poverty, children who are in care, in legal custody, subject to

abuse or neglect, homeless and children with disabilities. How are children valued in Ireland? This is difficult to measure but in economic terms the evidence suggests that they are not highly valued. For instance, Fahey (1998) noted that income tax allowances for children were abolished in 1986 and replaced by a universal child benefit. The value of this benefit, although increased in recent years, has over the long term been insufficient to compensate for the loss of tax-free allowances. Furthermore, the level of support for child dependants of those who are unemployed has been low and generally too little to keep children of unemployed parents out of poverty.

Gathering detailed and unambiguous information and statistics about children in Ireland is very difficult. This reflects the fact that policy relating to children and children's issues is fragmented and scattered across a variety of government departments. As a consequence, much of the policy — and associated information — is invisible as children's policy, and is subsumed under the broader policy headings of health, equality, education, justice and so on. The result is that, as a policy focus, children are also invisible.

The need for some degree of coordination with respect to policies about children has been recognised nationally. In reviewing international responses to the UN Convention, Ruxton (1998) noted some of the innovative actions in Ireland with respect to coordinating policy. The Human Rights Unit in the Department of Foreign Affairs acknowledged the difficulties in coordination across government departments on child policy. It noted that, "given Ireland's obligation under the Convention on the Rights of the Child, a Minister of State to the Departments of Health, Education and Justice, with special responsibility for children was appointed in 1996" (p. 32). It went on to detail the parameters of the appointment which "for the first time, brought together under a single Minister, responsibility for child protection, youth homelessness, school truancy and children in trouble with the law, areas which in the past have been the responsibility of three Government Ministers . . ." (p. 32). This development marked a new phase in approach to coordinating child policy and there are a number of points worth noting about the appointment. Although the appointment was only at junior ministry level it did have equal status across the three departments. The position was, however, clearly directed at the protection and welfare of vulnerable and troubled children and not at the development of a coordinated response to the rights of all children, a central principle of the UN Convention.

With the appointment of a new government in 1997 there were changes in the responsibilities of different government departments. These changes were captured, to an extent, in the new titles given to departments where some interesting changes were made. For instance the Department of Health became the Department of Health and Children and the Department of Social Welfare became the Department of Social, Community and Family Affairs. In a country that locates so much responsibility to the family with respect to children it is ironic that, administratively, children should appear to be so directly removed from family.

With its change of name the Department of Health and Children acquired an enhanced responsibility in respect of children. According to O'Dwyer (1998) it was a name change of considerable significance placing on the department:

> a responsibility to develop, monitor and review (on behalf of the government) an overall strategy in relation to children . . . and will require the development and implementation of much better processes than have heretofore been available to the department to influence policies and practices of other departments. . . . The main requirement is to see other departments as essential partners in achieving improvements for the good of the whole community (p. 40-42).

In 1997 the Department of Education was re-titled the Department of Education and Science by the incoming government. Through state support for the compulsory education system (6-15 years) this department has a profound impact on Irish children and childhood. While compulsory education can be seen as meeting a stated right for children under the UN Convention it emerged, in fact, from a different focus. There are some grounds for considering that education is directed more by economic factors than by the rights of children. Indeed, the increased investment in Irish education since the 1960s reflects a

shift from regarding education as personal development to-
wards viewing it in terms of a strategic investment in the future
(O'Sullivan, 1993). In an article on the relationship between the
State, the family and education, Fahey (1992) noted that:

> the idea of children's rights to schooling empowered the
> state not only to penalise parents who were negligent in re-
> gard to their children's schooling but also to incarcerate
> children who persistently resisted the exercise of that right
> on their own behalf (p. 391).

By balancing the right to education with other rights identified
in the Convention — such as participatory rights and leisure
rights — Irish educational policy could become more child-
focused and more explicitly respecting of children's rights.

The 1992 government established a new Department of
Equality and Law Reform. It had a wide remit including a responsibility for certain policy areas impacting on children. For
example, under Partnership 2000 this department, through its
responsibility for equality issues, became responsible for supporting the development of the childcare sector to assist parents in reconciling their work and family responsibilities. It was
also charged with coordinating an Expert Working Group on
Childcare. As the amalgamated Department of Justice, Equality
and Law Reform, following the 1997 departmental renaming
and restructuring, it published the report of this group in 1999
and is chair of the National Childcare Coordinating Committee
(2000-2006).

In the recent past there have been a number of positive and
innovative initiatives which were developed, with exchequer
and European Union funding, to address particular problems
such as educational disadvantage, childcare, drug abuse and
child abuse. However, many of these initiatives have been at a
pilot level only, targeted at a particular population and not developed within a wider policy for all children. Such "targeting
in a vacuum" is a short-sighted approach to improving the
quality of life for children. While such a targeted approach of
responding only to the needs and rights of vulnerable children
might be acceptable in a period of economic restraint, it is a

disappointment given the very healthy state of the Irish economy in recent years. This limited approach by government to
its obligations to children may reflect a particular interpretation
of the Irish Constitution but it is not in line with the spirit of the
Convention which is intended as a framework of rights for all
children (Article 2).

MONITORING THE CONVENTION

The UN Convention on the Rights of the Child has the potential to
be a valuable agent of change for children. However, for the
Convention to be more than mere rhetoric its implementation by
the various States Parties needs to be monitored. Under Article
44 of the Convention, States Parties are required to submit national reports describing progress towards implementation. An
initial report has to be submitted two years after ratification and
further "update" reports every five years thereafter. The reports
are examined by the UN Committee on the Rights of the Child, a
committee of ten experts. In addition to the national reports received the UN Committee also considers submissions from relevant NGOs in its assessment of a country's performance.

When countries ratify the Convention they commit to reviewing and harmonising domestic legislation to bring both
legislation and practice into full conformity with the principle of
the Convention. In preparing the *First National Report* Ireland
noted that it was "co-ordinated by the Department of Foreign
Affairs, [and] obliged all relevant Departments to reflect on
how the laws and policies within their sphere of competence
fulfilled the Convention obligations" (Ruxton, 1998, p. 25). Indeed, the *First National Report* (1996) acts as one of the first
government reports to give an overview of the status of Irish
children. Read in conjunction with the NGO report from the
CRA, *Small Voices, Vital Rights* (1997), the reader is provided
with a valuable basis from which to monitor Ireland's progress
in meeting its obligations under the Convention.

Ireland submitted the *First National Report* to the UN Committee on the Rights of the Child in April 1996. In preparing a
National Report countries are expected to facilitate the participation of the NGO sector. In a survey carried out for Save the

Children, Ruxton (1998) found that many countries ignored this expectation. He noted, however, that the Irish government did consult, informally and formally, with representatives of a cross-section of the NGO sector interested in the welfare of children. Ruxton cautions that there is a risk in this type of consultation as NGOs may be compromised, their views "watered down" or the consultation "used to legitimise otherwise ineffective policies" (p. 79). He goes on to point out that consultation by the government with the NGO sector does not preclude the sector from submitting an "alternative" report. This is what happened in Ireland, where the CRA was consulted in the preparation of the National Report and also submitted its own NGO report *Small Voices, Vital Rights* in May 1997.

Following receipt of the national and NGO reports the UN Committee holds a pre-sessional hearing where NGOs and international organisations are invited to present information about the performance of the country under consideration. At the conclusion of this hearing the Committee forwards a "list of issues" to the government concerned. This list identifies specific issues, under the different articles, where further information is required. Governments are requested to respond to this list, in writing, to the Committee one month in advance of the plenary hearing. At the plenary hearing the Committee rigorously reviews the country's national report and, using a question and answer format, analyses the country's progress in implementing the Convention. A statement of the Committee's findings and recommendations for action are then forwarded to the country as Concluding Observations. In addition, a Summary Record of the plenary session is issued. Both the Concluding Observations and the Summary Record are public documents and countries are expected to publicise them widely to encourage discussion and planning with regard to the actions proposed.

Following the plenary hearing in January 1998 the UN Committee issued its Concluding Observations on the state of children's rights in Ireland. The Concluding Observations (CRA, 1998) provide a valuable framework for action in furthering the implementation of the Convention. Among the principal recommendations are that Ireland:

- Adopt a comprehensive National Strategy for Children, incorporating the principles and provisions of the Convention

- Amend the Constitution of Ireland to accord specific recognition to the rights of children and to encompass all the principles of the Convention

- Consider the establishment of an independent monitoring body, such as an Office of Ombudsman for Children

- Strengthen co-ordination between government bodies dealing with children's rights

- Ensure the development of closer relationships between the statutory and non-governmental sectors

- Take immediate steps to address the problem of child poverty and ensure that all families have adequate resources and facilities

- Systematically promote and facilitate children's participation in decisions and policies affecting them (CRA, 1998, p. 5).

CONCLUSION

There can be no doubt that the Convention is influencing policy and has acted as a catalyst in policy developments for children in Ireland since ratification in 1992. For example, in 1996 the Irish Government made a commitment to the establishment of an Ombudsman's Office and the Department of Health and Children has confirmed the government's commitment to such an appointment on a number of occasions since. In October 1998 the Minister for Health and Children announced, in a speech delivered to the CRA Conference, that in response to the UN Committee recommendations his Department was drawing up a National Strategy for Children.

The National Children's Strategy was published in 2000. It is an ambitious ten-year policy plan which reflects the influence of the UN Convention on the Rights of the Child and emerged from consultation with interested parties, including children (NCS, 2000; Hayes, 2001). The strategy articulates a vision of an Ireland:

where children are respected as young citizens with a valued contribution to make and a voice of their own; where all children are cherished and supported by family and the wider society; where they enjoy a fulfilling childhood and realise their potential (p. 4).

This strategy has the potential to change the way children are viewed in Ireland and to strengthen their rights. It identifies six operational principles and sets three national goals for children. The principles are that the strategy will be child-centred; family oriented; equitable; inclusive; action oriented and integrated. The three goals are that (i) children will have a voice in matters which affect them, (ii) children's lives will be better understood and (iii) children will receive quality support and services to promote all aspects of their development. The effectiveness of the strategy will be determined by the structures that are developed to facilitate its implementation. Among the structures proposed are a National Children's Office, a National Children's Advisory Council and an Ombudsman for Children.

Despite considerable policy developments over the last decade we cannot afford to be complacent about the rights of children in Ireland. There is still a distance to travel before Irish legislation, policy and practice moves away from conceptualising children as dependants in need of protection towards developing strategies that encourage the protection of the rights of all children with their active participation in the process.

References

Archard, D. (1993) *Children: Rights and Childhood*, London: Routledge

Boyden, J. (1997) "Childhood and the Policy Makers: A Comparative Perspective on the Globalization of Childhood" in James, A. & Prout, A. (eds) *Constructing and Reconstructing Childhood*, p. 190-236, London: Falmer Press

Bronfenbrenner, U. (1979) *The Ecology of Human Development*, Cambridge, MA: Harvard University Press

Bronfenbrenner, U. (1993) "The ecology of cognitive development: Research models and fugitive findings" in Wozniak, R.H. and Fischer,

K. (eds) *Development in context: Acting and thinking in specific environments*, Hillsdale, NJ: Erlbaum, pp. 3-44

Bunreacht na hEireann: Constitution of Ireland, Dublin: Stationery Office

Child Care Act, 1991, Dublin: Stationery Office

Children's Rights Alliance (1997) *Small voices, Vital rights*, Dublin: CRA

Children's Rights Alliance (1998) *Children's rights, Our responsibilities*, Dublin: CRA

Constitutional Review Group (1996) *Report*, Dublin: Stationery Office

Corsaro, W. (1997) *The Sociology of Childhood*, London: Pine Forge Press/Sage Publications

Council of Europe (1997) *European Convention on the exercise of Children's Rights and explanatory report*, Strasbourg: Council of Europe Publishing; European Treaty Series No. 160

Cousins, M (1996) *Seen and Heard: Promoting and Protecting Children's Rights in Ireland*, Dublin: CRA

Department of Social, Community & Family Affairs (1998) *Strengthening Families for Life: Report of the Commission on the Family,* Dublin: Stationery Office

Droogleever Fortuyn, M. & de Langen, M. (eds) (1992) *Towards the Realization of Human Rights of Children*, Netherlands: Defence for Children International

Education Act, 1998, Dublin: Stationery Office

Fahey, T. (1992) "State, Family and Compulsory Schooling in Ireland" In *The Economic and Social Review*, Vol. 23, No. 4, pp. 369-395.

Fahey, T. (1998) "Family Policy in Ireland — A strategic overview background paper for the Commission on the Family" in *Strengthening Families for Life*, Dublin: Stationery Office, pp.384-403

Franklin, B. (1992) "Children and Decision Making: Developing Empowering Institutions" in Droogleever Fortuyn, M. & de Langen, M. (eds) *Towards the Realization of Human Rights of Children*, pp. 89-112, Netherlands: Defence for Children International

Freeman, M.D.A. (1992) "Beyond Conventions — Towards Empowerment" in Droogleever Fortuyn, M. & de Langen, M. (eds) *Towards the Realization of Human Rights of Children*, pp. 19-40, Netherlands: Defence for Children International

Gilligan, R. (1996) "Irish Child Care Services in the 1990's: The Child Care Act 1991 and other developments" in Hill, M. & Aldgate, J. (eds) *Child Welfare Services: Development in Law, Policy, Practice and Research*, London: Jessica Kingsley

Greene, S. (1994) "Growing up Irish: Development in context", *Irish Journal of Psychology*, 5, 2&3, pp. 354-371

Guardianship of Infants Act, 1964, Dublin: Stationery Office

Hayes, N. (1995) *Early Childhood Education: The Case for a National Policy*, Dublin: Combat Poverty Agency

Hayes, N. (forthcoming) "Participating in the Policy Process: Children's Rights in Ireland" in Crimmens, D. (ed) *Having Their Say: Young People and Participation in Europe*, Lyme Regis: Russell House

Investigation Team (1993) *Kilkenny Incest Investigation*, Dublin: Stationery Office

Ireland (1996) First National Report to the UN Committee on the Rights of the Child, Dublin: Stationery Office

James, A. & Prout, A. (eds) (1997) *Constructing and Reconstructing Childhood: New Directions in the Sociological Study of Childhood*, London: Falmer Press

National Children's Strategy (2000) Dublin: Stationery Office

O'Connor, P. (1992) "Childcare Policy: A provocative analysis and research agenda", *Administration*, 40, pp. 200-219

O'Dwyer, J. (1998) "Reflections on Future Structures in the Health Services" in Leahy, A.L. & Wiley, M.M. (eds), *The Irish Health System in the 21st Century*, Dublin: Oak Tree Press

O'Sullivan, D. (1993) "The Concept of Policy Paradigm: Elaboration and Illumination", *The Journal of Educational Thought*, Vol. 27, No. 3, pp. 246-272

Qvortrup, J., Bardy, M., Sgritta, G. & Wintersberger, H. (eds) (1994) *Childhood Matters: Social Theory, Practice and Policy*, Aldershot: Avebury

Ruxton, S. (1998) *Implementing Children's Rights: What can the UK learn from international experiences?* London: Save the Children

Task Force on Child Care Services (1981) *Final Report*, Dublin: Stationery Office

United Nations (1989) *Convention on the Rights of the Child*

United Nations Convention on the Rights of the Child: First National Report of Ireland (1996) Dublin: Stationery Office

Verhellen, E. (1992) "Children's Ombudswork: Motives and Strategies, even in Adler's time" in Droogleever Fortuyn, M. & de Langen, M. (eds) *Towards the Realization of Human Rights of Children*, pp. 60-65, Netherlands: Defence for Children International

Woodhead, M. (1997) "Psychology and the Cultural Construction of Children's Needs" in James, A. & Prout, A. (eds) *Constructing and Reconstructing Childhood*, pp. 63-83, London: Falmer Press

Chapter 2

Legal and Constitutional Rights of Children in Ireland

Valerie Richardson

INTRODUCTION

Concern to promote the rights of children has led to an increased codification of those rights in a number of international instruments, most notably the UN Convention on the Rights of the Child, supplemented by the UN Standard Minimum Rules for the Administration of Juvenile Justice (1985) and the UN Guidelines for the Protection of Juveniles Deprived of their Liberty (1990). The rights of children had already been guaranteed by the Universal Declaration of Human Rights and other human rights documents but the UN Convention on the Rights of the Child, for the first time, applied these principles specifically to children themselves and recognised that these rights are possessed by children by virtue of their human existence, independent of governments or adults granting them such rights.

While the importance of such conventions cannot be underestimated, the true recognition of children's rights requires implementation in practice, through the introduction of appropriate legislation and the provision of resources. However, it is important to note at the outset that children do not acquire their rights through legislation. Legislation can only protect and give expression to their rights. The UN Convention incorporates a range of rights that have been associated with children's welfare in the past such as the right to protection and to the provision of services. However, it is broader in its declaration in that it extends children's rights to that of participation in matters of importance to them, the right to be consulted about decisions concerning their care, rights to freedom of thought, to privacy and to assembly that bring their rights more into line with international legislation for adults (Burman, 1996). The Convention, therefore, represents an important development in the conceptualisation of children and their needs and rights. By ratifying the Convention, Ireland has made a public declaration of a commitment to work towards achieving those rights and to ensuring that all future legislation is in line with the letter and spirit of the Convention. In addition, the Convention provides for a clear and rigorous reporting process. It requires countries to produce a report on compliance within two years of signing and every five years thereafter. In accordance with this requirement Ireland submitted its First National Report in 1996. While there are guidelines issued to governments in the preparation of these reports there is no duty to include the views of non-governmental organisations and governments have failed to adopt a critical stance towards their own policies. (Harwin and Forrester, 1999, p. 122). The Irish report documented existing Government policies but the critical views were submitted as a separate document from the Children's Rights Alliance (Kilkelly, 1997).

Any examination of children's rights and legislation in Ireland inevitably starts with a consideration of the balance between the rights of children, the rights of parents and the rights of the State to intervene in family life. The UN Convention on the Rights of the Child asserts the inalienable nature of a child's rights while simultaneously accepting that children, by the nature of their physical dependence, require adult carers. Thus Article 5 states:

> States Parties shall respect the responsibilities, rights and duties of parents or, where applicable, the members of the extended family or community as provided for by local custom, legal guardians or other persons legally responsible for the child, to provide in a manner consistent with the evolving capacities of the child, appropriate direction and

guidance in the exercise by the child of the rights recognised in the present Convention.

If dependent children have rights as against their parents there has to be a third party to assert and assist in the achievement of such rights, and it is clear from the Convention that this responsibility must fall to the State. Therefore, any discussion around the issues of children's rights must revolve around the interplay between the rights and responsibilities of the child, of their parents and of the State. Any legislation enacted must, therefore, maintain the fine balance between these sets of rights. Ireland has traditionally maintained the principle of family autonomy which assumes that children are best left to the care and protection of their own parents and extended family, except where they seriously fail in their duty towards them. The Irish Constitution (*Bunreacht na hEireann*) places the family in a central position in Irish society, recognising it as the natural, primary and fundamental unit group of society with "inalienable and imprescriptible" rights (*Bunreacht na hEireann* Article 41.1). While children have rights under the Constitution by virtue of their human existence there is no specific declaration of the rights of the child. However, O'Higgins, J stated in *G. v. An Bord Uchtala* (1980.IR.32):

> The child also has natural rights. Normally these will be safe under the care and protection of its mother. Having been born the child has the right to be fed and to live, to be reared and educated, to have the opportunity of working and of realising his or her full personality and dignity as a human being. These rights . . . must equally be protected and vindicated by the State.

The Constitution Review Group (1996, pp. 336-337) recommended that the Constitution be amended to recognise the rights of the child as separate and independent of those derived from their membership of a family. They consider that any amendment should clearly spell out the rights of the child, incorporating the basic principles of the UN Convention on the Rights of the Child: non-discrimination (Article 2); the best interests of the child must be a primary consideration (Article 3);

every child has the right to life, survival and development (Article 6), and the child's view must be considered and taken into account in all matters affecting him or her (Article 12). Thus, the Constitution Review Group argued that if both the family and the child have rights which must be guaranteed it would be desirable if the Constitution made it clear which of these rights should take precedence in the event of a conflict between the two sets of rights. (Constitution Review Group, 1996, p. 330)

Within the limits of this chapter it is not possible to cover the full range of legislation concerned with children in Ireland. However, discussion of some of the current legislation relating to children in Ireland will be undertaken, in the context of the principles of the UN Convention on the Rights of the Child.

DEFINITION OF A CHILD

Under Article 1 of the UN Convention on the Rights of the Child, a child is defined as being under the age of 18 years. However, in Ireland the definition of a child varies depending on the particular circumstances under consideration. The Age of Majority Act, 1985 provides that majority is attained at the age of 18 years or on marriage and is the age at which citizens have a right to vote. In relation to child protection the Child Care Act, 1991 (S.) changed the definition of a child from under 16 years of age to that of being a person under the age of 18 years other than a person who is or has been married. Inconsistencies arise in other pieces of legislation, such as the Mental Treatment Act, 1945, as amended, which defines a child as a person under the age of 16 years.[1] Outside of marriage, 17 years is the age of consent for both heterosexual and homosexual intercourse. The age of criminal responsibility is 7 years, although there is a rebuttable presumption that a child between 7 and 14 years is incapable of committing an offence. Boys under 16 years and girls under 17 years of age cannot, except in exceptional circumstances, be sent to prisons or places of detention operated by the Department of Justice. In addition, the minimum age for recruitment to the Defence Forces is 15 years, 16 years for apprentices and 17 years for all other entry categories including the Air Corps and the Naval Service provided that parental consent is obtained. Under Social Welfare legislation financial support is provided for children under the age of 16 years with entitlement being extended to ages 18 or 22 according to the nature of the benefit or allowance where the child is in full-time education or undertaking training courses under the State's employment schemes, or has a physical or mental disability. If the legislative framework relating to children is to be in any way coherent it is essential that one standardised definition of a child be used in line with the accepted UN definition of childhood as being under the age of 18 years.

NON-DISCRIMINATION

Article 2 of the UN Convention states that all rights must apply to all children without exception and that the State has an obligation to protect children from any form of discrimination.

Historically, the common law in Ireland discriminated against children born outside marriage, particularly in the areas of succession and maintenance giving no rights in these areas to such children. Such discrimination was ended following the passing of the Status of Children Act, 1987, the main purpose of which was to abolish the concept of illegitimacy and to establish the principle of equal treatment of all children irrespective of the legal relationship between their parents. While it should no longer be necessary to distinguish between marital and non-marital children, in practice it is sometimes necessary to do this. It is mainly in the context of a father's guardianship rights to his child that some differences do remain. While the Children Act, 1997 has amended some aspects of the law in relation to the guardianship rights of certain fathers, in that it makes provision for unmarried parents to be made joint custodians and for unmarried fathers to be granted guardianship rights by agreement, the father of a non-marital child does not automatically become the guardian of his child, although he has a right to apply to the court to be appointed guardian and may become a guardian by agreement of the mother.[2]

One of the issues which arises in relation to this legislation and the relevant case law, is that of the child's right to know their parentage. At the present time children born outside of

marriage have no automatic right to have their paternity established and there is no requirement that the names of both parents be entered on the birth register. In addition, adopted children do not have a right to see their original birth certificate
(pending legislation will allow adopted children over 18 years
to see their birth certificate). The Report of the Constitution Review Group (1996, p. 328) has recommended that the Constitution should be amended to make provision for the child's right
to identity and this has been supported by the Children's Rights
Alliance (Kilkelly, 1997, p. 23).

The UN Committee on the Rights of the Child in its concluding observations on the Irish Report (CRC/C/15/Add.85: 1998)
made a number of criticisms of the Irish Government's response to the implementation of the Convention. Amongst them
were the problems of access to education and health services
experienced by certain minority groups, notably Traveller
children, children from poor families and refugee children. In
addition, it commented on the inadequate measures to ensure
the rights of children with disabilities (Kilkelly, 1998, p. 294).
The Minister for Education announced in November 1998 that
he was introducing a series of measures to assist children with
disabilities to participate in education in mainstream or special
schools and made available substantial financial resources to
address educational disadvantage (Gilligan, 1999, pp. 246-
249). The problem of discrimination and disadvantage for the
children of the Travelling community needs to be addressed
with early implementation of the recommendations of the Report of the Task Force on the Travelling Community (1995). The
Department of Justice, Equality and Law Reform has established
a committee to monitor the implementation of the recommendations of the Task Force on the Travelling Community, although Crowley (1999, p. 259) has argued that previous experience of monitoring committees in this area suggests that they
have little to offer in terms of promoting and supporting progress.

The recently enacted Equal Status Act, 1999 prohibits discrimination in the provision of goods and services and will allow
Ireland to ratify the International Convention on the Elimination

of All Forms of Racial Discrimination, which it signed in 1968. Ireland is currently facing the challenge of rapidly becoming a multi-cultural and multi-racial society with the arrival of refugees and asylum seekers, many of whom are children or unaccompanied minors. In 2000 there were 10,920 who sought asylum in Ireland averaging 910 individuals per month (Woods, 2001). Consequently, there is an increasing need to address the issues of racial integration and non-discrimin-ation. As Kilmurray and Richardson (1994, p. 126) have stated:

> considerable pride is often expressed in the relative homo-geneity of Irish society. In policy terms this can be trans-lated into a denial of the existence of individual or institu-tional racism.

Article 22 of the UN Convention on the Rights of the Child seeks to ensure that States take appropriate measures to ensure that refugee children receive appropriate protection and assistance in line with their human rights. Moran (1999, p. 282) has argued that Irish social policy for refugees has been ad hoc and lacking in strategic management or planning, although he comments that this is beginning to change, with efforts being made to re-spond to the needs of refugees. He states (1999, p. 282):

> Social policy for refugees should not be developed in isola-tion from general social policy. In fact the opposite should prevail, that social policy for refugees should be developed within the same framework as for society generally . . . based on the yardstick that all social policies for refugees respect (their) human rights and human dignity. . . .

The underlying principle of non-discrimination must, therefore, be at the very core of future policy initiatives.

PROTECTION OF CHILDREN

During the past ten years significant reforms have taken place in Ireland in terms of legislation, policies and services estab-lished to promote the protection and welfare of children. The main legislative framework now in place is the Child Care Act, 1991 which was drafted in line with the underlying principles of the UN Convention on the Rights of the Child. Promotion of the welfare of children is the paramount principle which underpins the Act, thus placing responsibility on the health boards to "provide child care and family support services" (S.3.3). Such a requirement is in line with the principle that it is generally in the best interests of a child to be brought up in their own family (S.3.2.c) Therefore, support for families which prevents family breakdown or the necessity to remove a child into the care of the State is of paramount importance.

Article 19 of the UN Convention on the Rights of the Child sets out the State's obligation to protect children from all forms of maltreatment perpetrated by parents or others responsible for their care and to undertake preventive and treatment programmes in this regard. While recognising the rights and duties of parents, the Child Care Act, 1991 enshrines the principle that the welfare of the child must be regarded as "the first and paramount consideration" (S3.2 (bi)). In addition, in accordance with Article 12 of the UN Convention, the Child Care Act, 1991 also clearly states that the court, in making a decision should, "in so far as is practicable, give due consideration, having regard to his age and understanding, to the wishes of the child" (S3 (bii)). Section 25 and Section 26 of the Child Care Act, 1991 are designed to fulfil this aspiration in so far as they empower the court to make a child a party to all or part of care proceedings and, where appropriate, to appoint a solicitor to represent the child (S.25), or to appoint a *guardian ad litem* for a child involved in care proceedings (S.26). In so doing, the legislation allows for a child's views to be heard independent of those of either their parents or the State, in the form of the health board. The National Guidelines for the Protection and Welfare of Children (1999, S8.19.1) also emphasise the importance of including the child in the Child Protection Conference where appropriate, during any investigation of abuse or neglect. In addition, in drawing up the Child Protection Plan the Child Abuse Guidelines state that any plan "is normally drawn up by the health board social worker in consultation with all parties involved, including the child and his or her parents/carers" (S.8.21.1). However, as Lavan (1998, p. 54) and

Whelan (1998) have argued, while involvement in and attendance at child protection conferences and review meetings is a
sound principle, it does not guarantee participation of the family and child. As Lavan states:

> While attendance is being heralded as good practice . . .
> (there is) need for research to answer a range of questions,
> for example whether children and young persons do par-
> ticipate and if so, how do they actually participate?" (1998,
> p. 54).

Part III and Part IV of the Child Care Act, 1991 provides for the
protection of children in emergencies and for care proceedings
to be instituted by the health boards. The grounds on which a
health board may obtain a Care Order (S.18) includes both
physical and sexual abuse and neglect, the definition of which
has, for the first time, been clearly set out in the National
Guidelines for the Protection and Welfare of Children (1999,
Ss.3.2-3.5).

The introduction of Supervision Orders in the Child Care
Act, 1991 (S.19) was an important innovation within the remedies for child protection. This section provides for the supervision of a child who is deemed to be at risk, while remaining
within their own family, thus preventing the necessity of removing the child into care while simultaneously receiving protection from the statutory services. The Report of the Commission on the Family (1998) highlighted the need for policies to
focus on prevention and support for families. It recommended
(*inter alia*) the development of family and community resource
centres, increased emphasis on the support functions of health
services and schools and special supports for vulnerable children and families.

While the Child Care Act, 1991 has provided the framework
for the protection of children, it relies heavily on the adequate
provision of resources designed to support families and promote the welfare of children. In its submission to the United Nations Committee on the Rights of the Child (First National Report of Ireland, 1996, p. 13) the government stated that it has
approved a range of developments to ensure that child protec-

tion services are strengthened and equipped to respond to the needs of children, intensive counselling and treatment is to be made available for victims of child abuse, special therapeutic care is provided for those damaged by abuse and neglect and that locally based services are available to assist families in difficulty. In June 1998 the Government launched 12 pilot projects, named "Springboard Initiatives", with funding of £2.4 million per year over a three-year period, which will focus on the most disadvantaged and troubled families (Gilligan, 1999, p. 240). Within their available resources, most of the health boards have responded to the challenge of providing a range of family support services.[3] However, there are not always sufficient funds available to resource the required facilities adequately. For example, in July 1999 the North Eastern Health Board, during the debate on the report of the Board's Child Care Advisory Committee stated that its resources were totally inadequate to deal with the 35 per cent increase in reported child abuse cases during 1998.

In relation to the protection of children from abuse, the UN Committee in reviewing the Irish submission suggested that appropriate measures should be taken, including legislation, to prohibit and eliminate the use of corporal punishment within the family environment. During 1997 the ISPCC ran an advertising campaign to raise awareness of the need to change the legislation to ban corporal punishment by parents. In 1994 the Law Reform Commission reviewed the issue of "reasonable chastisement" of children by parents and concluded that it would be premature to abolish the common law of chastisement exception before parents had been re-educated to use more appropriate methods of punishment, but they did state that the corporal punishment of children by parents should be abolished as soon as is feasible. The Children's Rights Alliance is also against the physical punishment of children by parents and advocates parent education programmes aimed at discouraging parents from slapping children and providing them with alternative ways of communicating with their children (1997, p. 34). However, there is no indication at present that the Government intends to change the legislation in this regard in the near future.

REPORTING OF CHILD ABUSE

At a national level, successive Programmes for Government have included commitments to the improvement of child care services. In 1996 the Department of Health issued a discussion document on the question of mandatory reporting of child abuse. This was followed by a consultation process and the majority view was against the introduction of a system of mandatory reporting. In 1997 a further document, *Putting Children First — Promoting and Protecting the Rights of Children,* was published which put forward a number of initiatives in place of the introduction of mandatory reporting. There has been considerable government ambivalence in relation to policies on mandatory reporting. As Gilligan has stated (*Irish Times*, 16 February 98):

> The absence of a clear strategy makes us more vulnerable to ad hoc policy lurches, shifts and reversals. Policy veers wildly, with announcements or promises often not followed through. Mandatory reporting of child abuse is a plank of government policy, later it is abandoned and then it stages a comeback as an element of the government's programme.

The UN Committee expressed considerable concern about the lack of mandatory reporting mechanisms for cases of child abuse. This despite the fact that a commitment to mandatory reporting was reintroduced, without any warning, during the oral presentation by the Minister at the hearing of the UN Committee in Geneva in January 1998.

While mandatory reporting has not been introduced other measures have been undertaken. In preparation for the introduction of new guidelines on the reporting of child abuse the Protection for Persons Reporting Child Abuse Act, 1998 was enacted. This act provides immunity from civil liability to any person who reports child abuse reasonably and in good faith to designated officers of health boards or the gardai. It also provides protection for employees who report child abuse and creates a new offence of false reporting of child abuse where a person makes a report of child abuse knowing that it is a false statement. In September 1999 the Government published the National Guidelines for the Protection and Welfare of Children which sets out practice and procedures to assist in the identification and reporting of child abuse. While mandatory reporting has not been introduced, the National Guidelines place great emphasis on the responsibility of professionals, voluntary organisations and individuals to report suspicions of abuse. They stress the importance of reporting on the basis that the safety and well-being of the child or young person must take priority and that any reasonable suspicion of abuse must elicit a response. The National Guidelines are clear and unequivocal on the practice and procedures to be followed in the reporting and assessment of cases. They outline procedures for a Child Protection Notification System, child protection conferences, child protection plans and review meetings. The involvement of parents/carers and children in any decision making process is stressed throughout the document.

As in all new initiatives the provision of adequate resources will be vital for the successful implementation of the National Guidelines. In 1998 the Minister for State admitted that £100 million would be needed over the following three years to put the child care system on a proper footing.

SUBSTITUTE CARE FOR CHILDREN

Despite the emphasis on prevention of family breakdown and attempts to support children within the family, increasing numbers of children are being received into the care of the statutory authorities. On 31 December 1996 (latest available national figures), there were 3,668 children and young people in the care of the health boards (Department of Health and Children, 1996). This represents approximately 3.2 per 1,000 children under 18 years (Gilligan, 1999, p. 235). Over the past 20 years there has been a gradual move from institutional care to community-based substitute care. This is shown by an increase in the numbers from 54 per cent in 1980 to just over 75 per cent of children now in substitute care being placed in foster care. Gilligan (1999, p. 235) has argued that Irish children remain in care far longer than in the US or the UK and he attributes this to limitations in the quality of care planning and reviews, his argument being substantiated by research carried out by the Irish Foster Care Association (Whelan, 1998; Kelleher & Kelleher, 1998).

The United Nations Convention on the Rights of the Child requires, under Article 3.3, that States Parties must ensure that the institutions, services and facilities responsible for the care or protection of children should adhere to appropriate standards, particularly in the areas of safety, health, the number and suitability of their staff as well as competent supervision. Article 9.3 provides for the preservation of the relationship between the child and their parent when a child has been received into the care of the State. The Child Care Act, 1991, Part 8, provides for a scheme for the regulation of children's residential centres. Following a number of investigations into the abuse of children in residential homes and the publication of the Report on the Inquiry into the Operation of Madonna House (Eastern Health Board, 1996), the Child Care (Standards in Children's Residential Centres) Regulations, 1996 and *Guide to Good Practice in Children's Residential Centres* (Department of Health, 1997) are the first comprehensive guidelines for this sector. They are based on the principle of respect for a child's dignity and individuality, the need to preserve the child's sense of identity and the child's right to be heard, together with the principle of partnership between the agencies and professionals and both the child and their parents. There is now a presumption of access for parents, friends and relatives and the health boards are under a statutory duty to provide reasonable access (Child Care Act, 1991, S. 37). Therefore, where children are in residential care there are implications for the residential sector in being party to or helping to facilitate that access. In March 1999 the Government set up a Social Services Inspectorate designed to regulate and advise on the provision of services and facilities within the child care system with its first priority to promote and ensure the development of quality standards in the personal social services.[4]

HOMELESS CHILDREN

Although the UN Convention on the Rights of the Child makes no specific mention in respect of children who are homeless, there are sections that suggest that the child's rights are being infringed if a child is homeless or is a member of a family which is homeless (Article 3(2), Article 9, Article 19(2) and Article 20). The UN Committee stated that it was particularly concerned about the incidence of child poverty and homeless children in the State and encourages it to strengthen measures and programmes for the protection of the rights of the most vulnerable children (Committee on the Rights of the Child, paragraph .21) Section 5 of the Child Care Act, 1991 places a statutory responsibility on health boards to provide appropriate accommodation for homeless children. Despite this requirement the provision of services to meet the needs of these children has been very slow and a number of cases have been taken in the courts to ensure that the Eastern Health Board fulfils its obligations under the Act (O'Sullivan, 1995; O'Sullivan, 1996; Kelleher & Kelleher, 1998). The numbers of children classified as homeless remains high, Focus Ireland reporting contact with up to 4,000 homeless young people and adults per year. Children leaving residential care have been found to be particularly vulnerable to homelessness because of the lack of adequate after-care services (Kelleher & Kelleher, 1998; Houghton, Kelleher & Kelleher, Chapter 4, this volume). It is obvious that this is an area which needs immediate attention and the response of placing homeless children in bed and breakfast accommodation is clearly inadequate.

ADOPTION

Under the Adoption Acts, 1952–1998, Ireland operates a full adoption system. On the making of an adoption order a natural parent loses all legal rights over the child and these are transferred to the adoptive parents. Legal adoption is permanent. The principle that the child is the most important person in the adoption process is fully embodied in the law and any decisions are based on the principle of the best interests of the child.

Ireland participated in the preparation of the Hague Convention on Protection and Co-operation in respect of Inter-country Adoption in 1993, which takes into account the principles set out in the UN Convention on the Rights of the Child. In 1998, the Law Reform Commission reported on the implementation of the Hague Convention the purpose of which was to make recommendations on the implementation of the Convention in Ireland. The Report endorses the belief that the entire inter-country adoption process must be child-centred in that at all stages the child's interests must be paramount. They state:

> The aim of inter-country adoption is to find the best parents for the child and not to find the best child for adoptive parents (1998, pp.2-3).

Furthermore, the Report recognises that inter-country adoption represents a subsidiary means of child care and that other options such as the child being cared for by relatives or in a family within their own country should be the primary approach (O'Brien and Richardson, 1999, pp. 9-12). Ireland is currently bringing forward legislation to enable the Hague Convention to be ratified.

CHILDREN IN CONFLICT WITH THE LAW

Several articles of the UN Convention deal with children who have come into conflict with the law (Articles 37-40). The Irish system of juvenile justice has been widely criticised for its lack of emphasis on prevention and its emphasis on a justice rather than a welfare model (Burke et al., 1981; Ring, 1991, O'Malley, 1992, O'Sullivan, 1998). In addition, the UN Committee was critical of the low age of criminal responsibility. The publication of the Children Bill, 1999 (which has superseded the Children Bill, 1996) represents an attempt to update the legislation on juvenile justice. The age of criminal responsibility is to be raised to 12 years with a rebuttable presumption that a child between the age of 12 and 14 is incapable of committing an offence.

The most important aspect of the Children Bill, 1999 is that it changes the emphasis to prevention and diversion from the criminal justice system in an attempt to move away from punishment and detention. It therefore proposes a comprehensive range of community-based sanctions with an emphasis on the needs of the child rather than the child's actions. For example, the introduction of Special Care Orders imposes a statutory duty on health boards to institute proceedings where the behaviour of the child is such that it poses a real and substantial risk to their health, safety, development or welfare and the child is unlikely to receive appropriate care and protection without the order of the court. These orders could, therefore, be used where a child is seen as being at risk of becoming involved in criminal activity. The Garda Diversionary Scheme is to be placed on a statutory footing and the scheme will aim to divert children who accept responsibility for offences from the courts. The Bill provides for the introduction of the Family Welfare Conference, a mechanism for early intervention at an interagency level for children at risk. It also introduces a range of orders to widen the range of dispositional alternatives available to the court, and detention can only be imposed as a last resort.[5] The Bill places an emphasis on parental responsibility by introducing Parental Supervision Orders (Ss 111-112), giving the Courts power to order a parent to pay compensation and also order a parent to enter a recognisance to exercise proper and adequate control over the child (Ss 114). For offenders under the age of 16 years detention is for a maximum of three years and must be in a children's detention school.

The original Bill (Children Bill, 1996) was received positively by professionals involved in the area of juvenile justice. As Tutt commented (1996, p. 8), "it is a serious attempt to implement the principles of restorative justice which invites and enables victims, offenders and the community to repair some of the injustices resulting from crime". It is an opportunity for children to be assessed and helped according to "needs" not "deeds" and for Ireland to move towards a welfare model of juvenile justice which is in line with a children's rights perspective.

CHILD ABDUCTION

Article 11 of the UN Convention on the Rights of the Child states that countries "shall take measures to combat the illicit transfer

and non-return of children abroad". In 1980 the Hague Conference on Private International Law recognised the increasing
problem of the abduction of children across international
boundaries. In order to provide for the prompt return of children to their country of residence the Convention on the Civil
Aspects of International Child Abduction was adopted. In addition, the European Convention on Recognition and Enforcement
of Decisions Concerning Custody of Children and on Restora-
tion of Custody of Children (the Luxembourg Agreement) was
adopted. The purpose of the Hague Convention is to resolve the
problem of child abduction by providing for the immediate return of the child. The Luxembourg Convention recognises and
enforces custody decisions made in other jurisdictions. Both
Conventions have been given legislative backing in the Child
Abduction and Enforcement of Custody Orders Act, 1991. The
removal of a child from the place of its habitual residence constitutes a breach of the custody rights of the parent who continues to reside in that place. However, children have a right of
access to both parents where they reside with only one of them
and concerns have been expressed by the Children's Rights
Alliance (1997, p. 30) regarding this issue. They argue that the
non-custodial parent may have difficulty in accessing the court
remedies available which can militate against them obtaining
access to their children.

Such difficulties can also arise for parents seeking access to
children who are in the care of the health boards. Although the
Child Care Act, 1991 requires health boards to facilitate reasonable access to a child in its care, such access may only be
provided on an irregular and inconsistent basis due to lack of
resources. This can frustrate attempts to maintain relationships
between the child and both parents, possibly militating against
rehabilitation and return to the family home.

CONCLUSIONS

The UN Convention on the Rights of the Child is a document
which has enormous potential in the protection of children
throughout the world. However, it is of limited value if the compliance of countries cannot be assessed. UNICEF (1998) is cur-

rently developing a number of indicators against which the performance of countries can be assessed. At this stage, their preliminary work has highlighted five indicators. Three indicators target the home environment and two focus on monitoring out of home care.

In the first category, the home environment, they suggest:

- Monitoring changes in family structures and teen parenthood on the basis that teen parenting correlates with lower levels of educational attainment for mothers, poverty and poorer prospects of employment (Moore, 1993)

- Monitoring the proportion of children living in poverty

- Monitoring the level of investment in children by the State on the basis of what proportion of GDP is spent in supporting children and families.

In the category of monitoring out-of-home care the indicators suggested are:

- The rate per 100,000 children under 18 living in institutional or foster care

- Measuring the quality of out-of-home care.

It is argued that by choosing indicators it is intended they should have a significant political impact. By monitoring teenage pregnancy it raises it as a social issue which is intended to lead to attempts to reduce the numbers by introducing prevention programmes. Asking countries if they have independent inspection of children's homes can actively encourage awareness for the improvement in standards. Finally, calculations on the percentage of GDP spent on children highlights the importance of adequate resources to meet the needs of children.

It is beyond the scope of this paper to undertake an in-depth assessment of these criteria within the Irish context. However, even a brief analysis can highlight the importance of such criteria. For example, most of the research on poverty in Ireland has highlighted the issue of child poverty. In particular, the *Living in Ireland Surveys* (ESRI, 1987–1998) have indicated that while there has been a drop in the percentage of children living in poverty over the last decade, a significant number of children still live in households below the 60 per cent relative income poverty line (Nolan, Chapter 11 of this volume). The number of children in the care of the State has been steadily rising and Gilligan (1999, p. 235) has calculated that on the basis of the latest available figures in 1996 approximately 3.2 per 1,000 children under 18 years are in the care of the health boards. While the total number of births to teenagers in Ireland has not changed significantly in the past 20 years the number of births to single teenage mothers has been rising. In 1998 almost 6 per cent of births were to women under 20 years of age of which 94 per cent were unmarried (CSO, 1999). The Eastern Health Board report on their Teenage Health Initiative (Acton and Hynes, 1998) highlighted the need for programmes to reduce teenage pregnancy. The shortfall between the demand for services in the child care sector and the resources available is rising. The residential care sector has been unregulated and has received much criticism (Focus Ireland, 1996; Department of Health and Children, 1996). The UN Committee on the Rights of the Child, in its concluding observations on Ireland (CRC/C/15/Add.85 1998) drew attention to a number of subjects of concern:

- Lack of a comprehensive national policy on children's rights and adequate promotion of the Convention, and adequate procedures to hear the views of children

- Welfare policies which do not adequately reflect the child rights base approach

- The lack of an independent inspectorate and an office of an Ombudsman for Children

- The low age limits set in the domestic legislation, in particular the age of criminal responsibility together with the treatment of children deprived of their liberty

- The difficulties faced by children from vulnerable and disadvantaged groups

- The level of child poverty and homelessness

- The disadvantaged situation of children born to unmarried parents

- Lack of adequate programmes addressing adolescent health problems.

Recent responses to these criticisms by the Irish Government gives some indication of the value of monitoring the performance of countries. In July 1999 the Government announced its intention to bring forward legislation for the appointment of an independent Ombudsman for children. A Child Care Commission, under the chairmanship of a member of the judiciary, has been set up to hear from victims of child abuse and the National Children's Strategy (2000) was published. The Strategy has three overall goals:

- To give children a voice in matters which affect them in accordance with their age and maturity

- To better understand children's lives through evaluation, research and information on their needs, rights and the effectiveness of services

- To provide quality supports and services to promote all aspects of their development.

The Strategy also provides a set of values which underpin it, and operational principles to guide action in pursuit of the national goals, together with new structures to ensure its implementation. These involve partnerships within and between the State, the voluntary and community sector and families and children themselves.

One final issue needs to be raised in relation to the framework for child care services in Ireland. Planning to meet the needs of children cannot be undertaken in a vacuum. The need for basic research on Irish children is vital if legislation and services which meet their needs and support their rights are to be implemented. Over many years calls have been made for a longitudinal study of children in Ireland (Richardson, 1985; McKeown, 1991; Morris, 1998). In December 2000, as part of the National Children's Strategy, the Government initiated the first stage of a longitudinal study of children by commissioning a design brief for such a study.

The National Children's Strategy (2000, p. 6) states that the publication of the Strategy is a major initiative to advancing, in Ireland, the implementation of the UN Convention on the Rights of the Child. At the present time much of the Strategy is aspirational. It will be vital that its implementation is closely monitored to ensure that the rights of children in Ireland are fulfilled and that every effort is made to enhance children's status and improve their quality of life.

Bibliography

Acton, M. and Hynes, M. (1998) *Teenage Health Initiative: Report and Evaluation of a Pilot Project aimed at Reducing Teenage Pregnancies in the Eastern Health Board Area, 1997-1998,* Dublin: Eastern Health Board

Bunreacht na hÉireann (1937) *Constitution of Ireland*, Dublin: Government Publications

Burke, H, Carney, C, and Cook, G. (1981) *Youth and Justice: Young Offenders in Ireland*, Dublin: Turoe Press

Burman, E. (1996) "Local, Global or Globalized? Child Development and International Child Rights Legislation" in *Childhood*, Vol. 3, No. 1, February, pp. 45-64

Burns, M. (1999) "Advancing the Rights of the Child" in *Poverty Today* September/October, No. 45

Committee on the Rights of the Child (1998) *Concluding Observations of the Committee on the Rights of the Child: Ireland*, Geneva: United Nations CRC/C/15Add.85

Cousins, M. (1996) *Seen and Heard: Promoting and Protecting Children's Rights in Ireland*, Dublin: Children's Rights Alliance

Crowley, N. (1999) "Travellers and Social Policy" in Quin, S., Kennedy, P., O'Donnell, A. and Kiely, G. (Eds) *Contemporary Irish Social Policy,* Chapter 11, Dublin: UCD Press

Department of Health and Children, *Report of the Enquiry into the Operation of Madonna House* (1996), Dublin: Government Publications

Department of Social, Community and Family Affairs, Report of the Commission on the Family (1998) *Strengthening Families for Life*, Dublin: Government Publications

First National Report of Ireland (1996) *Ireland: United Nations Convention on the Rights of the Child*, Dublin: Government Publications

Focus Ireland (1996) *Focus on Residential Child Care in Ireland*, Dublin: Focus Ireland

Gilligan, R. (1999) "Child Welfare Review 1998" in McCashin A., and O'Sullivan, E., (Eds) *Irish Social Policy Review* 1999, Administration, Vol. 47, No. 2, Summer

Harwin, J. and Forrester, D. (1999) "Measuring Child Rights around the World: The Potential of Global Indicators to Monitor the UN Convention on the Rights of the Child" *Representing Children*, Vol. 12, No. 2, pp. 121-135

Johnston, H. (1999) "Poverty in Ireland" in Kiely, G., O'Donnell, A., Kennedy, P and Quin, S (Eds) *Irish Social Policy in Context*, Dublin: UCD Press

Kelleher, P and Kelleher, C. (1998) *Out on Their Own – Young People Leaving Care in Ireland*, Dublin: Focus Point

Kilkelly, U. (1998) "In the best interests of the Child? An evaluation of Ireland's performance before the UN committee on the Rights of the Child" *Irish Law Times*, 19, pp. 293-300

Kilkelly, U. (1997) *Small Voices: Vital Rights*, Dublin: Children's Rights Alliance

Kilmurray, A. and Richardson, V. (1994) *Focus on Children: A Blueprint for Action*, Belfast and Dublin: Focus on Children

Lavan, A. (1998) "Social Work in Ireland", in Shardlow, S. and Payne, M., (eds) *Contemporary Issues in Social Work — Western Europe* Chapter 4, Aldershot: Arena

Law Reform Commission Consultation Paper on the Implementation of the Hague Convention on Protection of Children and Co-operation in Respect of Intercountry Adoption 1993 (1998), Dublin: Law Reform Commission

McKeown, K. (1991) *The Case for a Longitudinal Study of Children in Ireland*, Dublin: Combat Poverty Agency

Moore, K. (1993) *Teenage Childbearing: A Pragmatic Perspective*, Washington DC: Child Trends Inc.

Moran, J. (1999) "Refugees and Social Policy" in Quin, S., Kennedy, P., O'Donnell, A. and Kiely, G. (eds) *Contemporary Irish Social Policy*, Chapter 12, Dublin: UCD Press

Morris, M.(1998) *See How they Grow! The Case for a National Longitu-dinal Study of Children in Ireland*, Dublin: Treoir

National Children's Strategy (November 2000), *Our Children — Their Lives*, Dublin: Government Publications

National Guidelines for the Protection and Welfare of Children (1999), *Children First*, Dublin: Department of Health and Children

O'Brien, V. and Richardson, V. (1999) *Towards a Standardised Frame-work for Inter-Country Adoption Assessment Procedures*, Dublin: Gov-ernment Publications

O'Malley, T. (1992) "The United Nations Convention on the Rights of the Child: A Challenge for Ireland" in Berwick, P. and Burns, M. (eds) *The Rights of the Child*, Dublin: Council for Social Welfare

O'Sullivan, E. (1995) "Section 5 of the Child Care Act, 1991 and Youth Homelessness" in Ferguson, H. and Kenny, P. (eds) *On Behalf of the Child: Child Welfare, Child Protection and the Child Care Act 1991*, Dublin: A&A Farmer

O'Sullivan, E. (1996) "Adolescents Leaving Care or Leaving Home and Child Care Provision in Ireland and the UK: a Critical View" in Hill, M. and Aldgate, J. (eds) *Child Welfare Services: Developments in Law, Policy, Practice and Research*, London: Jessica Kingley Publishers

O'Sullivan, E. (1998) "Juvenile Justice and the Regulation of the Poor: Restored to Virtue, Society and to God" in Bacik, I. and O'Connell, M. (eds) *Crime and Poverty in Ireland*, Dublin: Round Hall, Sweet & Max-well

Report of the Constitution Review Group (1996), Dublin: Government Publications

Report of the Task Force on the Travelling Community (1995) Dublin: Government Publications

Richardson, V. (1985) *Whose Children?* Dublin: Family Studies Unit, UCD

Ring, M.E. (1991) "Custodial Treatment of Young Offenders", *Irish Criminal Law Journal*, Vol. 1, No. 1, pp. 59-67

Shatter, A. (1997) *Shatter's Family Law*, Dublin: Butterworths (Fourth Edition)

Tutt, N. (1996) "The Search for Justice: Home and Away" in *The Chil-dren's Bill 1966: Issues and Perspectives*, Dublin: Children's Legal Centre

UNICEF (1998) *Indicators for global monitoring of child rights*, International meeting sponsored by UNICEF February 1998 Summary Report and Background Papers, Division of Evaluation, Policy and Planning, New York

Whelan, P. (1998) "Care Plans — Are they happening? Are they working? Are you part of them?" *Newsletter of the Irish Foster Care Association*, No. 4

Woods, M. (2001) "Seeking asylum in Ireland: Comparative figures for asylum seekers and refugees in Europe and Ireland in 1999 and 2000 with a detailed breakdown for the Eastern Regional Health Authority", Dublin: Social Science Research Centre, UCD

Notes

---

[1] The Government has proposed in a White Paper on a new Mental Health Act to define a child for the purpose of mental health legislation as a person who has not yet attained their 18th birthday unless they have been married. This would bring the definition in line with child care legislation and with the age of majority.

[2] For a detailed discussion of relevant case law in relation to the rights of the father to apply for guardianship of his child born outside marriage see Shatter 1997, p. 982-986

[3] Under section 8 of the Child Care Act each health board is required to publish an annual report reviewing the child and family support services provided by them. These reports give details of the provision within the health board area and plans for the future.

[4] The functions of the Inspectorate are:

- Inspection of health board residential homes for children under the Child Care Act, 1991
- Monitoring of the organisation, operation and management of child care services
- Evaluation of the quality and responsiveness of services as experienced by users and carers and to improve standards
- Provision of professional advice and expertise to departments on the formulation, implementation and review of child care policy and the effective and efficient delivery of services
- Development of strategies to give effect to recommendations of relevant enquiry and review reports (Department of Health and Children, 1999)

[5] For example, Day Centre Orders, (Ss118-123) Suitable Person or Mentor Orders (Ss129-132) and Restriction on Movement Orders (Ss 133-136).

Chapter 3

"Mercy unto Thousands" — Constructing the Institutional Child

Eoin O'Sullivan

INTRODUCTION

On 11 May 1999, the Taoiseach, Mr. Bertie Ahern, TD made the following statement:

> On behalf of the State and of all citizens of the State, the Government wishes to make a sincere and long overdue apology to the victims of childhood abuse for our collective failure to intervene, to detect their pain, to come to their rescue.

Less than a fortnight later, the then Minister for Education, Micheál Martin TD, announced the establishment of a Commission on Childhood Abuse, chaired by Ms. Justice Mary Laffoy of the High Court, and in May 2000 the *Commission to Inquire into Child Abuse Act* was enacted. These dramatic developments followed a period of sustained debate on the treatment of children in residential institutions, funded and regulated by the State, but managed primarily by Catholic religious congregations. The treatment of children in such institutions came to the forefront most publicly with the showing of a documentary in early 1996 on the recollections of a former pupil in St. Vincent's Industrial School in Dublin (more commonly known as Goldenbridge) during the 1950s. The programme, entitled *Dear Daughter*, focused on the experience of Christine Buckley who alleged that the children in this institution were subjected to a regime of cruelty and neglect. This was followed in 1999 with a three part documentary shown on RTE entitled *States of Fear*. This was an in-depth analysis of the reformatory and industrial school system in Ireland. It generated considerable debate and led to the government apology mentioned at the beginning of the paragraph. In addition, the religious congregations that managed these institutions offered apologies to those who had been incarcerated in their institutions. In late 1999, a book based partly on the *States of Fear* series, but including more detailed information on the system was published which generated a heated debate.[1]

In one of the few theoretical accounts of the development of the child welfare system in Ireland, Denis O'Sullivan argues that it was only from the late 1960s that a "social risk" model of child care, which had influenced policy for the previous hundred years, became displaced by a more developmental model of child care. Prior to this period, child care intervention was viewed as "a means of social control rather than of individual fulfilment".[2] The primary facets of the emerging developmental model were a disenchantment with institutionalisation and the need to move beyond a narrow interpretation of child care. This chapter aims to explore the construction of this institutional mode of regulating children in Ireland. It focuses primarily on the first half of the 19th century and argues that it was in this period that the template of child welfare provision that was remarkably resilient until recently was stamped. The chapter firstly examines the relationship between organised religion and the development of welfare services, secondly, discusses the growth of the Catholic Church in Ireland, and thirdly, explores the role of the Catholic Church in Ireland in relation to the provision of services for children. It concludes that the longevity of the system of institutional provision of child welfare services provided by religious congregations in Ireland resulted from a heterogeneous ensemble of strategies and techniques, often not intentionally correlated but in effect intermeshed, which created the conditions that allowed for the construction and dominance of institutional regimes as the pre-eminent form of intervention into the lives of children in Ireland for most of the 19th and 20th centuries.

RELIGION AND WELFARE

The importance of organised religion in the development of welfare services cross-nationally has been identified by a number of authors.[3] James, for example, has argued that "non-profit schools, hospitals, and other social services are usually founded by organised religious groups, particularly proselytising religions, and others as defensive mechanisms". The rationale for religious organisations entering these particular fields of social activity is that their objective is to maximise adherents to the faith. Thus, schools, hospitals and other social services are key sites for the socialisation of populations and acquisition of desired moral norms.[4]

A similar line of argument has been developed by Valverde, who in her analysis of moral reform in English Canada between 1885 and 1925 argued that the objective of philanthropy was to seek moral profit or moral capital in the long term. Drawing on the work of Bourdieu, she argues that philanthropy, as opposed to charity, was concerned with investing in economic and cultural capital in order that the poor achieve moral gain, rather than giving money without being interested in how it is used, which she argues was characteristic of charity. The philanthropic agencies concerned with maximising moral capital should be viewed as agencies of moral regulation, who are concerned with "the maximisation of both the individual moral capital of the recipients and the aggregate moral capital of the nation state".[5] This work draws on the earlier analysis of Corrigan and Sayer on the formation of the English State.[6] However, their analysis focused primarily on the role of the State in the application of moral regulation, ignoring the multiplicity of agencies and authorities involved in the shaping of the conduct of individuals, families and groups. In addition, their analysis overemphasises the unity of the State.[7]

However, although the complexity of the State has been identified and its overlapping functions with other agencies noted, the complexity of philanthropy and religion has not yet been subjected to the same degree of historical interrogation. While work has been conducted on the differences between religions in the organisation and form of services provided, little work has been conducted on the differences in emphasis and delivery within particular organised religions. This chapter argues that, just as it is problematic to ascribe to the State a unified set of policies and practices, it is equally problematic to ascribe to the Catholic Church (and, no doubt, other churches) a unity and common *modus operandi* in the organisation, structure and delivery of welfare services. Although the end objective may be similar — the rescue of children from poverty and vice, or in the language used above, imbuing them with moral capital — a range of different tactics, often conflictual, are evident in achieving these objectives. This observation supports the assertion by Keogh that:

> The temptation to view Catholicism as a monolith is not a supportable historical proposition. It is important therefore to stress the existence of the different currents in Irish Catholicism.[8]

However, the thesis put forward by James does not assist us in explaining the variations within religions in the form of service developed, nor does it necessarily explain the longevity of such service providers when the conditions that led to the involvement and development of services by religious agencies disintegrated. With the advent of independence from Britain in 1921, Ireland became a predominantly Catholic country. Examining welfare service provision in Ireland in the latter half of the 20th century, one would be forced to conclude that the James' thesis had little applicability. However, by exploring the origins of such services, a clearer picture emerges. Valverde's concept of moral capital or moral profit assists us in explaining the persistence of particular forms of interventions by religious agencies, when the original stimulus for such actions has eroded. Religious agencies are concerned with profit, although not with monetary profit. They are concerned with the production of moral individuals, who, through the mechanisms of education, propaganda and enlightenment, would contribute to the moral capital of the nation.[9] However, Ruonavaara has argued:

> Why introduce a new concept; why not stick to good old "social control" claiming that moral regulation is only one form of "social control", the latter being "conventionally defined as control of behavior exercised in a community in order to make the members of the community conform to the dominant norms.[10]

However, one justification for utilising the concept of moral regulation rather than social control is that it avoids the state-centred manner in which the concept of social control has been largely utilised. Nor does it presuppose that power, whether in or out of the state, is a top-down and zero-sum process.

This chapter aims to explore the development of the system of child welfare in Ireland and attempts to explain the longevity of the system of institutional provision of child welfare services provided by religious congregations in Ireland. It traces the early development of orphan societies, their colonisation by Catholic religious congregations and their eventual incorporation into the system of reformatory and industrial schools established in the mid-19th century.[11]

THE GROWTH OF THE CATHOLIC CHURCH IN IRELAND

At the beginning of the 19th century, the Catholic Church in Ireland was highly fragmented and disorganised. Adherence to Catholic rules and rituals was minimal, particularly in the west and north of the country; the rank and file clergy were undisciplined and only a small number of religious congregations were active. One hundred years later, a highly centralised, disciplined Catholic Church is evident. Attendance at mass and adherence to the rituals of the Church was virtually universal amongst the Catholic population and earlier folk beliefs eroded. Irish Catholics had become Romanised. Through a phenomenal growth in native religious congregations of men and women, in addition to a number of congregations imported, primarily from France,[12] a comprehensive range of social services were in place, particularly in the fields of educa-

tion, health and child welfare.[13] Not only did these congregations dominate particular fields of welfare service provision in
Ireland, but also exported their regimes to America, Canada
and Australia.[14]

For example, there were only six female religious orders
with 120 nuns in eleven houses in 1800. By 1900, there were 35
religious orders and congregations with over 8,000 nuns in 368
houses,[15] with many established specifically to provide services to destitute women and children.[16] The Sisters of Mercy, for
example, had established 168 convents in Ireland by 1881.[17]
The role of the Hierarchy in instigating new female religious
congregations was highlighted by the biographer of Archbishop Murray of Dublin who argued that Murray found:

> at his accession to the prelacy, but one strictly regular
> community of females consecrated to God — he has left to
> his successors an additional TWENTY-NINE! (sic) — in all,
> thirty communities of holy women, each convent of them
> containing a numerous sisterhood, living, moving, breath-
> ing, day and night, for God and God only.[18]

The Christian Brothers also underwent an enormous growth
spurt during the 19th century. In 1831 they had only 45 Brothers, which had increased to almost 1,000 by 1900. By the 1960s,
there were 4,000 Christian Brothers in Ireland. This of course
was not unique to Ireland. In France over 400 female congregations and orders were founded or re-founded between 1800
and 1880 and attracted over 200,000 members during that period. In England, by 1900 there were some 600 convent houses
with between 8,000 and 10,000 sisters compared to only "a
score of nuns living covertly in two illegal houses" 130 years
earlier.[19]

Despite the centrality of the Catholic Church in Irish life
since the mid-19th century and its dominance in the educational
and health services in particular, much of the limited existing
research has tended to analyse its role in an abstract and total-
ising manner. Analyses of "the Catholic Church" in Ireland ig-
nore the significant differences that existed between agencies
linked to the church in Ireland. More importantly, the rationale

for agencies of the Catholic Church to become and remain involved in particular areas of welfare provision has yet to be fully explained and, as Cousins has argued, "the relationship between (Catholic) Church (and the State) is much more subtle than is sometimes portrayed".[20]

THE COLONISATION OF ORPHAN SOCIETIES

The first orphanage for Catholic children known to the author was the Patrician Orphan Society established in Dublin in 1750.[21] This orphanage was apparently established in reaction to the:

> appalling state of the Foundling Hospital (which) disgusted one decent minded unmarried mother who left her child at the door of "Adam and Eve'" chapel, off Cook Street. Some of the traders of the district combined to look after the foundling's welfare. The news spread abroad that Catholic foundlings were being taken charge of in Cook Street, and the deposited increased in numbers. The Charitable Catholics realising the advantage to the Church of the possession of the Catholic babes, began to deposit pennies for the foundlings in the poor box of "Adam and Eve" chapel. The pennies became so numerous that the Franciscan fathers formed a society for the protection of the foundlings, and called it the Patrician Orphan Society. It had for its motto: "Lend an Ear of Pity to the melancholy Tale of the Poor, and Pay with Cheerfulness the debt of Charity.[22]

The number of orphan societies grew during the latter half of the 18th and early 19th century, and particularly in Dublin after the Cholera epidemic of 1831-32.[23] The majority of these orphan societies were parish-based and were established and managed by local committees consisting of the parish priest and other notable locals,[24] often with the express aim of rescuing children from proselytising agencies.[25] The majority of these "orphanages" were non-institutional in orientation, rather they boarded-out orphan (or in contemporary parlance, foster care) children.[26] For example, the Malachean Orphan Society founded in 1822 adopted a system of boarding-out the children in the vicinity of Clondalkin, "under the care of decent, honest, virtuous housekeepers."[27] This system of boarding-out appeared to have operated for the majority of the "orphanages" under the management of the parish or lay bodies.

The small number of orphanages operated by the Religious Congregations, however, tended to operate an institutional form of care for the children under their supervision. One key exception to this rule was the St. Brigid's orphanage, established in 1857 by Margaret Aylward, which was to operate until the early 1970s:[28]

> The Association of St. Brigid in the few years of its existence has saved a large number of children from the fangs of proselytism. It has been able to perform so great a work of charity because its funds, though small, are managed with great economy. No expense is incurred in buildings, or for the rent of houses, or for a staff of masters and mistresses. . . . The poor orphans are sent to the country, and placed under the care of honest and religious families, who, for five or six pounds for each per annum, bring them up in the humble manner in which the peasants of Ireland are accustomed to live. In this way the orphans acquire that love for God, and that spirit of religion, for which the country is distinguished, and, at the same time, they become strong and vigorous like other inhabitants of the country, and are prepared to bear the hardships to which persons of their class are generally exposed in life. Were these children educated in large orphanages and in the smoky air of the city, they would perhaps be weak and delicate, incapable of bearing hard work, and likely to fail in the day of trial.[29]

With the growth of both male and female religious orders, particularly indigenous orders established to educate and care specifically for the children of the poor from the 1820s onwards, many of the parish or lay body orphanages were absorbed by these orders, amalgamated or they simply ceased to operate.[30]

For example, the female orphanage established in Dublin by Teresa Mulally in 1771 was taken over by the Presentation Sisters when they moved to Dublin in 1794.[31] In 1805, the Sisters of St. Clare took over the management of an orphanage that had been managed by a Ms. Maria O'Brien in Hendrick Street in

Dublin.[32] However, three female religious orders, in particular the Sisters of Mercy, the Irish Sisters of Charity and the Daughters of Charity, were to the forefront in establishing new orphanages or colonising existing orphanages and adapting them to fit their model of intervention with children of the poorer classes. For example, St. Joseph's Orphanage in Mountjoy Street, which was established by "two humble tradesmen in 1770", was taken over by the Sisters of Charity in 1866.[33] The Franciscan Orphan Society was amalgamated with the Society of St. Vincent De Paul Orphanage in Glasnevin in 1859 which, in turn, was to become managed by the Irish Christian Brothers in 1863.[34] The Sisters of Mercy in Cork city, in addition to establishing their own orphanage in 1839, took over the management of a further orphanage for "children of gentle birth who were left destitute" in 1877.[35] Prior to assuming full responsibility for the orphanage, the St. Patrick's Male and Female Orphan Asylum provided the sum of "eight pounds a year, per head, for their food and clothing" for 50 orphans placed under the care of the Sisters.[36]

Thus, by the mid-1850s the majority of the parish-based orphanages which had utilised the boarding-out or "outdoor orphanage" method of rescuing orphan and deserted children had been largely phased out. Virtually all orphanages were now operated by religious congregations,[37] primarily female congregations, and operated on an institutional model of "child welfare". Others at various stages closed their own institutions, but continued to provide funds to accommodate children in various other institutions. Very few new orphanages were established in the 20th century, but those that were, were managed by religious orders and usually instigated by the local bishop or archbishop.[38] Those orphanages that continued to operate received no funding from the State and depended on funding from relations of the children placed in the orphanages and on charity sermons.[39] Although a large number of these orphanages were certified as industrial schools following the Industrial Schools Act, 1868, a small number continued to operate outside of the State subsidised scheme of institutional child "welfare".[40]

Thus, both forms of institutional intervention in the lives of children were to co-exist until the 1960s, catering for quite distinct classes of children.[41] The total number of children catered for in both Catholic orphanages and those catering for children of other denominations in any given year is difficult to ascertain, and with the passing of the Industrial Schools Act in 1868, the numbers would have dropped substantially.

LEGISLATING INSTITUTIONALISM

The introduction of the reformatory and industrial schools legislation, in 1858 and 1868 respectively, further bolstered the institutional nature of the Irish child welfare apparatus.[42] By 1871 there were 51 certified industrial schools which grew to 70 by 1900 with a capacity for nearly 8,000 children. All the Catholic industrial schools were operated by religious orders,[43] many of them brought to Ireland specifically for the purpose of operating such schools.[44] For example, the Sisters of St. Louis were invited to Ireland on the request of Dr. McNally, the Bishop of Clogher, to establish a reformatory school for girls and later an industrial school.[45] Likewise, The Sisters of Our Lady of Charity came to Ireland in 1853 at the invitation of a priest of the Catholic Archdiocese of Dublin to run St. Mary's Magdalen Asylum in Dublin, and subsequently operated a reformatory school and a number of industrial schools.[46] The De La Salle Brothers were invited to Sligo from France by Bishop Gillooly of Elphin to establish what turned out to be a short-lived industrial school.[47] However, in the majority of cases it was the native congregations of brothers and sisters who managed the schools on the request of the local bishop. In Galway, Dr. McEvilly, Bishop of Galway, invited, initially, the Patrician Brothers to manage the newly built Industrial School for Catholic Boys in Salthill, and in 1876 he requested the Irish Christian Brothers to take over responsibility for the school.[48]

Many of the existing orphanages which had been either colonised by the female religious or established in response to requests from local bishops received certification. For example, on 29 September 1842, the Sisters of Mercy in Wexford had accepted management of an orphanage which had been founded by the Redmond and Talbot families of the town in 1829. It was certified as St. Michael's Industrial School for 106 places in 1869.[49] An orphanage established in Kinsale in 1848 by the Sisters of Mercy was certified as an industrial school in 1869, and their orphanage in Birr, established in 1865, was certified as an industrial school in 1870.[50] The Poor Clare Sisters established an orphanage in Cavan in 1865 on the request of Dr. Browne, Bishop of Kilmore, which was certified as an industrial school in 1869.[51] In Thurles, the Sisters of the Presentation established an orphanage in 1868, which was certified as an industrial school in 1869.[52] Likewise in Limerick, the Sisters of Mercy, having been invited to establish a foundation in 1838 by Dr. Ryan, Bishop of the Diocese of Limerick, established an orphanage in 1852, for which the Superior of the orphanage wrote to the Inspector of Reformatory and Industrial Schools seeking certification, which she duly obtained.

However, not all existing orphanages were certified. For example, the Sisters of Mercy orphanages in Castletownbere, Navan, Kells and Kilrush were refused certificates for industrial schools.[53] Their orphanage in Ennis, completed in 1875 for the reception of 100 children, was granted an industrial school certificate in 1880, and then only for 40 children.[54]

Likewise, efforts to establish new industrial schools were often rejected by the Office of the Inspector of Industrial and Reformatory Schools. The Sisters of Mercy were refused certification of a premises in Clondalkin, Co. Dublin for a girls' industrial school. The Inspector argued that there were sufficient places for girls and urged the Sisters to provide a school for junior boys. The Sisters agreed, but shortly afterwards closed the school.[55] Likewise, an attempt to establish an industrial school for boys in Clifden, Co. Galway, despite a vigorous campaign, was eventually rejected.

As the number of industrial schools rapidly grew, extensions to their certificates were frequently requested, a process that continued into the 20th century.[56] In some cases these extensions were granted, but by 1880 attempts were being made by the Office of the Chief Secretary to curtail the growth in numbers committed to industrial schools. From the 1870s onward, State expenditure on industrial schools was limited to a figure fixed by the Treasury from time to time; so, in addition to paying only for the number of children within the certified limit, it was decided to pay no grant whatever in relation to children under six — although no minimum age for committal was fixed by statute. The principle underlying this restriction on funding was that these children should be dealt with under the Poor Law. Until 1939, only the local authorities contributed to their support. However, the managers of the schools continued to accept children under six so as to have a reserve of children who could be put on the grant immediately when vacancies occurred in the certified numbers.[57]

The Treasury was particularly concerned that children who rightly should have been maintained in workhouses were being committed to industrial schools and condemned the liberal attitude of magistrates who were committing children to the schools without adequate reference to the legislation.[58] However:

> My Lords cannot say that much success has yet attended their efforts; but they believe that the Irish government is fully alive to their views, and is anxious to prevent any extravagant extension of the industrial school system.[59]

This theme was resurrected in 1896, when a circular was issued by the Lord Lieutenant claiming that:

> instances occur where children, who are not proper subjects for committal, are nonetheless brought by persons interested before magistrates in Petty sessions with the object of having them committed to industrial schools. The usual device adopted is to send out such children to beg in order ostensibly to qualify for these institutions. The magistrates are thus misled, and the result is that unproper committals are made which cast an unnecessary burden on the taxpayer, and, not infrequently, lead to the exclusion of children who would properly come within the Acts, and for whom these institutions were solely intended.[60]

In 1898 a further circular was issued urging magistrates to make orders of committal to industrial schools only when the children came within the strict scope of the Industrial School

Acts. Reaction to this circular from the managers of industrial schools, the Irish County Councils' General Council and various philanthropic bodies were uniformly critical, arguing that this policy would cause "grave injury to the industrial school system". In a pamphlet published by the Irish County Councils' General Council, letters from the managers of the majority of industrial schools on their experience of the implementation of the circular were reproduced. T.J. Butler, the manager of the largest industrial school in Ireland, and indeed in Britain, the Artane Industrial School, argued that while:

> A circular of one kind or other may have been called for, perhaps, to check some abuses in the committal of children to Industrial Schools. It is not, however, the correction of an abuse that is aimed at in the circular of October, 1898, but a total change in the administration of the system in this country, and the introduction of the English system instead.

He went on to highlight what he saw as the substantial differences between industrial schools in Ireland and industrial schools in England. Butler argued that (italics in original):

> The English Industrial Schools are *Semi-Reformatories* filled with juvenile criminals taken largely from the large manufacturing towns, and sent to those schools for some misdemeanour or breaches of the law. *This is not so* with our *Irish* Industrial schools. They are not to be found in any considerable numbers in this country. . . . Here in Ireland, we have, comparatively, very little juvenile crime, but we have much poverty and destitution, hence we require few reformatories but many Industrial Schools, for the very poverty of our orphans and guardianless children would soon lead them into evil ways, unless *rescued in time* under the Industrial Schools' Act, and this is what our Industrial Schools are accomplishing in Ireland. [61]

THE "MASTER BUILDERS"

Thus, rather than encountering a State-led expansion in the regulation and control of the errant young, we encounter the State desperately attempting to curb the growth in the number of industrial schools, reluctantly, if at all, increasing the certification level of the schools and imposing on magistrates strict guidelines to prevent excessive committals. The demand for the expansion of the industrial schools came from the religious managers of the schools themselves, allying themselves with local notables, local clergy and bishops. They viewed the function of industrial schools as embracing all poor, orphaned and destitute children, not simply those that came under the ambit of the Industrial School Acts. Such a policy ensured that children would not necessarily have to enter the workhouse and would be under the supervision of the Catholic Church. Despite the efforts of the Chief State Secretary's office to curb the growth in institutional provision for children and attempts to develop alternatives to institutionalisation, the system expanded throughout the 19th century and remained remarkably resilient until the 1960s. The domination of both the reformatory and industrial schools for Roman Catholic children by religious congregations is also significant, unlike the relatively small number of industrial and reformatory schools for Protestant children which were managed by lay committees. Table 3.1 shows the number of Catholic reformatory and industrial schools in Ireland in 1883 with regard to the congregation managing them.

Table 3.1: Distribution of Roman Catholic Reformatory and Industrial Schools by Order in 1883

	Industrial Schools	Reformatory Schools
Sisters of Mercy	30	1
Sisters of the Good Shepherd	4	1
Sisters of Charity	5	—
Christian Brothers	4	—
Sisters of St. Louis	2	1
Presentation Sisters	2	—
Oblate Fathers	—	2
Sisters of St. Clare	1	—
Presentation Brothers	1	—
Daughters of Charity	1	—
Order of Charity	—	1
Sisters of Our Lady of Charity of Refuge	—	1

Source: Report of the Inspector of Reformatory and Industrial Schools for Ireland, Dublin: Thom and Son.

Table 3.1 shows clearly that the Sisters of Mercy were responsible for the management of 60 per cent of all Catholic industrial schools. The Irish Sisters of Charity had responsibility for five, with the Sisters of the Good Shepherd and the Christian Brothers responsible for four apiece.[62] The other congregations had responsibility only for one or two schools. The male orders had responsibility for schools for senior boys and the female orders responsibility for all girls and boys under twelve. The rationale for giving responsibility for young boys to the female orders was that:

> Boys of these tender years who are ordered to be sent to an industrial school consist for the most part of orphans found destitute, and derelict children, who have acquired inveterate habits of vagrancy and a perfect contempt for law and order; the sons of abandoned characters also, and drunken

and dissolute parents, who never have known a mother's
care and solicitude, and who require the greatest attention
to wean them from their bad and filthy habits, and the evil
influences with which they have been surrounded. Under
the humanising management and training of women of a superior class, and formed to tidy habits, gentleness, order,
and strict cleanliness, these become susceptible of the best
impressions, which secretly and silently lead them to good;
and when transferred to the school where they are to labour
with the more adult boys, they will remember their former
teachers with affection, and will not easily forget the lessons
which they have been taught.[63]

THE POLITICS OF RELIGIOUS GOVERNANCE

Although the terms "religious congregation" and "religious order" are used inter-changeably in this chapter, there are theo-
logical differences between them. In essence, members of
congregations take simple vows, while members of orders take
solemn vows. Traditionally, members of religious orders were
perceived to have a higher social status than members of religious congregations. New Irish indigenous groups such as the
Sisters of Mercy and the Irish Christian Brothers are, strictly
speaking, congregations, rather than orders.[64]

A key issue for the bishops in their selection of congregations was the degree to which they could control them. As a result, this work fell to a relatively small number of congregations
whose constitution and rules gave primacy of control to the local bishop rather than to a centralised Mother House. Although
congregations, whose rules gave primacy of control to a centralised internal authority, were involved in this work, in relative terms their contribution was slight. A key factor in understanding the dominance of the Sisters of Mercy in the provision
of industrial schools is the structure of ecclesiastical authority.
As noted earlier in the chapter, local bishops were to the forefront in establishing orphanages and industrial schools in their
dioceses. The rules adopted by the Sisters of Mercy, an adaptation of the rules of the Presentation Sisters founded by Nano
Nagle, gave control over convents to the local bishop, rather

than to the superior of the congregation. According to the rule of the Sisters of Mercy:

> This Religious congregation shall be always subject to the authority and jurisdiction of the Bishop of the Diocese, and the Sisters shall respect and obey him as their principal Superior after the Holy See. If on account of his many avocations he should not have leisure to attend immediately to the direction of the community, a Priest shall be appointed by him on whose prudence, piety and experience he can depend to govern and direct under him and to whom he will give the necessary faculties. Nothing of importance related to the House or community shall be undertaken without the consent of the Bishop.[65]

The Irish Sisters of Charity, founded by Mary Aikenhead, on the other hand, gave primacy of control over their convents to the Mother Superior. As a biographer of Mary Aikenhead delicately put it:

> Up to this time convents in Ireland had been under the immediate control of the local bishop. Following the Institute at York, Mary Aikenhead established her Congregation with central government in Dublin headed by a Superior General. Local bishops had certain rights, but the overall control was in the hands of the Superior General and her Council. When the Sisters of Mercy were established in Cork, Mother Catherine McAuley gave the bishop executive authority over the community. This pleased him much more than Mother Aikenhead's central government.[66]

Thus, the issue of control by local bishops over these newly emerging congregations strongly influenced the expansion of the Sisters of Mercy in the provision of care for children. This issue of control by the local bishop over the superior of the congregation is exemplified by the experience of the Sisters of St. Louis. The Sisters of St. Louis, who had arrived in Monaghan from France in 1859, quickly found themselves in difficulty with the local bishop, Dr. McNally. He was unwilling to agree to allowing control over religious observance, internal discipline and the admission and formation of subjects to be retained by

the Abbé Buatain in Juilly, France, as he wished to have full
control over the affairs of the convent. Following a lengthy correspondence from France to Dr. McNally and having received
no reply from McNally, a decision was taken to "renounce the
direction of the Monaghan House. His Lordship is now its superior and may govern it as he thinks fit".[67] This decision was not
taken lightly and caused considerable anguish within the community in France as witnessed by the correspondence from
France:

> It is not without anguish of heart, my dear daughter, that I
> communicate this decision to you. But we cannot tolerate the
> present situation any longer. I regret to lose you for the sake
> of the community, but since we seek only to do good, and I
> think you are called to do it in your present situation, I
> should be sorry to see you leave it. No less than before we
> are united before God and in His Holy Spirit. Immediately
> on receipt of this letter, or as soon as possible afterwards,
> you are to read it for His Lordship, with whom you are to
> make the necessary arrangements. Then you are to commu-
> nicate the contents to the Sisters, and give them a few days
> to think the matter over. It is evident that we should gain
> nothing by further delay; the position in which we have
> been placed in Monaghan can be bourne no longer. Fare-
> well then my daughter; I do not know whether I shall ever
> see you again in this world. But it will always be consolation
> to me to have been instrumental in beginning the good
> work which you will accomplish in Ireland, and I hope that
> you will continue to pray for him who has been your father
> in Christ, and from the Community of St. Louis in which you
> were called.[68]

Thus, the growth of native religious congregations, both male
and female, in addition to those other congregations, primarily
French, invited to Ireland, provided the personnel, motivation
and structure to take full advantage of the newly emerging
structure of State funding for dependent children. The ability of
these congregations to operate was, however, highly condi-
tional on the support of the bishop in whichever locality they
wished to pursue their mission. The institutional nature of the

services they provided, be it for dependent children or fallen women, was a key feature of their work.[69]

Oates, in her study of the Catholic philanthropic tradition in America, has attempted to explain this Catholic predilection for institutions. She argues that initially, "the preference for explaining charity through institutions had reflected a concern to protect the poor, especially children, from evangelization by Protestant charities", but that this did not fully explain the persistence of the institutional model. She suggests that because of the different resource environment, in that labour was less expensive than other resources, "Religious Sisters and Brothers could care for large numbers in a single facility, minimizing costs of land, buildings and maintenance". She highlights that the Sisters of Charity preferred:

> the institutional setting to the foster home, not simply because of the real difficulties they confronted in finding suitable foster homes, but even more because the sisters could care for the children at a 40 percent lower cost, a saving that permitted the society to increase the work.[70]

She further argues that the bishops tended to be suspicious of lay charitable organisations that they did not control directly, and lay organisations "learned quickly that unless they worked closely with the clergy, their benevolent projects were doomed to failure".[71] Hazel, more recently, has argued that Belgium, whose child care services were primarily provided by religious orders which were mainly Catholic, had a situation whereby the majority of children in care were in residential care compared to the three other countries she surveyed, Sweden, England and Wales. Sweden had negligible numbers of children in residential care and, for those in residential care, their stay was minimal. England and Wales operated a more balanced system with approximately 40 per cent of children in need of alternative care in foster care. The reasons she put forward for Belgium having very high rates of children in residential care, and low numbers in foster care, were that the Catholic Church considered foster homes dangerous places, where controlling children was difficult and that it was only in large institutions that children could be adequately controlled and educated. Foster parents were not considered to have the expert skills needed to raise children and it was only within the institutional network that the range of expert interventions needed by the child could be provided.[72]

At the time of the construction of the child welfare apparatus, Irish society was riven by sectarian rivalries and nowhere was this more evident than in relation to the education of children. As a result, the various churches developed their own services, although considerable divergences existed in terms of the particular form of service provided. Within the Catholic Church divergences also existed, particularly between lay Catholic societies and Catholic congregations. This may, in part, be explained in terms of their respective organisational structures and their social class base. The congregations which dominated the field of child welfare were generally drawn from the respectable working classes, particularly from the 1850s onwards, and, within the structure of the Catholic church, were more amenable to hierarchical control and regulation than the longer established and more autonomous orders, such as the Jesuits.[73] Those involved with Catholic lay societies, such as the Catholic Protection and Rescue Society, tended to be from the merchant class. Crudely, the form of service provision reflected the internal organisational structure of the agency concerned.

ALTERNATIVES TO INSTITUTIONALISATION

In contrast to the institutional provision of child welfare services by Catholic bodies, orphan societies, operated either by the Established Church in Ireland or the Presbyterian Church in Ireland, generally adopted and continued to operate boarding-out orphanages. The Presbyterian Orphan Society established in 1866, provided for:

> the maintenance and education of children on the roll of the Society by continuing them under the care of their mothers or other suitable relatives, or by placing them with families in connection with the Presbyterian Church, residing within a convenient distance of a place of worship belonging to the said Church, and of a suitable school.[74]

Similarly, both the Protestant Orphan Refuge Society and the Protestant Orphan Society placed children in respectable families in the countryside rather than in institutional care.[75] While Protestant societies did manage institutional structures for orphan children and, certainly in Dublin, more than the Catholic societies or congregations did, nevertheless:

> the Roman Catholic ones are generally larger, far too large often, for individual care and the love these poor children so supremely need cannot be given where the numbers congregated together are very large. Moreover, to work large institutions much machinery is necessary; consequently when the inmates go out in the world they are at a loss how to do even ordinary housework, washing, &c, without the machinery to which they have been accustomed. The object of institution life should be to train the inmates that they may become good citizens and made fit for ordinary everyday life as speedily as possible, rather than the development of the military or drill system which is almost unavoidable in large institutions.[76]

Despite the overarching usage of institutional models for the provision of child welfare within Catholicism, dissenting views on the desirability of institutional care for children were evident. It was noted earlier in the chapter that St. Brigid's Orphanage managed by the Sisters of the Holy Faith resisted attempts to provide an institutional model for the care of orphan and dependent children and always provided a boarding-out scheme. However, with the congregations of the Catholic Church this was, by and large, unique.[77]

CONCLUSION

Over the past decade, the legacy of the institutional system constructed by a range of actors for the regulation of children has generated substantial debate. Recent television documentaries have resulted in the establishment of a Commission on Childhood Abuse, which will explore the extent of the alleged abuse in these institutions. Whatever the explanations for such an apparent record of abuse and neglect, it is important that we know how and why such a system developed.

The chapter argues that the growing power and influence of Catholic bishops in the post-Catholic emancipation period, allied with the growth of indigenous male and female religious orders and imported congregations, provided the necessary infrastructure and personnel for the development of a particular form of intervention into the lives of children. Fearful of the Established Church and seeking to physically demonstrate its growing power, bishops in virtually all dioceses of Ireland persuaded religious congregations to establish schools, hospitals, orphanages, industrial and reformatory schools in their bailiwick. A key issue for the bishops in their selection of congregations was the degree to which they could control them. As a result, this work fell to a relatively small number of congregations whose constitution and rules gave primacy of control to the local bishop rather than to a centralised Mother House. Although congregations whose rules gave primacy of control to a centralised internal authority were involved in this work, in relative terms their contribution was slight. This is not to suggest that these congregations of men and women were docile agents of the bishops, rather their origins and motivations coincided with the needs of the hierarchy who wished to develop the Catholic nation. They needed the sanction of the bishops to establish their schools and hospitals, and, in turn, the bishops needed them to provide the infrastructure of Catholic welfare provision. Although disputes between individual bishops and the congregations over the issue of ultimate control were evident, the relationship between them was largely symbiotic.

The role of the State in these developments was relatively marginal. The passing of the Industrial Schools Acts, in particular, simply provided a more stable basis for the funding of institutions already well established and allowed for an expansion of the model already dominant. Even with this funding, a considerable number of "orphanages" decided to remain outside of the industrial schools system and were entirely self-funding, and many of the certified industrial schools took in large numbers of children under the age of six who were not entitled to a capitation fee from the State. Despite this substantial subsidization of considerable numbers of children in the industrial schools and the separate system of "orphanage" care, the key concern for the Inspector of Industrial and Reformatory Schools and the Chief Secretary was an attempt to curb the number of children entering the schools and restricting the certification of new schools. Despite their efforts, the numbers of children in industrial schools continued to grow, while children catered for by means of boarding-out remained relatively slight.

Thus the development of the child welfare apparatus in Ireland was largely the creation of an increasingly powerful and numerically strong Catholic Church, actively providing a denominational system of institutional care for children deemed at risk, largely in their eyes from proselytisation. Mechanisms to provide for children that were outside of their direct control, in particular boarding-out, remained marginal in terms of the numbers of children catered for.

In summary, a range of discourses were evident during the formation of the child welfare apparatus in Ireland. The system of boarding-out children was gradually replaced, to a large degree, by sites of total institutionalisation. The role of the institutional Catholic Church was identified as the key agent in this transformation, but considerable divergences in discursive and non-discursive practices were observed within the Church (particularly between the religious congregations of the Catholic Church and Catholic lay agencies), and between the Catholic and the Established Church. These practices were, in turn, associated with the complex socio-political-religious transformations occurring in mid-19th century colonial Irish society.

Notes

[1] Raftery, M. and O'Sullivan, E. (1999) *Suffer the Little Children: The Inside Story of Ireland's Industrial Schools.* Dublin: New Island Books. For a detailed critique of the thesis outlined in the book, see Ferguson, H. (2000) "States of Fear, Child Abuse, and Irish Society". *Doctrine and Life,* Vol. 50, No. 1, pp. 20-31.

[2] O'Sullivan, D. (1979) "Social Definition in Child Care in the Irish Republic: Models of Child and Child Care Intervention", *Economic and Social Review*, Vol. 10, No. 3, p. 211. See also Gilligan, R. (1989) "Policy in the Republic of Ireland: Historical and Current Issues in Child Care", in Carter, P., Jeffs, T. and Smith, M. (eds) *Social Work and Social Welfare Yearbook 1*. Milton Keynes: Open University Press; Buckley, H. (1997) "Child Protection in Ireland", in *Child Protection in Europe: Towards a New Millennium*. University of Aalborg Press; McCullagh, C. (1992) "Reforming the Juvenile Justice System: The Examination of Failure". Paper presented to the Conference on the State of the Irish Political System, University College Cork, May, 1992; Ferguson, H. (1996) "Protecting Irish Children in Time: Child Abuse as a Social Problem and the Development of the Child Protection System in Ireland", *Administration*, Vol. 44, No.2, pp. 5-36 and Powell, F. (1992). *The Politics of Irish Social Policy, 1600-1990*, New York. Edwin Mellen Press.

[3] For a recent overview, see, Cormode, D.S. (1994) "Review Essay: Religion and the Nonprofit Sector". *Nonprofit and Voluntary Sector Quarterly*, Vol. 23, No. 2, pp. 171-182.

[4] James, E. (ed) (1989) *The Nonprofit Sector in International Perspective: Studies in Comparative Culture and Policy*. Oxford: Oxford University Press.

[5] Valverde, M. (1991) *The Age of Light, Soap and Water: Moral Reform in English-Canada, 1885-1925*. Toronto: McLellan and Stewart, and Valverde, M. (1994) "Moral Capital", *Canadian Journal of Law and Society*, Vol. 9, No. 1, pp. 213-232.

[6] Corrigan, P. and Sayer, D. (1985) *The Great Arch: English State Formation as Cultural Revolution*. Oxford: Basil Blackwell.

[7] Dean, M. (1994) "'A Social Structure of Many Souls': Moral Regulation, Government, and Self-formation". *Canadian Journal of Sociology*, Vol. 19, No. 2, p. 152.

[8] Keogh, D. (1996) "The Role of the Catholic Church in the Republic of Ireland, 1922-1995", in *Building Trust in Ireland: Studies Commissioned by the Forum for Peace and Reconciliation*. Dublin: Blackstaff Press, p. 118.

[9] Campos, for example, argues in relation to the Santiago Correction House for females, managed by the Sisters of the Good Shepherd, that the role of religion was viewed as crucial in the process of rescuing fallen women. For Campos, "the transformative power of religious discipline was also necessary to reform female delinquents. Praying and the imposition of Catholic sacraments were the principle instruments of reform and repentance". Campos, M.S.Z. (1996) "Vicious Women, Virtuous Women: The Female Delinquent and the Santiago de Chile Correctional House, 1860-1900", in Salvatore, R.D. and Aguirre, C. (eds) *The Birth of the Penitentiary in Latin America: Essays on Criminology, Prison Reform, and Social Control, 1830-1940*. Austin, TX: University of Texas Press, p. 95.

[10] Ruonavaara, H. (1997) "Moral Regulation: A Reformulation", *Sociological Theory*, Vol. 15, No. 3, pp. 286-7.

[11] Rather than viewing their engagement in this arena as occurring by default, as suggested by Fahey, this chapter suggests that a heterogeneous ensemble of strategies and techniques, often not intentionally correlated, but in effect intermeshed, created the conditions that allowed for the construction and dominance of institutional regimes as the pre-eminent form of intervention into the lives of children in Ireland from 1870 to 1970. The chapter also demonstrates that confining analysis to the institutions of the State conceals and misrepresents the range of discourses and practices that were and are evident in the construction of regimes for the regulation of children. Fahey, T. "Catholicism and Industrial Society in Ireland" in Goldthorpe, J.H. and Whelan, C.T. (eds) (1992) *The Development of Industrial Society in Ireland*. Proceedings of the British Academy No.79. Oxford: Oxford University Press.

[12] The most important new indigenous female congregations were the Presentation Sisters founded by Nano Nagle in 1775, the Irish Sisters of Charity founded by Mary Aikenhead in 1815, and the Sisters of Mercy, founded by Catherine McAuley in 1831. The most significant French congregations were the Daughters of Charity of St. Vincent De Paul, the Sisters of St. Louis, the Sisters of Our Lady of Charity of the Good Shepherd and the Sisters of Our Lady of Charity of Refuge. The Sisters of the Good Shepherd were established in 1835 following organisational difficulties with the Sisters of Charity of Our Lady of Refuge. The most significant male congregation was the Christian Brothers, founded in 1802 by Edmund Ignatius Rice. The Presentation Brothers also owe their origin to Rice, but split from him as a result of a conflict of interest that was initiated by the Bishop of Cork over the issue of Diocesan control. Also of importance were The Institute of Charity (Rosminians), which had been founded in 1828 by Antonio Rosmini (an Italian philosopher and priest), and the Oblates of Mary Immaculate, who were a French order, and had been founded in 1816.

[13] This growth in religious congregations in the early 19th century and the importation of a number of French congregations in the middle of the 19th century, in addition to adherence to Roman rituals, is linked to what Larkin has termed the "devotional revolution" in Ireland. Larkin has argued that between 1830 and 1870, the Catholic Church increased its wealth, the clergy were better disciplined and the ratio of priests to people declined significantly. Most importantly for Larkin, during this period the Irish became practising Catholics for the first time, with rates of church attendance increasing from approximately 33 per cent to near universal attendance. The key figure driving these changes was the Archbishop of Dublin, Paul Cullen. Larkin, E. (1976) "The Devotional Revolution in Ireland, 1850-75", in Larkin, E. *The Historical Dimensions of Irish Catholicism*. Washington, DC: Catholic University of America Press, p. 77. The Larkin thesis has been critiqued, in particular by Miller, Keenan, Whelan, Carroll and McGrath. Keenan, for example, attributes a far greater role to Archbishop Murray of Dublin in advancing the Catholic cause in Ireland than Cullen; Carroll has argued for a reconceptuali-

sation of popular Catholicism in pre-famine Ireland while McGrath, Whelan and Miller have questioned Larkin's figures on church attendance and his interpretation of them. Miller, D.W. (1975) "Irish Catholicism and the Great Famine", *Journal of Social History*, Vol. 9, No. 1; Keenan, D. (1983) *The Catholic Church in Nineteenth Century Ireland*. Dublin: Gill and Macmillan; Whelan, K. (1988) "The Regional Impact of Irish Catholicism 1700-1850", in Smythe, W.J. and Whelan, K. (eds) *Common Ground*. Cork: Cork University Press; McGrath, T.G. (1991) "The Tridentine Evolution of Modern Irish Catholicism, 1563-1962: A Re-examination of the 'Devotional Revolution' Thesis", *Recusant History*, Vol. 20, No. 2, pp. 512-523; Carroll, M.P. (1995) "Rethinking Popular Catholicism in Pre-Famine Ireland", *Journal for the Scientific Study of Religion*, Vol. 34, No. 3, pp. 354-365.

[14] O'Brien has estimated that by 1887, 57 of the 318 convents in England were of Irish origin. O'Brien, S. (1997) "French Nuns in Nineteenth Century England". *Past and Present*, No. 154, p. 156. For further information on the Irish religious diaspora see Hoy, S. (1995) "The Journey Out: The Recruitment and Emigration of Irish Religious Women to the United States, 1812-1914", in Hoff, J. and Coulter, M. (eds) *Irish Women's Voices: Past and Present*, Bloomington, IN: Indiana University Press; Gilley, S. (1984) The Roman Catholic Church and the Nineteenth-Century Irish Diaspora. *Journal of Ecclesiastical History*, Vol. 35, No. 2, pp. 188-207, and Bennett, J. (1950) "The Care of the Poor" Beck, G.A. (ed) *The English Catholics, 1850-1950*. London: Burns Oates.

[15] Clear, C. (1988) *Nuns in Nineteenth Century Ireland*. Dublin: Gill and Macmillan. See also Fahey, T. (1987) "Nuns in the Catholic Church in Ireland in the Nineteenth Century" in Cullen, M. (ed) *Girls Don't Do Honours: Irish Women in Education in the 19th and 20th Centuries*. Dublin: Women's Education Bureau.

[16] Entrants to the Sisters of Mercy, for example, "besides attending particularly to their own perfection, which is the principal end of all religious orders, should also have in view what is the peculiar characteristics of this congregation: i.e., the most assiduous application to the education of poor girls, the visitation of the sick, and the protection of women of good character". *The Rules and Constitutions of the Religious Called Sisters of Mercy*. (1863). Dublin: James Duffy, p. 4.

[17] Carroll, Sr. M.T.A. (1881) *Leaves from the Annals of the Sisters of Mercy. Vol. 1. Ireland*. New York: Catholic Publication Society.

[18] Meagher, W. (1853) *Notices of the Life and Character of His Grace, Most Rev. Daniel Murray, Late Archbishop of Dublin*. Dublin: Gerald Bellow, p. 36. This perception that the hierarchy was instrumental in establishing new female congregations in Ireland at the beginning of the 19th century has been challenged recently by Peckham Magray who argues that many convents were initiated independently of the bishops and it was only post-1850 that female congregations became subject to the control of the hierarchy. Peckham Magray, M. (1998) *The Transforming Power of the Nuns: Women, Religion, and Cultural Change in Ireland, 1750-1900*. Oxford: Oxford University Press.

[19] See O'Brien, S. (1997) "French Nuns in Nineteenth-Century England", *Past and Present*, No. 154. pp. 142-180, and O'Brien, S. (1988) *Terra Incognita*: The Nun in Nineteenth Century England, *Past and Present*, No. 145, pp. 110-140. On the feminisation of Catholic Europe more generally, see Ford, C. (1993) "Religion and Popular Culture in Modern Europe", *Journal of Modern History*, Vol. 63, March, pp. 152-175.

[20] Cousins, M. (1997) "Ireland's Place in the Worlds of Welfare Capitalism", *Journal of European Social Policy*, Vol. 7, No. 3., p. 230.

[21] Young, Rev. H. (1821) *The Catholic Directory dedicated to St. Patrick, Bishop, Apostle, and Patron of Ireland, which gives a useful and interesting information of the Dioceses of Ireland, also of the Parishes, Rev. Clergymen, Orphan Asylums, Catholic Schools, Pious Confraternities and all Charitable Institutions.* Dublin: John Coyle.

[22] Osler, T. (1834) Account of Catholic Orphanages in Dublin, including Statistics of numbers therein, 1789-1832. Ms. 640. National Library.

[23] O'Neill suggests that "the number of (Catholic) orphan societies doubled and the numbers of orphans trebled every fourteen years between 1789 and 1832". O'Neill, T.P. (1973) "The Catholic Church and the Relief of the Poor 1815-45", *Archivium Hibernicum*, Vol. xxxi, p. 144. This growth of orphanages for children was not unique to Ireland. In the United States there were only 5 orphanages in 1800 compared to over 1,000 by the end of the century. Smith, E.P. (1996) "Bring Back the Orphanages? What Policy Makers of Today can Learn from the past", in Smith, E.P. and Merkel-Holguin, L.A. (eds) *A History of Child Welfare*. New Brunswick: Transaction Publishers, pp. 107-134.

[24] See Ronan, M.V. (1944) *An Apostle of Catholic Dublin: Father Henry Young.* Dublin: Browne and Nolan, pp. 224-231, and Keenan, D.J. (1983) *The Catholic Church in Nineteenth Century Ireland: A Sociological Study.* Dublin: Gill and Macmillan, pp. 125-129 for further details on the management of these orphan societies.

[25] The Orphanage of Our Blessed Lady of Mount Carmel, in its first nine years of work, claimed that "four hundred children have been rescued from the snare of proselytisers" but that "there are many Catholic children in proselytising schools who are praying to-day for their deliverance, and we will never be content till the last captive is freed from a hateful bondage and restored to the bosom of the Church". *Addresses Delivered on Various Occasions by the Most Rev. Dr. Walsh, Archbishop of Dublin.* Dublin: Gill and Son, p. 146.

[26] The practice of boarding-out children from orphanages appears to have been relatively widespread. See Ingram, J.K. (1875) "Address at the opening of the Twenty-ninth Session: The Organisation of Charity, and the Education of the Children of the State", *Journal of the Statistical and Social Inquiry Society of Ireland*. Part xlviii, p. 460.

[27] Barrett, R.M. (1884) *Guide to Dublin Charities*. Dublin.

[28] Aylward was largely responsibly for the establishment of the Association of Ladies of Charity, which became the Sisters of the Holy Faith in 1866. Peader McSuibhne, the biographer of Archbishop Paul Cullen, has argued that Aylward "with the warm approval of Dr, Cullen offered the first systematic opposition to the advance of proselytism. From the beginning St. Brigid's orphanage battled bravely against the hideous device of kidnapping the souls of the forlorn and defenseless children of the poor. Its policy, unlike that of its opponents, has been a policy of protection. It strives to rescue the children of the Catholic Church from the enemies of the Catholic Church". MacSuibhne, P. (1961) *Paul Cullen and his Contemporaries*. Vol. 1. Naas: Leinster Leader Ltd., p. 46. The 19th Annual Report of the Orphanage showed that by 1876 1,340 orphans had been admitted. "337 remain in the orphanage. The remainder, that is, 1,010, minus about 50, who have died in the course of the past 15 years, have been reared, educated, and put out to earn their bread. 457 of them have been restored to their parents or guardians; 199 have been sent to trades or service; and 275 have been adopted by the families that nursed them, and are now as the sons and daughters of those good people". 19th Annual Report (1876) *St. Brigid's Orphanage for 500 Children*. Dublin: W. Powell, p. 8. See also Prunty, J. (1999) *Margaret Aylward, 1810-1889*. Dublin: Four Courts Press.

[29] St. Brigid's Orphanage.(1865) *Irish Ecclesiastical Record*, Vol. 1, p. 169.

[30] For an account of a similar process of colonisation in relation to deaf children, see Crean, E.J. (1997) *Breaking the Silence: The Education of the Deaf in Ireland, 1816-1996*. Dublin: Irish Deaf Society.

[31] Burke-Savage, R. (1940) *A Valiant Dublin Woman. The Story of George's Hill, 1766-1940*. Dublin: Gill and Son.

[32] The orphanage in Harold's Cross operated by the Poor Clares was originally established by three working men, Patrick Quarterman, James Auger and George Poland, who issued an appeal "to a benevolent and Charitable Public" proposing to "establish a Female Orphan Institution in this city, under the title of the Maria Female Orphans". The three gentleman had provided for a small number of female orphans prior to this appeal, but although "industrious men are reduced to the necessity of craving aid of the benevolent for their and others' future support". Following a donation of £500, a premises was purchased in Harold's Cross and in 1806, the children were "placed in the loving care of their new Mothers. A little later the children who were being boarded out in the country were also taken into the school". Concannon, T. (1930) *The Poor Clares in Ireland (A.D. 1929-A.D. 1929)*. Dublin: Gill and Son, pp. 123-128. This orphanage was to operate until the 1980s. Sisters of St. Clare (1985) *Sisters of St. Clare: A Brief History*. Dublin: Sisters of St. Clare, p. 21. See also A Loreto Sister (1961) *Joyful Mother of Children: Mother Frances Mary Teresa Ball*. Dublin: M.H. Gill and Son.

[33] Atkinson, S. (1879) *Mary Aikenhead: Her Life, Her Work, and Her Friends, Giving a History of the Foundation of the Congregation of the Irish Sisters of Charity*. Dublin: Gill and Son, p.447.

[34] *St. Vincent's Glasnevin. Centenary Annual, 1856-1956*. Dublin: Society of St. Vincent De Paul.

[35] Bolster, Sister M. A. (1987) *Mercy in Cork 1837-1987: A Sesquicentennial Commemoration*. Cork: Tower Books, p. 13.

[36] Murphy, J.N. (1873) *Terra Incognita or The Convents of the United Kingdom*. London: Longman, Green and Co., p. 189.

[37] Corish, P. (1985) *The Irish Catholic Experience: A Historical Survey*. Dublin: Gill and Macmillan.

[38] For example, St, Joseph's Orphanage in Bundoran, Co. Donegal, established in 1909 as a result of a legacy of £50,000 left by a Sara Crudden, was managed by the Sisters of St. Louis, despite competition from the Sisters of Mercy, until its closure in 1956. See Commins, M. (1990) "St. Joseph's Orphanage, Bundoran", *Clogher Record*, Vol. 13, No. 3, pp. 163-179 for further details. Madonna House was established in Dublin in 1955 by the Irish Sisters of Charity following a request from Dr. McQuaid, Archbishop of Dublin. Irish Sisters of Charity (1958) *Centenary Brochure, 1858-1958*. Dublin: Irish Sisters of Charity, p. 37. In the funeral oration for Paul Cullen, Archbishop of Dublin in 1878, Fr. Burke noted that under Cullen's reign "orphanages to the number of 16 were either established or enlarged". Quoted in Larkin, E. (1996) *The Roman Catholic Church and the Emergence of the Modern Irish Political System*. Dublin: Four Courts Press, p. 145.

[39] For example, Dr. Keane preached various sermons in aid of the Sacred Heart Home in Drumcondra, the St. Joseph's Orphanage, Mountjoy Street and the St. Vincent's Girls' Orphanage in North William Street. Keane, Dr. (1916) *Sermons Preached on Various Occasions*. London: Sands and Co. The Orphanage managed by the Daughters of Charity in North William Street received funds from the Vincentian Fathers and the Archbishop of Dublin contributed the sum of £25 for each Sister working in the orphanage. In 1933, for example, charity sermons in aid of St. Clare's Orphanage, St. Joseph's Orphanage, Sacred Heart Home, St. Vincent's Orphanage for Girls, St. Vincent's Orphanage for Boys, St. Brigid's Orphanage, St. Saviour's Orphanage and the Andrean Orphanage were authorised to be preached within the city of Dublin. *Irish Catholic Directory and Almanac* (1933) Dublin: Duffy and Co., pp. 672-673. Other orphanages such as George's Hill, managed by the Presentation Sisters sought £10 per annum from relatives of the orphans. Barrett, R.M. (1884) *Guide to Dublin Charities*. Dublin, p. 6.

[40] The St. Joseph's Orphanage in Dun Laoghaire established in 1860 by the Daughters of the Heart of Mary provided accommodation for 75 children where they were "trained for a number of occupations by the dedicated work of the sisters, without assistance from public funds and with a minimum of ap-

peals to public charity". (Anon, 1962, St. Joseph's Orphanage, Dun Laoghaire: 1860-1960. *Reportorium Novum: Dublin Diocesan Historical Record*, Vol. 3, No. 1, p. 215.

[41] A clear class distinction was evident between the industrial schools and the orphanages. The private orphanages catered for children of "good character from respectable families" while those children placed in industrial schools were the offspring of the disreputable classes. For example, the St. Joseph's Orphanage in Mountjoy Street operated by the Irish Sisters of Charity was "intended mainly for children whose parents occupied a good position in the world".[41] The object of St. Vincent's Orphanage in Glasnevin operated by the Christian Brothers on behalf of the Society of St. Vincent De Paul was "the education of boys of middle-class families who are orphans through the death of one or both parents". *Catholic Social Worker's Handbook*, 1947. Dublin: Society of St. Vincent de Paul., pp. 13-14 An exception to this comment appears to have been the St. Brigid's Orphanage in Eccles Street for whom "The orphan child of rich Catholic parents is not the subject for St. Brigid's orphanage, for though his faith may be in danger, he has friends to support and educate according to his rank. Neither is the orphan child of poor Catholic parents, whose Faith is secure, a special object of the charity. But the orphan and destitute child upon whom the double calamity of physical and spiritual destitution has fallen, he is the special object of St. Brigid's Charity". *12th Annual Report of St. Brigid's Orphanage for Five Hundred Children* (1869) Dublin: W. Powell, p. 1.

[42] For further detail on the establishment of reformatory and industrial schools, and the numbers contained within these schools, see O'Sullivan (1997) "'Restored to virtue, to society and to God': Juvenile Justice and the Regulation of the Poor" in Bacik, I. and O'Connell, M. (eds) *Crime and Poverty in Ireland*. Dublin: Roundhall Sweet and Maxwell.

[43] Although each reformatory and industrial school was certified under a committee of management, the Inspector of Schools reported in 1889 that "their meetings are very irregular, and in many schools I could find no evidence of their having met for years". The Inspector went on to argue that "This is open to great objection, and I would therefore argue that all committees should meet at stated intervals and keep regular minutes of their proceedings. And that they should visit the school frequently and look carefully after the details of its management". *Twenty-seventh Report of the Inspector of Reformatory and Industrial Schools* (1889) Dublin: Thom and Son, p. 28.

[44] An exception to this point was the Baltimore Fishery Industrial School established in 1887. The management of this school was vested in "the Most Reverend Roman Catholic Bishop of Ross, the Parish Priest of Baltimore, Lord Carbery, Sir Thomas Brady, Mr. Burdett-Coutts, M.P., Mr. W.T. Green, President of the Chamber of Commerce, Cork, Mr. Thomas Crosbie, Cork Examiner and two gentlemen who live in the neighbourhood". *Thirty-Second Report of the Inspector of Reformatory and Industrial Schools in Ireland.* (1894). Dublin: Thom and Son, p. 13.

[45] Pauline, Sr. M. (1959) *God Wills It! Centenary Story of the Sisters of St. Louis.* Dublin: Browne and Nolan.

[46] The Order of Our Lady of Charity of Refuge (1953) *A Centenary Record of the High Park Convent Drumcondra Dublin, 1853-1953.* Dublin: Three Candles Press.

[47] Towey, J. (1981) "Summerhill 1880". *Archivium Hibernicum*, pp. 26-33.

[48] Regan, T. (1993) *The Salthill Industrial School.* Galway: Galway Labour History Society.

[49] Burke-Savage, R. (1955) *Catherine McAuley: The First Sister of Mercy.* Dublin: Gill and Son.

[50] Hurley, F. (1995) *St. Joseph's Convent of Mercy, Kinsale: A Celebration of 150 Years! 1844-1994.* Kinsale; O'Brien, Sr. P. ((1994) *The Sisters of Mercy in Birr and Nenagh.* Killaloe: Congregation of the Sisters of Mercy, Mercy Generalate.

[51] Colcannon, H. (1930) *The Poor Clares in Ireland (A.D. 1629-A.D. 1929).* Dublin: Gill and Son. See also Kerr, D. (1983-4) "James Browne, Bishop of Kilmore, 1829-65". *Breifne — Journal of Cumann Seanchais Bhreifne*, Vol. vi, No. 22.

[52] Liguori, Sr. M. (1989) "Presentation Convent, Thurles, 1817-1917", in Corbett, W. and Nolan, W. (Eds) *Thurles: The Cathedral Town. Essays in honour of Archbishop Thomas Morris.* Dublin: Geography Publications. The same order also opened an industrial school in Cashel, Co. Tipperary. Luddy, M. (1992) "Presentation Convents in County Tipperary". *Tipperary Historical Journal*, pp. 84-95.

[53] St. Timothy's Orphanage, established in 1870 in Kilrush, was refused recognition as an industrial school, as the Inspector of Reformatory and Industrial Schools deemed that the industrial school in Ennis was sufficient for the county. The orphanage operated until 1944, catering for a small number of girls. O'Brien, Sr. P. (1997) *The Sisters of Mercy of Kilrush and Kilkee.* Killaloe: Congregation of the Sisters of Mercy, Mercy Generalete. The orphanages in Navan and Kells were later certified under Section 3 of the Pauper Children (Ireland) Act, 1898, which allowed local authorities to send to such homes children who were orphaned or deserted by their parents. See also Lunney, S. (1996) "Institutional Solution to a Social Problem: Industrial Schools in Ireland and the Sisters of Mercy". Unpublished MA Thesis, UCD.

[54] O'Brien, Sr. P. (1992) *The Sisters of Mercy of Ennis.* Killaloe: Congregation of the Sisters of Mercy, Mercy Generalate, p. 62.

[55] CSORP 1972/4523.

[56] For example, the Cappoquin Industrial School in Co. Waterford, certified in 1873, was certified initially for the accommodation of 36 children of the age of six years and upwards and 1 child under that age. In 1880 it was raised to 51 and 5 respectively. In 1912, accommodation was provided for 65 children, of

whom 51 were chargeable to the State grant. The accommodation limit of Cappoquin was increased from 51 to 65 on March 19th, 1928 and from 65 to 75 on the 26th of February, 1938. The school certificate number was 51 up to the date of the abolition of the certificate system, 1st July 1944. After this date the State Grant was payable for all children within the authorised accommodation limit, 75. D/Ed SpEd c 47. St. Michael's Cappoquin.

[57] For further details on the funding of Reformatory and Industrial Schools, see Raftery, M. and O'Sullivan, E. (1999) *Suffer the Little Children: The Inside Story of Ireland's Industrial Schools.* Dublin: New Island Books.

[58] Although the Treasury was primarily concerned with the cost of the escalating number of industrial schools, other commentators, such as the prolific contributor to a range of publications E.D. Daly, were concerned for other reasons. Daly argued that "our efforts should not run into a blind craze for establishing new schools. Schools, both reformatory and so-called industrial schools, are of vital importance for many cases; but it must be bad for any community needlessly to disturb the family as our social unit. State schools may be essential to rescue children whose parents are incorrigible or not forthcoming. But it is against common sense to hurry children into schools, as we are doing, without any adequate attempt first to persuade or coerce parents to take better care of them" Daly, E.D. (1897) "Crime, and How Best to Attack It", *Journal of the Statistical and Social Inquiry Society of Ireland*, Vol. 10, p. 338.

[59] CSORP 1881/3848.

[60] Circular to Magistrates at Petty Sessions. Improper Committal of Children to Industrial Schools. 22/5/1896.

[61] Letter from T.J. Butler, Manager Artane Industrial School, Co. Dublin 3/2/1900 to John Sweetman, Esq. Hon. Sec. County Council's General Council, in "Irish County Councils' General Council Publications", No. 1. *Industrial Schools.* Dublin: ICCGC.

[62] Nearly 100 years later, in 1980, of the 26 registered industrial schools in the country, 14 were managed by the Irish Sisters of Mercy, 5 by the Sisters of the Good Shepherd, 2 by the Irish Sisters of Charity, 2 by the Sisters of Our Lady of Charity of Refuge, 1 by the Daughters of Charity, 1 by the Irish Christian Brothers and 1 by the Presentation Sisters.

[63] *Ninth Report of the Inspector of Reformatory and Industrial Schools in Ireland* (1870) Dublin: Thom and Son, p. 25.

[64] A further distinction between female religious congregations was those that distinguished between lay sisters and choir sisters. Lay sisters were effectively domestic servants and were often working class, and it has been argued that it was "their domestic support which enabled middle-class sisters to develop a semi-professional life within the Catholic sub-culture as teachers, nurses, and social workers". O'Brien, S. (1990) "Lay Sisters and Good Mothers: Working-Class Women in English Convents, 1840-1910", in Sheils,

W.J. and Wood, D. (eds) *Women in the Church*. London: Ecclesiastical History Society/Basil Blackwell, p. 454. On these distinctions in Irish Convents see Clear, C. (1987) *Nuns in Nineteenth Century Ireland*. Dublin: Gill and Macmillan and Clear, C. (1987) "Walls within Walls: Nuns in Nineteenth Century Ireland" in Curtin, C., Jackson, P. and O'Connor, B. (eds) *Gender in Irish Society. Studies in Irish Society 3*. Galway: Galway University Press.

[65] *The Rules and Constitutions of the Religious Called Sisters of Mercy*. (1863). Dublin: James Duffy, p. 39. See Degnan, B (1958) *Mercy unto Thousands*. Dublin: Browne and Nolan, and Sullivan, M.C. (1995) *Catherine McAuley and the Tradition of Mercy*, Notre Dame, IN: University of Notre Dame Press, for the background to the adoption of this rule. This was also the rule adopted initially by the Irish Christian Brothers founded by Edmund Ignatius Rice in 1802. However, following the growth of the congregation, it was decided to adopt the rule of the De La Salle Brothers. This removed primary control from the local bishop and gave primary control to a Superior General. This development caused friction in the Diocese of Cork, where the Bishop Dr. Murphy insisted on retaining control over the congregation, resulting in the formation of the Presentation Brothers. See Fitzpatrick, J.D. (1945) *Edmund Rice: Founder of the Christian Brothers*. Dublin: M.H. Gill and Son, pp. 163-193 and Feheney, J.M. (1996) *A Time of Grace: School Memories*. Dublin: Veritas, for further details.

[66] Donovan, M. (1979) *Apostolate of Love. Mary Aikenhead 1787-1858*. Sydney: Sisters of Charity, p. 57.

[67] Pauline, Sr. M. (1959) *God Wills It! Centenary Story of the Sisters of St. Louis*. Dublin: Browne and Nolan, p. 152.

[68] ibid. p. 153.

[69] For example the Sisters of the Good Shepherd, who provided "care" for three separate classes of subjects; the penitentiary class, the reformatory class and the preservation class, were "kept severally quite distinct, their houses and exercise grounds being divided by high walls, and, in fact, as completely separated as if they were several miles distant from each other". Murphy, J.N. (1873) *Terra Incognita or the Convents of the United Kingdom*. London: Longmans, Green and Co., p. 197.

[70] Oates, M.J. (1995) *The Catholic Philanthropic Tradition in America*. Bloomington, IN: Indiana University Press, pp. 28-32. Dekker in his study of reformatories in the Netherlands also notes that the "Roman Catholic reformatories were larger than the Protestant ones, and there were large deviations from the average". Dekker, J.J.H. (1990) "The Role of Temporary Marginalisation. Reformatories and Insane Asylums: The Netherlands in the Nineteenth Century". *Paedagogica Historica*, Vol. 26, Pt. 2, pp. 125-146.

[71] Oates, M.J. (1995) *The Catholic Philanthropic Tradition in America*. Bloomington, IN: Indiana University Press, p. 26.

[72] Hazel, N. (1976) "Child Placement Policy: Some European Comparisons", *British Journal of Social Work*, Vol. 6, No. 3, pp. 315-326.

[73] See Gannon, T.M. (1980) "Catholic Religious Orders in Sociological Perspective" in Scherer, R.P. (ed) *American Religious Organisations*, for an overview of the different forms of organisation and structure within the Catholic Church. On female congregations and orders, see CitaMalard, S. (1964) *Religious Orders of Women*. New York: Hawthorn Books.

[74] Barkley, J.M. (1966) *The Presbyterian Orphan Society, 1866-1966*. Belfast: BNL Printing Co., pp. 116-117.

[75] Barrett, R.M. (1884) *Guide to Dublin Charities*. Dublin.

[76] Barrett, R.M. (1902) "Introduction to section v. Orphanages and Homes for the Young", in Williams, G. *Dublin Charities*. Dublin: The Educational Depository, p. 123.

[77] Notwithstanding this preference for institutional structures within Catholicism, as new Catholic lay societies emerged from the beginning of the 20th century, the boarding-out model of child welfare provision rather than the institutional model was favoured. For example, the Catholic Protection and Rescue Society, established in 1913, endeavoured to place children in foster homes rather than in industrial schools or orphanages, a view also endorsed by the Catholic Social Welfare Bureau, established by the Archbishop of Dublin, John Charles McQuaid in 1942, and the Legion of Mary. Thus, there was not necessarily a homogeneity of views within the agencies of the Catholic church on the most appropriate manner to deal with children. A range of Catholic lay agencies were opposed to the institutional method of dealing with children, and developed their own informal methods of placing children with respectable families, often a form of informal adoption. Yet, even within these agencies, there was a diversity of views on how this system of informal adoption should be regulated.

Chapter 4

Children Out-of-Home in Ireland

Frank Houghton, Patricia Kelleher and Carmel Kelleher

In many ways children are marginalised members of society. Their relative lack of power spans many areas of life including the all important economic and political dimensions. Children out-of-home constitute a particularly "at risk" group within Irish society. Such children are a heterogeneous group which includes both children in care and homeless children. Perhaps the most disturbing aspect of the growing problem of homelessness in Ireland is the increasing number of homeless children. Once on the streets these children often become immersed in street culture, which can involve begging, petty crime and prostitution. Drug misuse is an additional element in the lives of many homeless children, leading to chaotic and dangerous lifestyles. Children in care are probably equally marginalised and, like many homeless children, may have experienced abuse and neglect. Both groups of children may effectively have been homeless, that is, without the support of a nurturing home environment, long before they physically became homeless or went into care. This chapter will focus on recent research carried out in Ireland which has identified significant links between these two groups of children.

As O'Sullivan (1996a, p. 212) reports, homeless children are "increasingly becoming a feature of urban landscapes across Western Europe". Ireland, and particularly Dublin, are no exception to this international trend. Old stereotypes, often defining the homeless as ageing males, are increasingly inaccurate in contemporary Ireland. It is generally agreed that there is a growing number of homeless children in Ireland. There has been a debate about exact definitions of homelessness, given the extent of hidden homelessness which can include people having to stay with friends or relatives through lack of alternative accommodation. Gilligan (1991, p. 50) has pointed out that homelessness does not only include those without their own accommodation, but "is a broad concept which ranges from sleeping rough to living in highly insecure or unsatisfactory conditions". Putting definitional questions aside, a significant number of studies have charted the developing problem of homeless children in Ireland over the last decade or so (McCarthy and Conlon, 1988; Focus Point and the Eastern Health Board, 1989; Harvey and Menton, 1989; Dillon et al., 1990; Dillon, 1992; Keane and Crowley, 1990).

It is unfortunate that most studies conducted on youth homelessness in Ireland have attempted to do little more than quantify the extent of youth homelessness. However, even in this field, national counts are rare and most investigations tend to be local affairs (Keane and Crowley, 1990; Dillon, 1992). The only routinely available information on youth homelessness in Ireland is produced by the health boards, who under The Child Care Act, 1991 are obliged to produce annual reviews of the adequacy of child care services. However, this information provides little more than counts which may or may not even be broken down by age and gender.

There is no one simple answer as to why people, particularly children, become homeless. Presenting problems such as family breakdown are underpinned by deeper explanations. O'Sullivan (1996b, p. 105) argues that youth homelessness is a manifestation of the structural inequalities inherent in Irish society:

> Youth homelessness arises from a complex set of structural inequalities, poor familial relations often exacerbated by poverty, illness and unemployment, lack of adequate aftercare for those leaving institutional care, poor educational opportunities leading to reduced employment prospects,

and the lack of low-cost accommodation, either local authority or private rented, or the reluctance of landlords in the private rented sector to accept those in receipt of social welfare.

O'Brien (1988) reports that Focus Point identified three primary causes of youth homelessness. The primary element identified is family conflict and a breakdown in communications. Such conflict, O'Brien (1988, p. 46) states, is often related to such factors as "behaviour, attitudes, or where there are issues of conflict — such as violence, sexual or drug abuse, pregnancy, delinquency, unemployment". The second cause identified is migration in search of employment and/or independence. Most young people make this transition successfully, however a minority do not. This particularly affects those with poor educational standards, few social networks or financial back-up. The third risk factor for homelessness identified by O'Brien (1988) is leaving residential child care.

This chapter will focus specifically on the relationship between those leaving institutional care and deprivation and homelessness, noting the frequent lack of adequate after-care. As noted above, children out-of-home may be seen to be constituted of two separate groups, homeless children and children in care. However there is now a growing wealth of literature which demonstrates that these two groups not only have strong similarities, but are often the same individuals at different points in their out-of-home careers.[1] As Crowley (1997, p. 62) comments:

> the post-care lifestyle of significant percentages of children who have been in care are very similar to those of adolescents who drift from their dysfunctional or abusive families and eventually present to the developing youth homeless services.

The findings drawn on in this chapter are predominantly from the report *Out On Their Own* commissioned by Focus Ireland and produced by Kelleher Associates (1998).[2] This study, as well as including an examination of practical and policy developments in relation to foster care and residential care, also involved a longitudinal study of young people leaving care. In recent years a number of studies on "leaving care" and "after-care" have been undertaken in England, Scotland and Northern Ireland (Morgan-Klein and Murdoch, 1985; Stein and Carey, 1986; Stone, 1990; Garnet, 1992; Biehal et al., 1995; Pinkerton and McCrea, 1996; Stein, 1997). These studies, dating from the mid-1980s, are the result of what has been described as an "awakening of leaving care in the professional and political consciousness" at that time (Stein, 1991). Until the *Out On Their Own* report (Kelleher Associates, 1998) little research on leaving care had been conducted in the Republic of Ireland. The only prior substantial piece of research on this issue was conducted by McCarthy (1990). This research examined the difficult experiences of young people leaving St Joseph's Special School, Clonmel and led to the establishment of the Slievenamon Project.

The importance of preparation for leaving care and aftercare support should not be underestimated. It is important to remember that the transition to independence is often an intimidating and difficult process for young people leaving their family homes with the support of their family. The experience for those without such support and care has been described as:

> When you come out (of care) it's hell after. You don't know what you're doing or where you're going. It's just like taking you from one country and putting you into another (quoted in Biehal et al., 1995, p. 3).

Upon leaving care young people are somehow expected to achieve instant maturity. The often abrupt end of care with an absence of adequate aftercare which many young care-leavers experience is contrary both to the recommendations of the Kennedy Report (1970) and much of the recent research on good leaving care practice. It is now widely acknowledged that preparation for leaving care should begin on admission and not just prior to departure. The abruptness of the departure has been vividly captured in a quote from one care worker who explained:

You help them to pack their bags and take their posters down from the wall and you say goodbye and tell them to keep in contact, to ring you (quoted in Kelleher Associates, 1998:8).

OUT ON THEIR OWN (KELLEHER ASSOCIATES, 1998)

The research population for this project was comprised of three distinct sub-groupings: Young people leaving the care of the country's five special schools for young offenders over an 18-month period; young people leaving the care of the two Dublin probation hostels over a six-month period; and young people leaving the care of three health boards, also over a six-month period (the Eastern, North-Eastern and North-Western Health Board regions). The circumstances and case histories of young people leaving care from these three services over the respective periods were ascertained. This was followed by an examination of the circumstances of the young people six months after leaving care.

YOUNG PEOPLE LEAVING SPECIAL SCHOOLS

Excluding centres for remand and assessment, there are five special schools for young offenders funded by the Department of Education and Science in the Republic of Ireland (St. Joseph's, Clonmel; St. Laurence's, Finglas; Oberstown Boys' Centre, Lusk; Oberstown Girls' Centre, Lusk; and Trinity House, Lusk). First information was collected on all 103 children who left the care of these five centres in the study time frame. This group was predominantly male, consisting of only 5 females and 98 males. The demographic profile of these children was striking. A third had between three and five siblings, another third had between six and eight siblings, while more than one in seven had nine or more siblings. Just over a third of these children came from families in which the marital status of the parents was that they were either married or living together. The remainder came from single parent families.

The adversity these children had already suffered before ever coming into residential care was overwhelming. Almost three-quarters of these children had serious relationship diffi-

culties with their parents and about a quarter had similar difficulties with their siblings. Over half had one or more parents
addicted to alcohol and domestic violence was a feature of the
family household in almost half of cases. Mental health problems of parents were reported in about one in ten children,
while parental drug abuse was reported in about one in twelve
children. These findings illustrate a similar level of trauma to
that reported by Fahy-Bates (1996) in her study of young offenders in open centres in Ireland.

In addition to those listed above, the young people themselves also had a significant number of other difficulties. This
cannot be seen as surprising given the propensity for violence
within many of the young peoples' families combined with
other adverse environmental factors. Approximately nine out of
ten of the children had only attended school on an irregular basis and four out of five had delayed learning due to irregular
school attendance. The vast majority (85 per cent) of children
were known to have been involved in criminal activity, about
half had a problem with drugs, solvents or glue while approximately three in ten had problems with alcohol. Almost one in
five of these children had been or was thought to have been
sexually abused, while other problems included learning disability (17 per cent), physical ill-health (11 per cent), mental
health problems (9 per cent) and gambling problems (4 per
cent). The vast majority (81 per cent) of children were placed in
care because of criminal behaviour, while about a third were
thought to be out of control.

Only 17 per cent of young people in this element of the
study had never been in care before their current admission.
For over half it was their second admission, almost another
quarter were in their third care placement and approximately
one in eleven had four or more admissions. Upon leaving care
only 12 per cent had been in care for less than one year. Over
half had been in care for between one and two years, while
substantial proportions had been in care for between two and
five years (20 per cent) and over five years (15 per cent).

Twenty-one per cent of the young people interviewed were
identified by staff to be inappropriately placed in a Special
School. It was felt that some young people who were in secure

units could be transferred to more open centres or half-way hostels and the need for short-stay specialised units for young people with addiction problems was identified. Three of the young people surveyed required placement in a residential centre that could respond to the specific challenges of learning disability. There is a need for a range of placement options for young people whose primary issue is not criminal behaviour. The current practice in special schools of mixing these young people with young people who are engaged in persistent criminal activity is a serious cause for concern.

At the point of leaving care, staff were of the opinion that for 38 per cent of young people leaving these special schools there were important issues which had not been addressed. The reasons cited for this were a lack of appropriate services and difficulties in engaging the young people. Upon leaving care, 63 per cent of the young people returned to either their family or relatives. Ten per cent of the young people absconded and 18 per cent were placed in detention centres. The remainder went to either hostel accommodation (3 per cent), supported lodgings (5 per cent) or were placed in foster care (1 per cent). In 50 per cent of cases where individuals returned to their families, it was felt this environment had improved. This included instances where, for example, parents addressed their own addiction issues. However, for the other 50 per cent of young people who returned home, there was no improvement in family circumstances. In a number of cases it was felt that returning home was not the most advisable course of action. However, given the absence of suitable alternative accommodation, many young people were forced to return home to extremely adverse circumstances.

At the point of the six month follow-up, 93 of the original 103 were traced. One young person had died of a drug overdose, three were in England and the whereabouts of the remaining six was not known. Of those who could be traced, the number living with relatives had declined from 63 per cent upon leaving care to 48 per cent at the six-month point. Whereas 18 per cent had gone to detention centres upon leaving care, 39 per cent of this sample were in such centres six months later. A further 13 per cent had been in a detention centre at some stage during the six months since leaving care. This means that over 51 per cent of the young people in this sample had been in a detention centre at some point during the six-month period after leaving care. The situation of the young people at this stage was even more bleak, as those committed to detention centres are no doubt only a subset of those involved in crime. Staff were of the opinion that a further 31 per cent of young people were involved in crime. This means that more than eight out of ten (83 per cent) of young people were known or suspected to be involved in crime six months after leaving the special schools.

The work status of the young people at the six-month mark reflected their early school leaving age and low educational achievement. Twenty per cent were unemployed, 5 per cent either at school or in further education. Only 15 per cent were in employment, while 20 per cent were on training courses (the remaining 39 per cent, as noted above, were in detention centres). Only six of the 93 young people traced had an income in excess of £100 per week.

At least 30 per cent of the young people had experienced homelessness during the six months since leaving care. Many of the young people were experiencing difficulties regarding alcohol, drugs, anger management and familial relationships.

All 93 young people followed-up at the six-month point were assessed by care staff in terms of their progress since leaving care. It should be noted that as Biehal et al. (1995, p. 252) state "in the field of social care, outcomes are rarely clear cut". Assessment of the young people involved examining the young person's ability to develop a stable lifestyle. This involved either staying out of crime or committing less serious crime, attending school, a training course, further education or work. Fourteen per cent of the young people were assessed as having made "very good" progress. An equal number were assessed as having made "good" progress, 26 per cent of young people were felt to have made "fair" progress and 40 per cent were felt to have made "poor" progress (there was no information on 7 per cent).

Care staff were of the opinion that 58 per cent of the young people were not getting the aftercare they urgently required. In a further 20 per cent of cases staff were not able to make such an assessment due to inadequate information. Only about 21 per cent of young people were considered to have the appropriate level of help.

YOUNG PEOPLE LEAVING PROBATION HOSTELS

Young people leaving Lionsvilla Hostel and Sarsfield House, the two probation hostels located in the Eastern Health Board (EHB) Region constituted the study population of the second part of the research project. The two hostels are relatively small, catering for only 11 and 18 people respectively, all of whom are males. It is not surprising, therefore, that only a small number of young people (seven) left the hostels in the six-month data collection period between April and September 1997. Information was collected on six of these seven young people. Given the small number involved, it is not constructive to look in great detail into family and personal circumstances. However, it is important to note a similar pattern to that observed in young people in the special schools. Only two of the six children had parents living together and only one family was in the owner-occupied sector. Other problems were also prevalent among the young peoples' families in this group. These included domestic violence (in five out of six families), relationship difficulties (in four out of six families), and addiction problems to either alcohol (in three out of six families) or drugs (in one out of six families).

All of the six young people leaving the probation hostels in this period displayed socially disruptive behaviour. All six were known to be involved in criminal activity and each had a criminal record. Five of the six children had an irregular pattern of school attendance, while half had problems with drugs, solvents or glue. Half also had a problem with alcohol and the same number had delayed learning due to irregular school attendance. Other problems included learning disability (two out of six), physical ill-health and having been, or suspected of having been, sexually abused (both one out of six). All of these young people had been in care for more than one year upon leaving and two also had siblings in care.

All six of the young people were in the hostels for less than one year. Five of the young people left because their placements broke down, either because the young person breached the rules of the hostel or as a result of new convictions. The sixth person was returned to court and convicted of assault. Upon leaving care, two of the young people were remanded to juvenile detention centres and one was committed to such a centre. Two of the young people returned home, while another returned to a special school.

Examination of the circumstances of the six young people, six months after leaving care, revealed one young person was in prison, while another had absconded to England from an open prison. Two young people were living in the family home, one was living in emergency hostels for young people out-of-home and one was living independently in the private rented sector. Four of the young people had either been in prison or a juvenile detention centre within six months of leaving care. Overall, three of the young people were assessed as having made good progress since leaving care. Two of these were in employment, while the third had returned to education. However, the remaining three young people must be assessed as having made only poor progress.

YOUNG PEOPLE LEAVING HEALTH BOARD CARE

In order to achieve both an urban and a rural sample, the North Eastern Health Board (NEHB), the North Western Health Board (NWHB) and the EHB were included in the study. The study population was designed to include young people of 13 years or older in foster care, residential care, supported lodgings or semi-independent living arrangements in the three health board regions listed and discharged from care during the six-month study period.

Only 56 young people leaving care were identified during the study period. This is probably a gross underestimate, but reflects the absence of a database or records on young people leaving care in the EHB region. The 56 young people identified were exactly equal in terms of the number of males and females identified (28 of each sex). Twenty-nine per cent left care aged

16 or under, the majority (48 per cent) leaving aged 17 or 18 years. Almost 36 per cent of these young people had also been admitted to care on a previous occasion.

Once again the socio-demographic profile of this group was very noticeable. There can be little doubt that reception into care is closely associated with poverty and deprivation. Just over 3 per cent of mothers and 20 per cent of fathers of the young people were in full-time employment. Almost six in ten of parents were living in local authority accommodation, while 17 per cent lived in the owner-occupied sector and 9 per cent in the private rented sector. This contrasts with the general population of which 79 per cent live in the owner-occupied sector and just 10 per cent live in local authority housing. Six of the remaining seven families were effectively homeless, while one lone parent was in a psychiatric hospital. Following a similar pattern to that observed above, only about four in ten parents were living together, either married or unmarried.

The problems associated with the family circumstances of young people in care were again mirrored in this group. Four out of ten came from families experiencing domestic violence. Nearly half of the children came from families where one or more parents had an alcohol addiction. Three in ten families had one or more parents with mental health problems, while about one in ten families had one or both parents experiencing difficulties with drugs.

The young peoples' own difficulties were equally marked. Just over half had been irregular school attenders, while 45 per cent displayed socially disruptive behaviour. Approximately four out of ten had been, or were thought to have been, sexually abused, while about three in ten had problems with drugs, solvents or glue. Two in ten had mental health problems, while the same number had a criminal record. Other difficulties included problems with alcohol (16 per cent), physical ill-health (14 per cent) and learning disability (13 per cent).

Perhaps one of the most startling aspects of this study group was the significant proportion (21 per cent) who entered care when they were less than one-year-old. Upon leaving care, 46 per cent had been in care for over five years and a further 11 per cent had been in care for between two and five years. Only

13 per cent had been in care for less than six months. During their time in care, 32 per cent of young people did not have a placement move, 36 per cent had between two and four placement moves. A further 19 per cent had between five and ten placement moves and 13 per cent had ten or more placement moves. Included in this last figure are three individuals who had 40 or more placement moves. Social workers contacted as part of this research felt that over one-third of the placements were unsuitable.

The destination of the young people was recorded upon leaving care. Almost one-third returned either to their families or to relatives, while over a quarter moved into private sector accommodation. One in eight remained in their foster home, while 5 per cent each went to hostels and supported accommodation. Two individuals became homeless, while another went to prison. The remaining seven young people whose whereabouts are unknown were all in care placements which broke down.

Six months after leaving care 49 of the original population were contacted and their progress was assessed. Of the seven who were not contactable, one young person had died, one had emigrated to England and the whereabouts of the remaining five were unknown. At the six-month point eight individuals (16 per cent) were homeless. Even more alarmingly, twice this number had experienced some form of homelessness during the six-month period after leaving care. Ten per cent of young people reported at this point that they had no form of family contact or support. Even in those situations where young people were receiving support, the relationship between the two parties was only considered to be satisfactory and important in 61 per cent of cases. Information on school-leaving age was available on 46 of the 49 young people contacted. This revealed that three-fifths had left school aged 15 years or younger. Only about a fifth of this sample remained in school until aged 17 or more. It is not surprising, therefore, that almost half had no qualifications on leaving education, that a further 30 per cent had only taken subjects in the Junior Certificate and that a mere 10 per cent had taken the Leaving Certificate. This contrasts with the general population in which as few as 4 per cent leave school without qualifications. Just three of these young people had, at this point in time, progressed to third-level education.

Only 24 per cent of the 49 young people traced six months after leaving care were at work, 20 per cent were on state-sponsored training courses and 39 per cent were unemployed. The reality was worse than that depicted above, as only 14 per cent of the young people were earning in excess of £100 per week. Six months after leaving care, these young people experienced a range of difficulties, which included problems regarding drugs, alcohol, and anger management difficulties. Forty-seven per cent of young people had difficulties in relation to accommodation and social workers were of the opinion that 37 per cent were involved in crime. Eighteen per cent had been arrested and four had spent time in prison (one individual was currently in prison).

Social workers were of the opinion that 53 per cent of these young people were not getting the aftercare help which they needed. In a further 10 per cent of cases, social workers were unable to assess whether or not the young people were getting the help they required, as they did not have sufficient information on which to make such an evaluation.

As in the other parts of the study social workers were asked to make an assessment of the progress of the young person six months after leaving care. Thirty-nine per cent were considered to be making "good" or "very good" progress, while 57 per cent were considered to be making only "poor" or "fair" progress.

Young people who were making "good" or "very good" progress tended to be in the older age groups and to have educational qualifications (see Table 4.1). In addition, they tended not to be involved with drugs and not to have had a breakdown in their care placement. Interestingly these young people also tended not to have returned home and to have had a planned transition from care.

Table 4.1: Characteristics of Young People Rated as Making Good Progress after Leaving Health Board Care

Characteristics	Percentage of Young People Making Good Progress	Percentage of Health Board Leaving Care Population
No educational qualification	26	50
Placement breakdown	11	48
Living with family	11	35
Past involvement in drugs	11	30
	N=19	N=49

Source: Kelleher Associates (1998)

CONCLUSIONS

The link between young people leaving state care and becoming homeless has been clearly identified. This research demonstrates that young people leaving care are at a considerable social disadvantage compared to similar young people who do not have a care background. Care-leavers also leave school at an earlier age than the general population and with less educational qualifications than their contemporaries. One per cent of young people leaving the care of special schools and four per cent of those leaving Health Board care had sat the Leaving Certificate. These statistics contrast with those of the general population where 82 per cent sat the Leaving Certificate (Williams and Collins, 1997). Young people leaving care also predominantly come from very economically deprived backgrounds. Significantly higher than average unemployment rates and rates of local authority housing tenure clearly demonstrate this pattern. It is also important to note that Stein (1997) has identified that, in addition to the poor socio-economic backgrounds of many young people in care, the legacy of care has an independent negative effect on disadvantage experienced in later life.

Care-leavers are also highly likely to have experienced a greater level of emotional trauma than non-care-leavers. Between 40 and 50 per cent of care-leavers had experienced violence in the home compared with estimates of the national incidence of domestic violence which put the figure at 18 per cent (Kelleher Associates and O'Connor, 1995). Addiction issues, separation and bereavement all contribute to the high level of emotional trauma care-leavers experience.

In effect, children leaving care can be categorised as being socially disadvantaged and often hold only rudimentary education qualifications, if any. In addition, as well as possibly being traumatised by the effects of separation, the majority have suffered severe emotional trauma through the adverse conditions experienced before entering care. This profile obviously highlights the need for substantial help for this population both during and following care. However, as demonstrated in the *Out On Their Own* (Kelleher Associates, 1998) report, these children, who are obviously in need, are failing to receive the aftercare services they require. It is unacceptable that an estimated 58 per cent of children leaving special schools and 53 per cent of children leaving health board care required an aftercare support which was not available. Therefore, it is not surprising given the trauma many of the young people have experienced and the lack of appropriate aftercare supports, that the young people leaving care fare as badly as they do. The individual commitment of staff to these issues cannot be blamed. One finding of this research is that aftercare is often provided by staff in their own time. The fault lies in the lack of resources allocated to aftercare services.

An overview of the results of the *Out On Their Own* research makes for depressing reading. Upon leaving care those more likely to progress well tend to be older and hold educational qualifications. In addition, the more successful leaving care groups are less likely to have been involved in drugs, not have had a breakdown in their care, and to have had a planned transition from care. Interestingly, the groups making good progress also tend not to have returned home after being in care.

ADDRESSING THE ISSUES OF YOUNG PEOPLE IN CARE

The issue of young people in care requires urgent government attention. The development of an overall policy or strategic plan for young people in care is a priority. A central feature of this plan should be the integration of the current care facilities operated by the three Departments of Health and Children, Education and Science, and Justice, Equality and Law Reform into one unified system of child care. In addition, the current legislation relating to aftercare is either absent or weak. There is no provision for special schools to undertake aftercare and both the Child Care Act, 1991 and the Children Bill, 1996 are particularly weak on the aftercare issue. This legislation is enabling in relation to aftercare, rather than enforcing. There is a need for a clear written policy to develop an adequate aftercare service which should address the needs of young people in regard to finances, employment, training and education, accommodation, health and therapeutic services. Given the age and vulnerability of care-leavers, a comprehensive range of accommodation options is essential. These could include priority access to local authority accommodation, furnished flats, supported housing in local areas, half-way homes in local areas and an increased number of probation hostels.

The *Out On Their Own* report (Kelleher Associates, 1998) revealed a considerable level of ambiguity over what exactly constitutes a care plan. Some care plans are not even written down, while others often constitute nothing more than a few notes. A minority of care plans are the result of careful and constructive work including a lengthy statement, an analysis of aims and objectives, as well as formal agreements, or "contracts", between the child and care staff. Given the importance of such plans, as enshrined in the Child Care Act, 1991, there is a need for the Department of Health and Children to develop national guidelines on care plans.

Further investigation is also required into what appears from this research to be a substantial rate of inappropriate placements and the significantly high rates of placement breakdown. This research also revealed the effective criminalisation of homelessness through the use of remand/assessment centres for housing some girls because of a lack of suitable health board accommodation. The use of such centres in this way is unacceptable and alternative accommodation needs to be provided as a matter of priority.

This research has also identified the lack of information on young people in care and young people leaving care. Accurate and timely data on information relating to children in care and leaving care is an important element in strategic planning and the management of child care services as well being the foundation of an evidence-based approach on which to evaluate child care and aftercare services.

Significant resources must be invested in the Community Care service in the three health boards of what constituted the Eastern Health Board area. At the time the *Out On Their Own* research was conducted, there were 2,400 cases on waiting lists in the EHB region awaiting the allocation of social workers to undertake an assessment.

The Department of Health and Children should provide financial support for the Irish Association for Young People in Care (IAYPIC). It is a support group for young people in care which aims to empower these young people to have their voice heard and to provide an input into government policy on foster and residential care. Equally, there is need for support for an organisation which would focus on leaving care. For example, First Key is an organisation which specialises in leaving-care policy and practice in the UK.

It is widely acknowledged in the Republic of Ireland that The Child Care Act, 1991 has meant that there have been considerable advances in the State's provision for children. However, O'Sullivan (1996b) has argued that the implementation of Section 5 of the Act has succeeded in marginalising homeless children within a secondary child care system. Some children may be classified as "runaways" or "intentionally homeless" and may then be excluded from the benefits and protection of the Act. Given the intense vulnerability of children out-of-home, and the responsibility of the state to protect its weakest members, this is an area in need of immediate remedial action.

References

Biehal, Nina, Clayden, J., Stein, M. and Wade, J. (1995) *Moving On: Young People and Leaving Care Schemes*. London: HMSO.

Crowley, G. (1997) "A Health Board Worker's Perspective", in Focus Ireland's *Transition from Care* conference proceedings, pp. 61-63. Dublin: Focus Ireland.

Dillon, B, Murphy-Lawless, J. and Redmond, D. (1990) *Homelessness in Co. Louth. A Research Report*. A SUS Research for Dundalk Simon Community and Drogheda Homeless Aid.

Dillon, C. (1992) *A Survey of Youth Homelessness in Co. Clare*. Clare Youth Centre.

Eastern Health Board (1987) *Homeless Young People*, unpublished report.

Eastern Health Board (1994) *Homeless Young People*, unpublished report.

Fahy-Bates, B. (1996) "Aspects of Childhood Deviancy: A Study of Young Offenders in Open Centres in the Republic of Ireland". PhD Thesis, Dublin: Department of Education, University College Dublin.

Focus Point and Eastern Health Board (1989) *Forgotten Children — Research on Young People Who Are Homeless in Dublin*. Dublin: Eastern Health Board and Focus Project Limited.

Garnet, L. (1992) *Leaving Care and After*. London: National Children's Bureau.

Gilligan, R. (1991) *Irish Child Care Services — Policy, Practice and Provision*. Dublin: Institute of Public Administration.

Harvey, B. and Menton, M. (1989) "Ireland's Young Homeless", *Children and Youth Service Review*, 11, pp. 31-43.

Keane, C. and Crowley, G. (1990) *On My Own: Report On Youth Homelessness In Limerick City*. Limerick: Mid-Western Health Board and Limerick Social Service Centre.

Kelleher Associates (1998) *Out on Their Own. Young People Leaving Care in Ireland*. Dublin: Focus Ireland.

Kelleher Associates and O'Connor, M. (1995) *Making the Links*. Dublin: Women's Aid.

Kelleher, P., Kelleher, M. and Corbett, M. (2000) *Left Out on Their Own. Young People Leaving Care in Ireland*, Dublin: Oak Tree Press is association with Focus Point.

Kennedy, E. (1970) *Reformatory and Industrial Schools Systems* (also known as The Kennedy Report). Dublin: Government Publications.

McCarthy, M. (1990) *Research Project for a Through-Care/Aftercare Support Service, St. Joseph's Special School.* Clonmel, Tipperary: Ferryhouse.

McCarthy, P. and Conlon, E. (1988) *A National Survey on Young People Out of Home in Ireland.* Dublin: Streetwise National Coalition.

Morgan-Klein, B and Murdoch, M (1985) *Where Am I Going? A Report of Young People Leaving Care in Scotland.* Edinburgh: Scottish Council for the Single Homeless.

O'Brien, J. (1988) "Youth Homelessness", in J. Blackwell & S. Kennedy *Focus on Homelessness: A new look at Housing Policy*, pp. 45-54. Dublin: Columba Press.

O'Sullivan, E. (1996a) "Adolescents Leaving Care or Leaving Home and Child Care Provision in Ireland and the UK. A Critical View", pp. 212-224 in M. Hill and J. Aldgate (eds), *Child Welfare Services- Developments in Law, Policy, Practice and Research.* London: Jessica Kingsley Publishers.

O'Sullivan, E (1996b) *Homelessness and Social Policy in the Republic of Ireland.* Department of Social Studies Occasional Paper No. 5. Dublin: University of Dublin, Trinity College.

Pinkerton, J. (1997) "Key Messages from Research on Leaving Care in Northern Ireland", pp. 10-13 in Focus Ireland, *Transition from Care.* Dublin: Focus Ireland.

Pinkerton, J. and McCrea, R. (1996) *Meeting the Challenge? Young People Leaving the Care of the Social Services and Training Schools in Northern Ireland.* Belfast: Centre for Child Care Research, Department of Social Work, QUB.

Southern Health Board (1996) *Review of Adequacy of Child Care and Family Support Services.* Kilkenny: Southern Health Board.

Stein, M. (1991) *Leaving Care and the 1989 Children Act: The Agenda.* Leeds: First Key.

Stein, M. (1994) "Leaving care, education and career trajectories", *Oxford Review of Education*, 20(3), pp. 349-360.

Stein, M. and Carey, K. (1986) *Leaving Care.* Oxford: Blackwell.

Stein, M. (1997) *What Works in Leaving Care?* Barkingside: Barnardos.

Stone, M. (1990) *Young People Leaving Care: A Study of Management Systems Service Delivery and User Evaluation.* Redhill: Royal Philanthropic Society.

Task Force on Child Care Services (1980) *Final Report.* Dublin: Government Publications Office.

Williams, J. and Collins, C. (1997) *The Economic Status of School Leavers: 1994-1996: Results of the School Leavers Survey.* Dublin: Department of Education and Science.

---

[1] Estimates of the proportion of homeless youths who have previously been in residential care vary considerably. Estimates have ranged from 22.7 per cent (Eastern Health Board,1987) to 40 per cent (found by both the EHB [1994] and Kelleher Associates [1998]).Within this range a study conducted in the MWHB reported a figure of 29 per cent (Keane and Crowley, 1990), while a similar study in the EHB reported that 38 per cent of homeless youths had previously been in long-term care (Focus Point & EHB,1989). A recent analysis conducted by the Southern Health Board (1996) found that 35 per cent of young people out-of-home had previously been in care.

[2] Published as *Left Out on Their Own: Young People Leaving Care in Ireland* (2000), by Kelleher, P., Kelleher, M. and Corbett, M., Dublin: Oak Tree Press in association with Focus Ireland.

Chapter 5

Children and Political Violence: The Northern Ireland Conflict

Ed Cairns and Frances McLernon

BACKGROUND TO THE "TROUBLES"

Although it is 800 years since England began to consolidate its control over Ireland, thus planting the seeds of the "Troubles" in the northern counties, it could be argued that the current political situation in Northern Ireland is a direct result of the invasion in 1649 by Oliver Cromwell, when England began to settle Scottish Protestants along the north coast of Ireland. Since then, intermittent periods of conflict have occurred between the Protestant "settlers" and the Catholic "natives". The current period of violence, which began in 1969, has been endured by the people of Northern Ireland for over 30 years, has relentlessly disrupted the daily lives of both Catholic and Protestant people, and has cost the lives of over 3,000 of them.

Two separate states have existed in Ireland since 1921, when the country was divided into the Republic of Ireland, which has 26 counties and a population of approximately 3.5 million, and Northern Ireland, which has 6 counties and a population of approximately 1.5 million, about 40 per cent of whom are Catholic and 60 per cent Protestant. Until 1960, most of the social institutions in Northern Ireland were controlled by the Unionist Stormont government. Because non-unionists were mistrusted politically, they were deemed unsuitable to participate in political affairs, and were excluded from holding place in government. This led to considerable resentment amongst the nationalist population of Northern Ireland, resulting in a mounting tension between the two communities which culminated in the 1960s in frequent protest marches which were often accompanied by street violence, rioting, house burnings, intimidation and terror. In 1966 the UVF (Ulster Volunteer Force) was formed, for the express purpose of protecting the interests of the Protestant people in the north and combating the IRA. In August 1969, amid growing Republican support for the IRA (Irish Republican Army), the Stormont Parliament asked Westminster to send the British army to Northern Ireland. Although both Protestants and Catholics initially welcomed the British soldiers, they quickly came to be perceived by the Catholics as "pro-unionist", and hence the tools of the Unionist Government, operating solely in the interests of Unionism. With the introduction in 1970 of internment without trial, this view was strengthened, leading to widespread riots, arson attacks, and a consolidation of Catholic support for the IRA. As a result, Northern Ireland resorted in 1971 to direct rule from Westminster.

THIRTY YEARS OF CONFLICT

Over the last three decades, the conflict in Northern Ireland has not been constant in its intensity. After rising to a high of 467 deaths in 1972, the level of violence dropped to an average of 250 deaths in each of the next three years, then fell in subsequent years to a mean rate not exceeding 100 deaths per annum. The violence in Northern Ireland also varied along the dimensions of intensity (the number of deaths and personal injuries, and the extent of environmental destruction); quality (the type of violence; for example, car-bombs, murders of civilians and of security forces); and location (Belfast and Derry suffered most of the destruction, but other towns and villages were also targeted in dramatic ways)(Cairns and Toner, 1993). Widespread strikes by workers in the key industries occurred at times of particular tension, together with almost constant assassinations, riots, ambushes by paramilitaries and arson attacks. People felt a sense of danger because of the random and unpredictable nature of the violence. Everyday activities such as going to the shops, to school or out for a drink to a local pub involved the risk of being caught in an explosion, ambush or shooting. As a result, many people felt intense fear, and the experience of terrorism by both security forces and civilians was extensive, with adults and children equally likely to find themselves exposed to scenes of violence on the streets. Life could be disrupted on a daily basis by personal, house and vehicle searches by the army and police. Public transport services were often sporadic and unreliable, with buses often hijacked and set on fire to form barricades, especially in the cities of Belfast and Derry. Shops and schools were at times forced to close because of the violence, but the residents of Northern Ireland went on with their daily lives. Babies were born into the violence, and children grew up having known no other way of life.

By 1992, the violence had abated somewhat, although the two communities remained polarised, and Catholic support had risen considerably for Sinn Fein, the political wing of the IRA. The signing, by the British Government, of the Anglo-Irish agreement in 1985 infuriated Protestants, who reacted with street violence and an upsurge in the number and strength of minor loyalist paramilitary groups, offshoots of the outlawed UVF. Between the signing of the Anglo-Irish agreement and the cease-fire announcement of 1994, paramilitary groups from both sides of the religious divide continued to initiate sporadic outbursts of violence. In addition to this, the loyalist tradition of Orange marches provoked extreme reactions from a growing number of nationalists, particularly in the flashpoint areas of Lower Ormeau Road (Belfast) and Garvaghy Road (Portadown). This exacerbated the Protestant sense of insecurity and intensified the feeling of threat from the Catholic community. It is in this climate of mistrust, the result of generations of conflict, that almost half a million children in Northern Ireland have grown up.

GROWING UP WITH THE CONFLICT

It is important to recognise that the violence in Northern Ireland has been sporadic, concentrated in certain areas, while others have enjoyed a relatively trouble-free existence. For this reason, the experience of violence by the children in Northern Ireland has been varied. As Cairns (1987) has pointed out:

> . . . this must always be kept in mind, even when research-ers make the mistake of talking about "the children of Northern Ireland" as if they were some homogeneous mass who all had in common the fact that they had been exposed to "the violence" (p. 24).

However, even though all children in Northern Ireland did not suffer the same degree of disruption to their lives because of the violence, it has been shown that most of the children were, from a very early age, aware of the violence going on around them, and that this knowledge increased as the children grew older. This was consistently found in the first two decades of the troubles. A study carried out in 1973 in two areas of Belfast, one Catholic and one Protestant, showed that compared with similar children in Edinburgh, Belfast children were more acutely aware of the potential for everyday objects such as a cigarette packet, a letter, a milk bottle and a parcel to be used in bomb-making than were the Scottish children (Jahoda and Harrison, 1975). Further studies carried out in 1976 and 1977 supported the conclusion that Northern Irish children are aware of the violence around them. In these studies, 90 per cent of five- to six-year-olds living in a relatively trouble-free area of Northern Ireland when shown pictures of a train crash or a derelict house suggested an explosion as the cause, compared with only 20 per cent of five- to six-year-olds from a London suburb who did so (Cairns, Hunter and Herring, 1980).

This theme continued into the 1980s, when a series of studies confirmed the extent of the knowledge of the troubles held by children both in areas of high violence, and those where sectar-ian violence is relatively infrequent (Taggart, 1980; McIvor, 1981; McWhirter, 1982). In addition, studies by Cairns in 1972 and 1982 suggested that not only were children in Northern Ireland more knowledgeable about the violence than their counterparts in the Republic of Ireland, but that the knowledge of those in the north was increasing as the violence continued (Cairns, 1982a; 1983a; 1984). A further study carried out during the paramilitary cease-fires in 1994-96 asked Protestant primary school children the question, "What was happening in Northern Ireland when there was no peace?" It was clear from the children's responses that the paramilitary groups played a major role in the children's awareness of the conflict (McLernon, 1998).

Not only did children in Northern Ireland possess relatively sophisticated knowledge of the conflict, but in some areas, particularly in Belfast, many children had first-hand experience of sectarian violence. For example, a paper by McKeown (1973) reported that of 178 secondary schools who responded to a survey on harassment of pupils going to and from school, 51 per cent reported harassment in the form of verbal abuse, assault or in one case the death of a pupil. Children's experience has not been limited to sectarian violence perpetrated by others, however. Cairns (1987, p. 26) has reported that in the early 1970s, press reports described the arrest of children as young as ten years of age who were charged with rioting offences. Neither was children's involvement in the conflict confined to the early years of the troubles. A study by McGrath and Wilson (1985) found that in a random sample of 522 children in Northern Ireland, 20 per cent had been in or near a bomb explosion, another 20 per cent had had a friend or relative killed or injured, and 12 per cent felt that the area they lived in was not safe.

EFFECTS OF THE CONFLICT ON CHILDREN'S BEHAVIOUR

Based on the experiences of Northern Irish children such as those described, who suffered directly or indirectly from the effects of the troubles, many pessimistic and gloomy predictions were made concerning the future mental health of these children. Some researchers felt that behaviour learned during the period of unrest in the province would be difficult to eradicate:

> When peace returns to Northern Ireland there will be a continuing epidemic of violence and anti-social behaviour amongst teenagers (Lyons, 1973).

Others were concerned about the damaging effects of the troubles on children:

> The violence that the children learn in the street spills over
> in the schools and into the home, toward all authority fig-
> ures. Once you are patterned to violence it is hard to get
> unpatterned (Fraser, 1974).

Lyons (1973) and Fraser (1974) both predicted that children
would become uncontrollable in law, and would never conform
even if a peaceful situation became the norm:

> But what will happen when a political settlement is eventu-
> ally achieved and these young people no longer have li-
> cence to commit anti-social acts? It is only to be expected
> that acts of violence and anti-social behaviour will continue
> because of the conditioning of previous years (Lyons, 1973).

Fraser also noted, however, that a certain amount of psychological resilience existed in Belfast children, and when emotional disorders did occur they tended to be short-lived. Further, those who did suffer from some form of emotional disorder tended to be those who were already vulnerable (for example, children of psychiatrically disturbed parents) and the
degree of emotional disturbance was found to be related to
facets of the child's personality, rather than to experiences of
violence or fear of the troubles.

In spite of these predictions that Northern Irish society was
raising a generation of anti-social and irresponsible children to
whom human life was cheap, evidence soon began to emerge
of the questionable accuracy of these predictions. One of the
problems with this early research on children in Northern Ireland is that it tended to focus only on children who had been
involved in violent acts, such as street rioting, and to see this
behaviour as indicative of the future behaviour of children in
Northern Ireland generally. In a review of research on children
in Northern Ireland, Harbison (1983) remarked:

> Evidence reviewed reflects the relative normalcy of most
> children — the social, economic, security and political
> problems are real, severe and damaging, but in spite of
> that, the children and young people are proving encourag-
> ingly adaptive.

In order to test the level of normalcy of children living in troubled areas of Northern Ireland, Whyte (1983) asked 173 children from West Belfast to complete a revised and adapted version of the Manchester Scales of Social Adaptation (1966). Measures included the assessment of leisure activities and family interaction. Whyte found that in this highly troubled area of Belfast, life progressed in a non-reactive way for almost all the children, with the Troubles "not really impinging on their daily leisure activities" (p. 102). In addition, it was found that 68 per cent of 12-year-old girls and 53 per cent of 12-year-old boys in the area belonged either to sports clubs or to youth clubs run by the parish or the education authority. Whyte interpreted this as evidence of the continuance of normal life. With regard to family interaction, the pattern found was described by the author as a "traditional" structure, in which no evidence existed that children had ceased to respect parental authority, but rather a picture emerged of normal, traditionally functioning family life on which the violence did not impinge. Both Jenvey (1972) and Bell (1990) have suggested that the overall result of the influence of polarisation and sectarianism which prevails in Ulster is to divert children and young people away from direct rebellion against their parents towards conformity with their ideology as expressed in their group identities. In support of this view, Halla Beloff (1980) said:

> The Northern Ireland situation may not be as special, deviant, sensational as some observers would have us believe . . . young people in Ulster are not as a group qualitatively different from their peers in large cities and other areas of deprivation like Scotland.

EFFECTS ON THE MENTAL HEALTH OF CHILDREN

It might be expected that exposure to the social conflict in Northern Ireland would have had a detrimental effect on the mental health of children living there. However, Cairns, Wilson, Gallagher and Trew (1995) have pointed out that although a proportion of people in Northern Ireland have become psychiatric casualties, most of those affected by the troubles, whether children or adults, have tended to suffer from milder stress-related illnesses which have been relatively short-lived. Cairns and Darby (1998) have interpreted this as evidence that people have adapted and learnt to distance themselves psychologically from the political violence and its associated stress. Further, although suicide figures for the decade 1976 to 1986 show a rise from 4 in 1974 to 7 in 1985 in the incidence of suicide of young people aged between 10-20, no evidence of psychiatric disturbance was found. In a study which examined case notes of Belfast children referred to the Regional Child Psychiatry Department in Belfast in the years 1968 (n=610), 1972 (n=381), 1976 (n=563) and 1980 (n=561), McAuley and Troy (1983) attempted to identify any relationship between social violence and psychiatric disorder in children. No relationship was found, however, between child psychiatric disorder and the troubles. Furthermore, using the Rutter Teacher Questionnaire (Rutter, 1967), Fee (1980) found that although Belfast children were more "psychiatrically disturbed" than children on the Isle of Wight (Rutter et al., 1970), they showed less evidence of psychological disturbance than those in an inner London Borough (Rutter et al., 1975).

McWhirter (1983b) points out that:

> After a further decade of civil strife, it would seem that we can still remain reasonably optimistic about the mental health of the young in Northern Ireland.

EFFECTS ON CHILDREN'S MORAL REASONING, EDUCATION AND CRIME

Levels of moral reasoning and moral behaviour may also be considered indicators of the effect on children of social conflict and disruption. Research has shown, however, that the moral reasoning of children in Northern Ireland is in fact likely to be generally no different from children in other parts of the UK. One exception was a study by Lorenc and Branthwaite (1986) which found no significant differences in levels of moral reasoning between Catholic and Protestant children in Northern Ireland, but they did find differences between Northern Irish

and English children. English children tended to be more critical than Northern Irish children of a teacher who applied corporal punishment to a child who had not done homework. Lorenc and Branthwaite interpreted this as evidence that the
Northern Irish children are more prepared than the English
children to succumb to authority. Although it could be argued
that this result perhaps indicates a familiarity with the "para-
military-style" punishment beating, and the greater acceptance
of violence as a way of life rather than as a greater respect for
authority, ample evidence exists to suggest that the moral reasoning levels of children in Northern Ireland are no different
from those of children in other parts of the UK. A review of research in this area by Heskin (1981) concluded that there was
no evidence that society in Northern Ireland was suffering from
a disintegration of moral standards of its young people as a result of growing up with the troubles. Furthermore, McLernon,
Ferguson and Cairns (1996) found a wish for peace on the part
of Northern Irish adolescents, shown by their eagerness to turn
to alternatives to violence such as disarmament. Even younger,
primary school children in Belfast were aware of the need for
all members of the community to work towards peace, and
were not content to leave it to politicians or others to bring
about peace.

A further indicator of anti-social behaviour amongst children
is the incidence of truancy. A report on truancy in Belfast
showed that between 1968 and 1977, when some of the worst
levels of violence were occurring in the province, truancy levels remained constant at around 9 per cent in primary schools,
and 16 per cent in secondary schools (Caven and Harbison,
1978). In the same decade, the number of Northern Irish children leaving school with no GCE or CSE qualifications fell from
27 per cent in 1979 to 22.4 per cent in 1984. By 1994, this figure
had fallen to 6 per cent, compared with 3.2 per cent in the Republic of Ireland in the same year. These figures can also be
compared with figures for England and Wales which showed a
drop of 12.2 per cent in 1979 to 9.5 per cent in 1984 for English
children, and 25.1 per cent in 1979 to 17.7 per cent in 1984 for
Welsh children. It appears therefore that school-leavers in
Northern Ireland were showing a similar rise in the standard of

educational attainment to that observed in other parts of the UK, further evidence of the normalcy of children in Northern Ireland generally.

Discipline within Northern Ireland's schools was also at this time perceived as better than in British schools. Knox (1982) said:

> Despite the troubles we do not hear of the breakdown of individual institutions, as in England, and one can but wonder at the surprising normality of life here. Examiners from across the water have commented favourably on the behaviour of Ulster's school children as follows: "A pupil actually opened the door for me, a thing you would never find in England. There, you would hardly dare to show your face".

Likewise, figures for juvenile crime during the period of the troubles show an encouraging time-related drop and are also favourable for Northern Irish children when compared with similar rates in other parts of the United Kingdom. In 1979, 2,646 juveniles (i.e. aged 10-17 years) were found guilty of a crime in Northern Ireland compared with 1,611 in 1986 and 742 in 1992. This figure was 133 (15 per cent) fewer than in 1991. This is the lowest total for over ten years, the downward trend being greater than that which would be attributable to demographic factors (Northern Ireland Office, 1993). By 1993 this figure showed a further fall, to 725. Northern Ireland has always had a significantly lower rate of juvenile involvement in crime than elsewhere in the UK (for a detailed analysis see Coleman, 1996). For example, the crime rate for Northern Ireland in 1994 was 42 per 1,000. The corresponding figure for England and Wales was 98 per 1,000. Further, the Northern Ireland figure was lower than that of any single police force area in England and Wales.

ATTEMPTS AT RECONCILIATION

During the 1970s and 1980s, various schemes were implemented which were designed to facilitate reconciliation between children from Catholic and Protestant backgrounds. Cairns & Darby (1998) describe what is known as "the contact hypothesis" as a means to overcome social division (Allport, 1954; Amir, 1969). This hypothesis suggests that social contact between members of opposing groups will allow the development of better understanding of one another's values and attitudes, and of improved respect for each other's lifestyles. Most attempts at promoting contact between the groups in Northern Ireland have taken two forms. The first is the organisation of holidays for religiously mixed groups of children from Catholic and Protestant backgrounds, usually from areas of Northern Ireland which have experienced the worst of the violence. Venues for holidays tend to be countries such as the United States, Great Britain, Holland and the Irish Republic, all of which possess strong historical links with Northern Ireland. These holidays provided the opportunity for the fostering of cross-community relationships amongst children who were accustomed to segregation in education, play and housing. Although some difficulties were initially encountered in the introduction and promotion of structured community relations work within the "holiday" format, the development of training programmes and the production of written guidelines for holiday staff and volunteer helpers resulted in the inclusion of the issue of conflict resolution and prejudice reduction in practically all mixed community holiday programmes. In the early 1990s researchers began to turn their attention to assessing the impact and effect on children of planned reconciliation programmes. As Wilson and Tyrrell (1995) have commented, the success of these schemes "can be measured to some extent by their contribution to the development of current official structures and strategies on community relations within Northern Ireland" (p. 241).

The second attempt to promote contact between Catholic and Protestant children was the development of more formal curriculum-based activities, such as EMU (Education for Mutual Understanding) or Cultural Heritage, which are government-funded attempts to encourage schools to initiate contact between Catholic and Protestant pupils. A study published in 1984 by Dunn, Darby and Mullan had provided evidence of the lack of contact between "controlled" schools, most of which were Protestant, and the "maintained" system of mostly Catholic schools. As a result, a scheme was introduced by which Catholic and Protestant primary school pupils in the same town worked together on curriculum-based activities during normal school hours: for post-primary or secondary pupils programmes were created during which Catholic and Protestant children came together to carry out joint field work in the study of Irish history. A subsequent evaluation of these programmes (Smith and Dunn, 1990) showed that not only had cross-community contact become an accepted feature of the school curriculum amongst pupils and teachers, but also that the programme attracted an encouragingly high level of support amongst parents. By 1995, a third of primary schools in Northern Ireland and over half post-primary schools were involved in some form of inter-school contact to bring Catholic and Protestant pupils together (Smith, 1995).

In addition to curriculum-based cross-community contact in segregated schools in Northern Ireland, the creation by the Education Reform (NI) Order 1989 of a statutory Government responsibility for the funding, support and promotion of religiously integrated schools further promoted contact between children from different religious and cultural traditions in Northern Ireland. Research is currently in progress on the impact of integrated primary and post-primary schools, although some studies already exist on the impact of integrated schools on parental choice of school (Cairns, 1989; Morgan et al., 1993); the views of parents (Agnew et al., 1992); the role of parents and teachers (Morgan et al., 1992; 1993; 1994) and friendship patterns (Irwin, 1991; 1993).

CONCLUSION

It has been seen in this chapter that children in Northern Ireland are not only aware of the violence going on around them, but in many cases have direct experience of this violence, or in some instances, have taken part in it. Despite these experiences, and despite the pessimistic predictions of researchers of the 1970s, children in Northern Ireland who have grown up during the worst of the violence in the 1970s and 1980s show little sign of abnormality in comparison to children in other parts of Great

Britain or the Republic of Ireland, in their levels of moral reasoning, juvenile crime, educational attainment and psychiatric disorder. It should be borne in mind, however, that researchers in Northern Ireland have not claimed that children do not suffer emotionally or behaviourally because of the troubles:

> Researchers . . . must examine . . . the vitally important distinction between individual case studies and group studies. Conclusions, by their nature, tend to be made in group terms, and all generalisations can mislead unless fringed with qualifications (Anthony, 1974, p. 147).

Anthony has further stated that:

> . . . stress as experienced or anticipated by the child and the stress as estimated by the adult observing the impact of the stress on the child are frequently of very different orders of magnitude (p. 106).

More recently, Palme (1991) pointed out that childhood trauma induced by war, social conflict or other extreme experiences can affect the individual and society for decades, yet children's suffering is consistently denied by educated thought. Instead, it is assumed that children can cope under all conditions provided they are not separated from close adults. Further, many adults believe that children do not have the capacity to fully understand war and social conflict, and so are protected from anticipatory stress and not significantly affected by war experiences. From the evidence of the research in Northern Ireland, there is no reason to doubt that the majority of the children of the province have coped and that many of them cope very well even when facing the reality of violence. The relevant question, however, is how children cope, and at what psychological cost? The relationships between the short- and long-term consequences of dealing with the threat of violence must be explored, as must the relationship between immediate coping mechanisms and their long-term after-effects. What, for example, is the "price" exacted in psychological terms for staying seemingly unaffected and showing no emotional signs of stress?

In 1990 the United Nations General Assembly approved the Convention on the Rights of the Child. Article 39 of the convention states:

> State parties shall take all appropriate measures to promote physical and psychological recovery and social re-integration of a child victim of any form of neglect, exploitation, or abuse; torture or any form of cruel, inhuman or degrading treatment or punishment, or armed conflict. Such recovery and reintegration shall take place in an environment which fosters the health, self-respect and dignity of the child.

These new rights incorporate not only physical and psychological recovery, but also social integration. It is vital, therefore, that the processes of recovery already begun in Northern Ireland take account not only of the rebuilding of the physical environment of the Northern Irish children, but also of the voices of the childhood victims of trauma.

This is particularly important in Northern Ireland considering the results of a study by McLernon (1998) which suggested that Northern Ireland children develop the ability to recognise the emotional and consequential aspects of war younger than children of other countries such as Holland and Sweden, where no social conflict exists, and that this may be a result of their close experience of the emotional anguish which accompanies the conflict in Northern Ireland. Furthermore, McLernon et al. (1996) found that once a cessation of violence had been achieved in Northern Ireland after the paramilitary cease-fires, young adolescents (14-15 years) were inclined to be hesitant about accepting the reality of peace, particularly as the cause of the conflict had not been satisfactorily resolved. For this reason it is of paramount importance not only that the extent of children's trauma is recognised, but that Northern Irish society provides its children with the reassurance and re-integration recommended by the United Nations Convention.

References

Agnew, U., McEwan, A., Salters, J. & Salters, M. (1992) *Integrated education: the views of parents.* Belfast, Queen's University School of Education.

Allport, G. W. (1954) *The Nature of Prejudice.* Cambridge, MA: Addison-Wesley.

Amir, Y. (1969) "Contact hypothesis in ethnic relations" *Psychological Bulletin,* 71, pp. 319-42.

Anthony, E. (ed.) (1974) *The Child in His Family (Vol. 3: Children at Psychiatric Risk),* New York: Wiley Interscience

Bell, D. (1990) *Acts of Union: Youth Culture and Sectarianism in Northern Ireland.* London: Macmillan.

Beloff, H. (1980) "A Place not so Far Apart: Conclusions of an Outsider" in Harbison, J. (ed.) A *Society Under Stress: Children and Young People in Northern Ireland.* Somerset: Open Books.

Cairns, E. (1982a) "Northern Irish children's perceptions of the level of neighbourhood violence". Unpublished paper.

Cairns, E. (1983a) "Children's perceptions of normative and prescriptive interpersonal aggression in high and low areas of violence in Northern Ireland." Unpublished paper.

Cairns, E. (1984) "Television news as a source of knowledge about the violence for children in Ireland: a test of the knowledge-gap hypothesis." *Current Psychological Research and Reviews,* Winter, 32-8.

Cairns, E. (1987) *Caught in Crossfire: Children and the Northern Ireland Conflict.* Belfast: Appletree Press.

Cairns, E. (1989) "Integrated education in Northern Ireland; the impact of real choice." *Education North,* 2.

Cairns, E. & Darby, J. (1998) "The conflict in Northern Ireland: Causes, consequences and controls." *American Psychologist,* 53, (7) pp. 754-760.

Cairns, E. & Toner, N. (1993) "Children and political violence: from riots to reconciliation", in Leavitt, L. A. & Fox, N. (eds) *Psychological Effects of War and Violence on Children,* New York, Lawrence Erlbaum.

Cairns, E., Hunter, D. & Herring, L. (1980) "Young children's awareness of violence in Northern Ireland: The influence of Northern Irish television in Scotland and Northern Ireland." *British Journal of Social and Clinical Psychology,* 19, pp. 3-6.

Cairns, E., Wilson, R., Gallagher, T. & Trew, K. (1995) "Psychology's contribution to understanding conflict in Northern Ireland", *Peace and Conflict: Journal of Peace Psychology*, 1 (2), pp. 131-148

Caven, N. & Harbison, J. (1978) *Persistent school non-attendance. Report of a survey and discussion of the links between absenteeism and various environmental factors.* Paper presented to the Northern Ireland Regional Office, British Psychological Society Conference on children and young people in a society under stress, Belfast, September.

Coleman, C. (1996) *Understanding crime data: haunted by the dark figure.* Buckingham: Open University Press.

Dunn, S., Darby, J. & Mullan, K. (1984) *Schools Together?* Coleraine, Centre for the Study of Conflict, University of Ulster.

Fee, F. (1980) "Responses to a Behavioural Questionnaire of a Group of Belfast Children" in Harbison, J. (ed.) *Children of the Troubles: Children in Northern Ireland.* Somerset: Open Books.

Fraser, M. (1974) *Children in Conflict.* Middlesex: Penguin.

Hadden, T. & Boyle, K. (1989) *The Anglo-Irish Agreement: Commentary, Text and Official Review.* London, Sweet and Maxwell: Dublin, Edward Higel.

Harbison, J. J. (1983) "Children in a Society in Turmoil" in Harbison, J. (ed.) *Children of the Troubles: Children in Northern Ireland.* Belfast, Stranmillis College Learning Resources Unit.

Heskin, K. (1981) "Societal disintegration in Northern Ireland: fact or fiction?" *The Economic and Social Review*, 12, 2, pp. 97-113.

Irwin, C. (1991) *Education and the development of social integration in divided societies.* Belfast, Queen's University.

Irwin, C. (1993) "Making Integrated Education Work for Pupils" in C. Moffatt (ed.), *Education Together for a Change*, Belfast: Fortnight Educational Trust.

Jahoda, G. & Harrison, S. (1975) "Belfast children: Some effects of a conflict environment." *Irish Journal of Psychology*, 3, 1, pp. 1-19.

Jenvey, S. (1972) "Sons and haters: Youth in conflict", *New Society*, 21:512, pp. 125-7.

Knox, H. M. (1982) Graduation Address. *QUB Bulletin*, No. 82. 6th Sept., 6-7. Belfast: Queen's University.

Lorenc, L. & Branthwaite, A. (1986) "Evaluations of political violence by English and Northern Irish school children". *British Journal of Psychology*, 25, pp. 349-352.

Lyons, H. A. (1973) "The psychological effects of the civil disturbances on children", *The Northern Teacher*, Winter, pp. 35-38.

McAuley, R. & Troy, M. (1983) "The impact of urban conflict and violence on children referred to a child guidance clinic" in Harbison, J. (ed.) *Children of the Troubles: Children in Northern Ireland*. Belfast: Stranmillis College Learning Resources Unit, 1983.

McGrath, A. & Wilson, R. (1985) *Factors which influence the prevalence and variation of psychological problems in children in Northern Ireland*. Paper read to the Annual Conference of the Development Section of the British Psychological Society, Belfast.

McIvor, M. (1981) *Northern Ireland: A preliminary look at environmental awareness*. Paper presented at the Sixth Biennial Conference of the International Society for the Study of Behavioural Development, Toronto.

McKeown, M. (1973) "Civil unrest: Secondary Schools' Survey". *The Northern Teacher*, Winter, pp. 39-42.

McLernon, F. (1998) "The effects of the conflict on Northern Irish children's concepts of peace and war". Unpublished D.Phil Thesis. Coleraine: University of Ulster.

McLernon, F., Ferguson, N. & Cairns, E. (1996) "Comparison of Northern Irish children's attitudes to peace and war before and after the paramilitary ceasefires", *International Journal of Behavioral Development*, 20 (4) pp. 715-30.

McWhirter, L. (1982) "Northern Irish children's Conceptions of Violent Crime", *The Howard Journal*, 21, pp. 167-77.

McWhirter, L. (1983b) "Looking back and looking forward: An inside perspective" in Harbison, J. (eds.) *Children of the Troubles: Children in Northern Ireland*. Belfast: Stranmillis College Learning Resources Unit.

Morgan, V., Dunn, S., Cairns, E. & Fraser, G. (1992) *Breaking the mould. The role of parents and teachers in the integrated schools in Northern Ireland*. Coleraine, Centre for the Study of Conflict, University of Ulster.

Morgan, V., Fraser, G., Dunn, S. & Cairns, E. (1993) "A new order of cooperation and involvement — relationships between parents and teachers in the integrated schools", *Educational Review*, 45 (1) pp. 43-52.

Morgan, V., Dunn, S., Cairns, E. & Fraser, G. (1993) "How do parents choose a school for their child — an example of the exercise of parental choice". *Educational Research*, 35 (2), pp. 139-148.

Morgan, V., Dunn, S., Fraser, G. & Cairns, E. (1994) "A different sort of teaching, a different sort of teacher — teachers in integrated schools in Northern Ireland". *Comparative Education.* 30 (2), pp. 153-163.

Northern Ireland Office (1993), Criminal Justice Services Division.

Palme, L. (1991) "Personal Reflections on the new rights for children in war" in *Reaching Children in War.* by Dodge, C. & Raundalen, M. (eds) Norway: Sigma Vorlag.

Rutter, M. (1967) "A child's behavioural questionnaire for completion by teachers: preliminary findings", *Journal of Child Psychology and Psychiatry,* 8, pp. 1-11.

Rutter, M., Cox, A., Tupling, C., Berger, M. & Yule, W. (1975) "Attainment and adjustment in two geographical areas: the prevalence of psychiatric disorder", *British Journal of Psychiatry,* 126, pp. 530-33.

Rutter, M., Tizard, J. & Whitmore, K. (1970) *Education, Health and Behaviour.* London: Longman.

Smith, A. (1995) "Education and the conflict in Northern Ireland" in S. Dunn (Ed.) *Facets of the conflict in Northern Ireland.* London: Macmillan.

Smith, A. & Dunn, S. (1990) *Extending inter school links: An evaluation of contact between Protestant and Catholic Pupils in Northern Ireland* Coleraine: Centre for the Study of Conflict, University of Ulster.

Taggart, G. (1980) "Social awareness and social reasoning in a sample of Northern Ireland children and adolescents". Unpublished B.A. Thesis, Queen's University, Belfast.

United Nations General Assembly: World Summit for Children, New York, 30 September 1990.

Wilson, D. & Tyrrell, J. (1995) "Institutions for conciliation and mediation: The origins of community reconciliation groups in Northern Ireland" in Dunn, S. *Facets of the Conflict in Northern Ireland.* London; Macmillan.

Whyte, Jean. (1983) "Control and supervision of urban 12-year-olds within and outside Northern Ireland: a pilot study", *Irish Journal of Psychology,* 1983, 6, pp. 37-45a.

Part 2:
Children in Education

Chapter 6

Some Aspects of Quality in Early Childhood Education

Mary Horgan and *Francis Douglas*

INTRODUCTION

Woodhead (1996) has noted that the pursuit of an all-embracing definition of quality is analogous to:

> ... trying to find the crock of gold at the end of the rainbow. We may make progress in the right direction, but we never quite get there. ... As with the rainbow, we may be able to identify invariant ingredients in the spectrum of early childhood quality, but the spectrum itself is not fixed, but emerges from a combination of particular circumstances, viewed from particular perspectives (pp. 9-10).

In similar vein, Jensen (1994), in his analysis of the Danish system, has referred to its elusiveness, concluding that "true quality, like true art, cannot be reduced to simple statements" (p. 156). With respect to questions of "quality" in early childhood education and care services, it is important to realise that concepts of quality are reflective of the particular mixture of socio-historical and political perspectives within any given culture. These include conceptions of:

> children's potential, their civil rights and position in society, but also our own understanding of the past, the present and the future and how we should meet the requirements and challenges of the modernization process with its struggles

between ideas and social forces (Dahlberg and Åsén, 1994,
p. 164).

However, Woodhead (1998), while accepting this stance, further argues that quality, although relative, is not arbitrary. It
thus has limits, "boundaries of adequacy . . . defined by children's basic needs and rights" (p. 16). Kellmer-Pringle (1975)
argued that there were four fundamental psychological needs
— the need for love and affection, new experiences, praise and
recognition, and responsibility. Brüner notes that one of the
most significant features of *homo sapiens* is the relative immaturity of the human infant and the protracted period of childhood relative to other animals (Brüner, 1972). It is, thus, human
society that structures and determines to a large extent how
children's needs are expressed and satisfied.

Nevertheless, the analysis of child development throughout
the 20th century has underscored the importance of nurturing,
supporting and promoting the personal development of each
child. Furthermore, this is reinforced by psychological and
neurobiological studies which show that major aspects of this
process of development are culturally invariant, beginning *in
utero* before there can be any conscious or unconscious attempts at socialisation.

> Such a concept of development, then, must be regarded as
> natural rather than as socially constructed. And childhood
> must be seen as a biological, and psychological reality.
> What is, or may be, socially constructed is the way in which
> we view this developmental process, and the way in which
> we set about supporting it (Kelly, 1994, p. 9).

The concepts of both childhood and child development which
are inherent in the philosophies of both State and voluntary
providers of early years' education and care in the Republic of
Ireland underpin the notion of the developmentally appropriate
curriculum, the education of reflective practitioners and the
necessity of parental involvement. All are predicated on a view
of education as a process involving conversation and collaboration between all those involved and as one centrally con-

cerned with empowerment and the facilitation of individual autonomy.

The resultant common factors of good practice have been encapsulated as follows: clear aims and objectives; a broad, balanced and developmentally appropriate curriculum; a variety of learning experiences which are active, relevant and enjoyable; warm and positive relationships; a well planned, stimulating, secure and healthy environment; a commitment to equal opportunities and justice for all; systematic planning, assessment and record-keeping; satisfactory adult:child ratios; continuity of care and consistent staff development; partnership with parents and family and liaison with the community; and effective procedures for monitoring and evaluating the quality of practice (Ball, 1994).

It is of significance that, despite the caveat that "developmentally appropriate practice" may vary from region to region due to differing cultural contexts (e.g. Vygotsky, 1978; Nunes, 1994), research on the quality of the curriculum has been amazingly consistent cross-culturally. The results of a US longitudinal research study, for example, which followed children from three different curricula into primary school, secondary school, and finally into adulthood, demonstrated that children who had participated in a "constructivist" curriculum, centred on active learning (high/scope[1] or traditional nursery) had better outcomes as 23-year-olds than children who had attended a programme based on adult-dominated, formal teaching, i.e. direct instruction or an environment with a *laissez-faire* ethos (Schweinhart and Weikart, 1993, 1997). A replication of this study in Portugal (Nabuco and Sylva, 1995) which followed children through to the end of first class in primary school yielded results which were:

> in complete agreement with those of Schweinhart and Weikart; since at primary school, children from the High/Scope nurseries showed significantly higher educational attainment (reading and writing), higher self-esteem (Harter Assessment of Perceived Competence and Acceptance) and lower anxiety than the matched control children (Sylva, 1996, pp. 3-4).

Indeed, the long-term educational benefits would appear to stem not primarily from what children are specifically taught but from effects on their attitudes to learning, on their task orientation and also on their self-esteem (Rutter, 1985). Further longitudinal research in the German Democratic Republic (Ewert and Braun, 1978; Winkelmann et al., 1979; Tietze, 1987) also resonates the fact that a preschool curriculum which is too formal too soon can have serious negative long-term repercussions. Other research by Osborn and Milbank (1987), Katz (1987), and Kärrby (1990) further substantiates the fact that programmes which embrace a more holistic and dynamic notion of child development are more successful. It would, thus, appear to be of major significance that attempts to determine quality provision should focus on the qualitative, dynamic, interactive and rather elusive facets of provision such as the developmental appropriateness of activities and expectations in all areas of growth and the nature of adult-child interaction, rather than being fixated on more quantifiable dimensions such as space, ratio and equipment to the exclusion of all else (a lacuna which is evident in Section VII of the 1991 Child Care Act in this country).

RESEARCH ON EARLY YEARS EDUCATION

During the past decade, successive studies have investigated the extent to which the child-centred philosophies/recommendations of the various preschool providers have, in effect, been realised (i.e. the level of quality achieved in the implementation of their curricula).

These establishments include playgroups (home/community), Montessori preschools, *Naíonraí* (i.e. Irish-medium playgroups), the junior infant classes of standard primary schools and junior infant classes in *Gaelscoileanna* (Irish-medium primary schools). Indeed, junior and senior infant classes in primary schools (catering for children aged 4-6 years approximately) constitute the largest sector providing preschool education in Ireland since the compulsory school starting age is 6. (Since 1994, "Early Start" classes for 3-year-olds have also been initiated in 40 primary schools in designated disadvantaged areas — see INTO, 1995.)

Many community playgroups are situated in disadvantaged areas where they often act as a focus for community development, and although Montessori education is commonly associated with the middle class, there are, in fact, some excellent examples, such as the "Before 5 Centre" in Churchfield, Cork, catering for the needs of deprived children. Nevertheless, there is as yet a lack of research regarding the social composition of preschools in the voluntary sector.

Currently, some 316 primary schools qualify for inclusion in the Disadvantaged Areas Scheme covering a population of up to 76,000 pupils. These schools (about 10 per cent of the total) are primarily concentrated in Dublin with two per cent of designated disadvantaged schools in rural areas. In December 1999, the Minister for Education proposed the "New Deal — A Plan for Educational Opportunities" which aims to target disadvantaged pupils in a more flexible manner. Differing supports will be available to individual schools according to the level of pupil disadvantage identified therein. These will result from a proposed primary pupil database which will allow the tracking of each pupil's progress throughout the primary system (Murphy, 2000).

In research conducted in University College Cork from 1987 to 1998, 477 children in 60 randomly-selected institutions were evaluated, during more than 176 hours of continuous observation. (This constituted approximately 50 per cent of the time spent in these classrooms as an equal amount of time was devoted to the collection of supplementary information, interviews, etc.) The ethnographic research strategy utilised involved a plurality of approaches, such as, A Target Child Study (Sylva et al., 1980 (amended by Jowett, 1981)); interviews with teachers/preschool leaders; Brown's Interaction Analysis System (BIAS; Brown, 1975); an analysis of classrooms — timetables, layout and equipment; a nationwide questionnaire survey.

Horgan, M. (1987) observed 150 children in 15 junior infant classes of primary schools. Dunlea (1990) observed 60 children in 10 Montessori schools. Douglas (1993) observed 157 children in 24 preschools (11 community playgroups (78 children); eight home playgroups (44 children); two preschools for Travelling children (14 children); one parent and toddler group (7 children); two Montessori classes (14 children)). Horgan, S. (1995) observed 60 children in five junior infant classes in *Gaelscoileanna*, and Dwane (1998) observed 50 children in five *Naíonraí*. (Note: In the State sector the average pupil:teacher ratio observed was 33:1, whereas in the voluntary sector the average recorded was 10:1). The findings presented below illuminate practice in the cognitive, linguistic and social domains.

In recent years, the importance of play in the child's cognitive development has been addressed by many. The most influential have been Piaget (1962), Vygotsky (1962), Brüner et al. (1976) and Sutton-Smith (1979). Each argues that the child cannot move towards abstract structure and reasoning without a broad base of direct sensory, dramatic and manipulative experience from which they can generalise and extrapolate.

The Target Child technique offers 42 coding categories to encompass all possible types of activity in the preschool setting (Sylva et al., 1980; Jowett, 1981). Categories 1-12 concern play which can either be deemed by the observer to be of high or low cognitive challenge. Categories 13-28 contain 3R activities which are considered to be highly cognitively challenging by definition. Finally, categories 29-42 outline what are known as "inscrutable" activities, where the observer cannot determine whether or not the child is being cognitively challenged.

In both standard primary schools and in *Gaelscoileanna*, certain factors revealed themselves as obstacles to the cognitive development of junior infant class children through play. These included the teacher's attitude to play, pupil-teacher ratio, and the availability of equipment. However, when other factors were held constant, the teacher's attitude was found to be the factor most highly correlated with the provision of play experiences. Results obtained from the classroom studies showed that a low level of cognitively challenging play was found in classrooms where the teacher followed an inflexible timetable and taught the class as a whole. Furthermore, the questionnaire results indicated that class instruction was the most frequently used instructional method. While most teachers agreed in theory with the importance of play and the manipulation of concrete objects in the enhancement of cognitive development, the majority of participants revealed that, in practice, they followed a reverse of this order.

Table 6.1: Summary of Main Findings of Recent Research in Cork City and County Regarding the Behaviour of Target Children and Cognitive Challenge

Category	Horgan (1987) Junior Infant Classes n = 15	Dunlea (1990) Montessori Schools n = 10	Douglas (1993) Community Playgroups n = 11	Horgan (1995) Junior Infant Classes in Gaelscoileanna n = 5	Dwane (1998) Naíonraí n = 5
Challenging 3Rs activity	9%	18%	3%	13%	6%
Activities 1-12 High cognitive challenge	8%	41%	19%	15%	14%
Activities 1-12 Low cognitive challenge	13%	13%	37%	11%	20%
Inscrutable activities which contained no visible challenge	70%	28%	41%	61%	60%

Note: These are average figures and mask the fact that the range between preschools/infant classes in each category varies considerably between the highest and the lowest.

In contrast, a flexible timetable and teacher awareness of the importance of dramatic, manipulative and structured play usually resulted in an environment where cognitive challenge was high. Waiting, watching or group repetition cannot be said to stimulate the child. Even if one were to concede that such behaviour contained some level of cognitive stimulation, it could hardly be equated with the high challenge and rich stimulation which accrues from direct sensory experience by the child. The evidence from the literature is overwhelming on this point (Piaget, 1962; Brüner, 1975; Sutton-Smith, 1967; Hutt, 1979; Johnson, 1976, Johnson et al., 1982).

Community playgroups, which have a far better staff/pupil ratio, suffer from the children wandering aimlessly around and from these results, even when playing, they are not being challenged at a high level. In other words, they are not being sufficiently goal-directed. This is almost certainly due to the lack of training received by these preschool personnel. The *Naíonraí* are similar but with a slightly lower level of high cognitive challenge. Montessori schools, in contrast, have a highly-structured environment with well-trained staff and because of the ascending level of complexity and self-correcting nature of their system, they provide the highest level of cognitive challenge for their pupils.

In summary, junior infant classes have a high level of structure which results in little freedom or choice for the child. Playgroups offer the child a great deal of freedom but lack structure, while Montessori schools provide freedom *within limits* in a highly structured environment. It is only the last which leads to high cognitive challenge.

The findings concerning play and linguistic development are interesting because every preschool programme prioritises the fostering and development of language. Moreover, research has highlighted the link between linguistic fluency and competence and cognitive development (Vygotsky, 1962; Luria, 1963; Cazden, 1976; Donaldson, 1978; Brüner, 1984; Wells, 1987).

The main finding to emerge was the very small percentage of time during which the child actually spoke in the majority of the situations observed.

As can be seen from Table 6.2, the target children spoke for less than 15 per cent of the total observed time in ordinary junior infant classes. However, one cannot conclude from this that these children were engaged in the silent unquestioning assimilation of knowledge. This would only be partly true — adult-imparted information was accepted without question but silence did not always prevail (for example, in adult-led group activities). The key factor was that the content was frequently determined by the adult.

Table 6.2: Summary of the Behaviour and Language of the Target Children

Category	Horgan (1987) Junior Infant Classes n = 15	Dunlea (1990) Montessori Schools n = 10	Douglas (1993) Community Playgroups n = 11	Horgan (1995) Junior Infant Classes in Gaelscoil-eanna n = 5	Dwane (1998) Naíonraí n = 5
Initiations to the teacher/ responses to the teacher.	5%	11%	10%	22%	10%
Initiations to other children	6%	1%	4%	10%	16%
Dialogue	2%	2%	3%	6%	2%
Egocentric speech	1%	1%	5%	5%	5%
Total language	14%	15%	22%	43%	33%

Note: These are average figures and mask the fact that the range between preschools/infant classes in each category varies considerably from the highest and the lowest.

A similar picture emerges with the Montessori classes, but for different reasons. Here the individualistic nature of the structured apparatus, which involved each child working primarily in isolation, curtailed linguistic interaction. This is perhaps the "pay-off" for the very high levels of cognitive challenge afforded by these self-same activities.

Playgroups lacked adult stimulation and interaction. With such an advantageous staff/pupil ratio these practitioners could have engaged in linguistic scaffolding to a much greater extent than was evident.

All the above have to be contrasted with the results from the junior infants in *Gaelscoileanna*, which exhibit a staggering amount of language for each child, considering the adverse teacher:pupil ratio. This ratio is as bad, or almost as bad, as in the standard primary school junior infant classes, and far worse than in Montessori classes or playgroups, yet the individual child speaks, on average, two to three times more frequently.

During the course of the study, several language-promoting factors were discovered. These included: the importance of a relaxed classroom atmosphere which is conducive to communication; the use of methodologies which exploit the child's natural fascination with the "new" language; the utilisation of an immersion rather than a submersion approach to language teaching; and above all, the teacher's commitment to and enthusiasm for the promotion of language in the classroom. It is also interesting to note that a similar ethos prevails in *Naíonraí*, where children, although younger, were found to speak for twice as much time as those in standard junior infant classes.

The social settings of the target children are summarised in Table 6.3.

Table 6.3: Social Settings of the Target Children

Category	Horgan (1987) Junior Infant Classes n = 15	Dunlea (1990) Montessori Schools n = 10	Douglas (1993) Community Playgroups n = 11	Horgan (1995) Junior Infant Classes in Gaelscoileanna n = 5	Dwane (1998) Naíonraí n = 5
Sitting passively side-by-side in large groups.	47%	5%	12%	26%	14%
Sitting side-by-side in large groups while interacting.	16%	2%	1%	36%	13%
Sitting passively side-by-side in small groups.	15%	1%	6%	1%	6%
Sitting side-by-side in small groups while interacting.	2%	3%	2%	2%	10%
In a pair	15%	38%	34%	22%	34%
Alone	5%	51%	45%	13%	23%

Note: These are average figures and mask the fact that the range between preschools/infant classes in each category varies considerably from the highest and the lowest.

During any class day, a variety of activities will be undertaken which will require different types of social grouping. However, empirical research has isolated interaction in pair or small group settings as the most advantageous for cognitive, linguistic and social development (Moore et al., 1974; Roper et al., 1978).

The table shows that the results for the children in both ordinary schools and *Gaelscoileanna* were disappointing in this respect. Indeed, children did not really interact with each other very much. In the junior infant classes, prescribed educational tasks and teacher-directed activities precluded social interaction — over 60 per cent of the total time was spent in large groups. (The *Gaelscoileanna* achieved a significantly higher level of interaction in large groups but not in small.)
In Montessori classes and playgroups, it was noticeable that the children spent a large percentage of their time alone. In Montessori classes this perhaps was not so unusual as the children worked individually with the structured activities but it was more surprising in playgroups where they had the freedom to interact if they so wished. However, in all types of voluntary sector preschool, interaction in pairs and small groups was significantly higher than that found in state-sector classes.

The following two case studies represent a major state and voluntary sector provider of preschool education. Junior infant classes in primary schools cater for approximately 32,000 four- and five-year-olds (Department of Education Statistics, 1997) while community playgroups are attended by over 10,000 children aged three and four (IPPA Statistics, 1996).

A CASE STUDY OF AN OUTSTANDING JUNIOR INFANT CLASS

The school has a staff of nine teachers — three males, one of whom is the school principal, and six females. The most recently qualified of these women teaches the junior infant class. Thirty-six children of both sexes are under her care, all aged between four and five years. (Approximately half of these children come from single-parent homes and unemployment is high in the catchment area.) One reaches their "pre-fab" classroom by climbing the make-shift steps which are really just a stack of cavity blocks.

The door of the junior infant classroom has been painted bright blue. A large cardboard rainbow stretches across it while white fluffy cottonwool clouds are glued on at random. Underneath are about 40 little scraps of paper. On closer inspection I observe that each contains a badly-written child's name. Laughter escapes from within the confines of this horse-box-like structure.

The classroom appears to be very crowded as children move ant-like in every direction around me. It measures approximately seven metres by seven metres, and this is exacerbated by the very low ceiling. The two side walls have full length windows which are almost one metre in height, thus making the room very bright inside. The floor has no covering and the original timber floorboards are discoloured and noisy.

The teacher is in her early twenties. This is her second year teaching and she neither requested nor was offered an alternative class. During the third year of her B.Ed. degree course, she attended lectures which specialised in infant education. Although she views these as an excellent foundation for anybody who is confronted with a class of "sobbing infants" in September, she is quick to add that her style of teaching is totally spontaneous:

> I just get ideas as I go along. . . . I rarely plan ahead. The way I teach something usually depends on how the children are that particular day.

She does not adhere to a fixed timetable but has a "rough guideline" which is followed every day.

> I always try to include Irish, English, Reading, Mathematics, Religion and either Drama or PE.

However, these are not allocated any special time with the exception of Reading and Mathematics which she usually takes in the morning as "the children are more alert before lunch". The remainder of the day contains a mélange of Music, Singing, Art, Rhymes and Stories. Social and Environmental Studies are taught entirely through stories but the children are taken on a nature walk to the adjoining sports field at least once a fortnight. Most of the Physical Education classes are also conducted in this field as the school does not have a hall or an "all purpose room". Although each day's activities follow a haphazard schedule, their unpredictability is tempered by the use of fastidiously planned schemes. These schemes of work are compiled every two weeks by the teacher. They include her intended content in each subject for this period and also take cognisance of any areas which need to be strengthened since the previous fortnight. How and when the fragments therein are imparted troubles her little provided that the majority of the class has assimilated them before the next scheme is due. Her one methodological tenet, however, is that the children should enjoy what they are doing:

> If they get turned off school at this age, what hope have they afterwards?

This attitude is reflected in the freedom which the children here enjoy. In the first instance they are allowed to move freely within the room, whether to look at a friend's activity, to collect something from the shelves or to show something to the teacher. Secondly, there is no restriction on their use of language — children are allowed to talk to their friends during activities. They are actively encouraged to volunteer information or comment to the teacher and a vocal (i.e. singing) accompaniment to their "work" is a common occurrence.

Due to the large number of children and the obvious lack of space, the class is taught quite frequently as a unit. However, this in itself was quite unlike the passive adult-led situations with which I was *au fait*. A synopsis of one such class fails to appreciate its inherent vitality and complexity. Instead, I hope that the following extract, which is based on one of my observations in this classroom, will illuminate the diversity of approach involved.

> The children have just come back from their morning break which allowed them ten minutes' freedom in the school yard. Arm-in-arm, Marie Thérèse and her friend Claire skip to their chairs. After their prayer they smile at one another while the teacher writes "Our News" on the blackboard.

Claire looks at the child who shouts, "Goodie, I knew we forgot it today, Teach". Claire jumps up on her chair and waves her right hand as she says, "*A mhúinteoir, a mhúinteoir*, I know what day today is". She is duly allowed up to the blackboard where she announces, "Today is Thursday. It's a sunny day." She runs back to her place while the teacher writes this on the blackboard. Alan says that he can spell "today" with his eyes closed. "I bet you can't!" says Claire. When he succeeds she gives him a hug and says, "*Buachaill maith* (good boy), Alan, that was hard". The remainder of the class clap. Eileen suggests that he should be in charge of the pencils for the remainder of the day. Teacher smiles and says, "Okay, *Tá go maith*". Just then Seán, whose attention has been riveted by the "*go maith*", stands up and begins to sing an Irish version of the "Birdie Song", complete with feather ruffling actions and claps and waddles. The class and teacher laugh. They then join him and continue: "*Tá mé go maith, tá mé go deas, tá mé ag crith* . . ." (I am good, I am nice, I am shaking). Teacher then suggests that they all sit down and "*Téigh a chodhladh*" (go to sleep) while she gets ready for a word game. "Henrietta" (teacher's talking doll) signals them to wake up. The game begins. Teacher has written several words from the Pre-Reader Approach Book on the blackboard. Duplicates of these have been placed on her desk. The teacher selects individual children to call out a word for Henrietta, who attempts to point it out and match it to the flashcard. If she fails, the child must correct her and come out "to slap her bottom". Elaine asks the doll to find "this". Henrietta the doll fails to do so. Claire runs up to her and says "Don't worry, Henrietta, a "t" is just like "f" turned the wrong way . . . I'll show you". She does and is given a kiss by the "magic doll".

The teaching style outlined here is quite difficult to pinpoint. However, its results speak for themselves. The interaction analysis indicated that pupils spoke for over 56 per cent of the time, the majority of which was devoted to pupil comment. The teacher spoke for 38 per cent of the time and this included instructing, questioning and responding to pupils. These findings were substantiated by the target child study which recorded a significantly higher percentage of pupil utterances than the average. The children's social interaction patterns represented a wide variety of setting. The "large group" was the most common as almost half of the total time observed was spent interacting in such a group. A further quarter of the total time (approx.) involved large group parallel activity (i.e. where children sat side by side without interacting), while they were on their own, in pairs or in a small group, for the remaining period.

Analysis of the target child categories also showed that children spent almost a third of recorded units engaged in free-play activities. Five and a half percent of this involved dramatic play tutoring, which surpassed the other 15 classes observed, as did the 11.5 per cent segment which Art received.

Furthermore, most of the instruction in the three R's was introduced informally during games. Children spent only 9 per cent of their time actively involved in individual reading, writing or mathematical activities.

The merits of this albeit idiosyncratic approach to the implementation of the junior infant programme stem from many diverse techniques. Firstly, this teacher is a firm believer in the power of "magic". As a result, "magic circles", "magic thinking caps" and "talking dolls and puppets" are very much in evidence. Secondly, she is convinced that young children need freedom of movement and expression, the lack of which stultifies their confidence and intelligence. Music and pretend also figure prominently in daily activities. Apart from their inherent value which she says is "to develop the children's imagination and creativity", they arouse interest and foster concentration. She regrets the fact that her class is taught as a unit for such a large percentage of school time but has failed to improve this due to the very high pupil:teacher ratio and the unavailability of equipment. What is important, however, is her recognition of the need to equate play with fun:

> Discovery methods aren't much good if the children can't laugh and enjoy themselves.

This was the reasoning behind reducing her status from that of the omniscient pedagogue to that of collaborator with the children. However, it would be remiss to conclude that this was a classroom in which mayhem reigned. On the contrary, a mutual tolerance and respect was very much in evidence.

In the course of this study, certain factors revealed themselves as obstacles to the education of junior infant class children through play and experiential learning. These included the teacher's attitude to play, pupil:teacher ratio, and the availability of equipment. However, when other factors were held constant, the teacher's attitude was found to be the factor most highly correlated with the provision of heuristic, play-based experiences. It was found that the few teachers who were positively disposed to play (such as the practitioner profiled above), believing in its unique potential as a learning medium, succeeded in overcoming many of the obstacles which were the stumbling blocks of several of their colleagues. Nevertheless, failure to take cognisance of the obstacles which exist is both naive and dangerous.

A CASE STUDY OF A COMMUNITY PLAYGROUP WHICH EXCELLED

This community playgroup is situated in a purpose-built building in a modern Corporation housing estate some five miles from the centre of Cork city. The general impression is of poorly kept surroundings, which is epitomised by the general disarray surrounding the caravans of the travelling people who camp out on the "green" area half a mile away. Most of this area was indeed "green fields" ten years ago, but the balance of private and public housing originally intended has not been achieved as the latter now predominates. The families who live here have mostly moved out from the inner city and facilities such as shops are few and far between. (Approximately 90 per cent of the children's fathers are unemployed.)

The centre houses two playgroups — one for three- to four-year-olds and the other for four- to five-year-olds. An idea of the four- to five-year-old group can be gained from the notes taken on the researcher's second visit. There are 13 children present, and Mary is the Playgroup Leader.

From 9.30 a.m. to 11.00 a.m. there is free play but small groups are extracted to do "writing" in their copy books (as they did during the first visit). Free play consists of water play, sand play, drawing with crayons and playing with stickle bricks. There are a very large number of "constructional toys" with few ordinary toys in evidence. At 11.30 a.m. lunch finishes and is followed by a story.

"Who's going to tell me about the story? Who's in the story?"

The children all shout "The Mooney Fellow!"

"What was the Mooney Fellow's name? . . . Sit down in your chair!"

The children all shout, "He keeps whinging!"

"That's right, he keeps whinging. What's his name?"

"His name is Eeyore. He's always giving out . . . he's always whinging".

"Tell me about Winnie-the-Pooh. When Winnie-the-Pooh went to Piglet's house, what happened?"

One of the children says, "They were looking for each other in Piglet's house". Mary holds up the book so that the children can see the pictures and starts reading. She "reads" very well... she doesn't look at the book but tells the story in her own words while the children look at the pictures. In concluding her story, Mary says "So I'm cold . . . I can't go anywhere". "Thank you very much Christopher Robin." "Come on Ee Orr. Show me exactly where your house is said Christopher Robin". "Stop whinging and hurry up."

"What do you think is happening?" Mary asks the children. Mary uses her eyes in a wonderful and effective way and she has the children's complete attention.

There is a very high incidence of questions which are phrased in such a manner as to make the children think. Mary uses "pausing" very effectively to control the children, being a master in the use of non-verbal cues to add extra meaning to her questions. She spends a great deal of time encouraging individual children to verbalise and she has imposing discipline.

Mary herself believes in structured play. She believes in preparing the environment as she argues that the children can only play with what is available. They thus learn different things by playing with different equipment.

This equipment is graded in terms of complexity and, when a child has mastered a given level, they are encouraged to try something a little more difficult. If the children appear to be doing nothing, they are given something to work with.

The children are constantly assessed, as a written report is kept of every activity undertaken by each child — individual record cards are compiled after the children go home. This system allows Mary to identify any areas where a child needs extra practice.

In essence, Mary believes that it is her job to prepare children for primary school but she is deeply concerned about what happens (or what doesn't happen) when they get there. In a letter sent to the author, she says:

> A lot more could be achieved by children attending a playgroup if the educational system, i.e. the junior level in national schools and playgroups, was restructured. But one has to work within the system that exists, for the benefit of the child. To create a playgroup environment that is totally contradictory to that which the child will encounter on entering junior infants in primary school would be of no benefit to the child at all. Therefore, one has to take the best of both systems and try and work within that structure.

The children in this community playgroup were engaged in cognitively stretching tasks for 43 per cent of the total time observed (13 per cent of this was spent in pre-reading, pre-writing and pre-arithmetic activities and 30 per cent in highly challenging play-based activities). They spent 51 per cent of their time alone and 28 per cent with the playgroup leader (they were in pairs and large groups for only 6 per cent). Finally, they each spoke to the playgroup leader for 8 per cent of their time there. (They spoke to no-one for 82 per cent, while other children received 2 per cent, leaving 8 per cent for speaking to themselves!)

From Brown's Interaction Analysis, it was found that this playgroup leader spent 20 per cent of her time addressing the group as a whole, 19 per cent asking questions and 5 per cent responding to the children's questions.

It is interesting to note that, according to Mary, make-believe and drama were used very frequently in her group while in the least stimulated group, of the eleven community playgroups observed, the playgroup leader said that make-believe and drama were *never* used.

It is also worth noting that, even with the use of a timetable, Mary's group allowed a great deal of time for child-chosen activities while children in the least stimulated group were only permitted to choose their own activities "sometimes". The perception of these two leaders, as evidenced by the interview and the questionnaire, forced the conclusion that the former, despite her structured curriculum, was much more child-centred in approach.

From the eleven community playgroups visited in this research, it was established that the normal pattern of curriculum activity was for the children to spend the first hour in free play, choosing what to do themselves, followed by lunch. After lunch, organised whole-group activities were engaged in.

Analysis of the coding sheets regarding the curriculum, as observed in these eleven centres, revealed that activity was limited largely to manipulative play, small-scale construction and structured materials (which can provide high or low levels of challenge to the children concerned). In addition, a significant amount of low level art activity was engaged in.

The most important variable in providing a highly stimulating environment for the children observed was undoubtedly the expertise and attitude of the playgroup leader. The staff/child ratio was also significant. However, the total lack of training for parents on rota had a strong negative effect.

In contrast to the remuneration of the fully qualified primary teachers in junior and senior infant classes of the primary schools, the pay of the playgroup leaders was low. Most of the latter worked a maximum of 15 hours per week and were normally not paid during the Christmas and Easter holidays. They were never paid during the summer holidays.

In general, there was a rich diversity of provision within the community playgroups of Cork city and county. Almost without exception, there was a desire by those involved to make them function. Enthusiasm and hard work characterised them all. However, there was an enormous discrepancy in terms of their physical provision — some of them were cold, damp and dangerous for small children while others were in very good purpose-built accommodation. The grants given by the Southern Health Board were awarded on an *ad hoc* basis and, in servicing them, a lot seemed to depend on the competence and responsibility of the community worker.

It must be stressed that cognitive challenge provides only one criterion by which to measure merit. Community playgroups by their nature have other objectives. The community playgroup, in this research study, which provided no high-level challenging activities at all still served as a meeting place for young mothers who otherwise would not have met and who, in its absence, undoubtedly would have been left at home lonely, despondent and constrained by young children. The three- and four-year-olds in this non-stimulated group were happy and gained much from their walks, visits and games. On the other hand, children who have learned to concentrate on their own and are used to being cognitively and linguistically stretched will excel in the formal school system, as presently structured.

CONCLUSION

In the Republic of Ireland, the pursuit of quality in early years education and care has been stymied and stultified by several factors. The UN Committee on the Rights of the Child, in its report of January 1998 on Ireland's implementation of the Convention, pinpointed lack of co-ordination as the main obstacle to progress (UN, 1998). Lack of communication and collaboration, not only between the nine government departments with involvement in the area of early childhood but sometimes even within individual departments, has resulted in much frustration, fragmentation and dissipation of time and resources. This is further reflected in the voluntary sector where, historically, there has been little communication or co-ordination of effort between the various providers of early years care and education and is significantly exacerbated by the artificial divide between the voluntary sector and the statutory and governmental sector. Therefore, although improved co-ordination at national and local levels, in itself, is not the panacea for improving provision of early childhood services, it can expedite the realisation of that aspiration by rendering more effective and efficient existing resources, thus optimising the value of the services.

The complexity of preparing personnel for early childhood environments is common to many countries of the world. Issues and stumbling blocks include duration of courses, prerequisites for entry, core curriculum content, the age range covered in courses, and practicum requirements. Moreover, definitions of "quality teaching" like those of "good practice" are difficult to find as most authors tend to be unwilling to identify exactly what constitutes a "good early years teacher". However, the research studies described above, undertaken over a period of more than ten years, isolate the attitude of the early years practitioners as a further critical correlate of quality.

Notwithstanding the diversity of provision, it must be appreciated that all workers with young children require support and, while acknowledging the different levels of expertise involved, there needs to be some coherence and standardisation in the training offered to those working in State, private and voluntary settings.

In the State sector, in this country, the curricular pendulum since 1831 has oscillated back and forth from the traditional, didactic approach to child-centredness. The latter is the underpinning ideology of the 1971 curriculum and of its recent revision by the NCCA. However, its potential has been compromised by environmental constraints such as inadequate space, high adult:child ratios and by attitudinal negativity partly resultant from lack of education at pre-and in-service levels (Horgan, 1987, 1995). Within all areas of the voluntary sector, the child-centred philosophy is also espoused. However, lack of training, State recognition and funding has again curtailed its implementation (Douglas, 1993).

The research in UCC focused attention on the value of a highly structured, child-centred curriculum, which correlates significantly with cognitive development. However, it further revealed the urgent need for programmes which enable children to maximise their potential in the areas of linguistic and social development. These methodological issues need to be addressed.

Preschool children represent one of the most powerless and vulnerable groups in our educational system. The range and quality of life experiences to which they are exposed, whether at home or outside the home, is dependent upon those with more power than themselves. Therefore, it is imperative that those of us involved in working in or promoting early years education should seriously question current provision and practice.

References

Ball, Sir Christopher (1994). *Start Right, the importance of early learning*, Oxford: Gower Publishing for RSA.

Brown, G.A. (1975). *Microteaching — A Programme of Teaching Skills*. London: Methuen.

Brüner, J.S. (1972). "The nature and use of immaturity." *American Psychologist*, 1972, 27, pp. 687-708.

Brüner, J.S. (1975). "From communication to language: a psychological perspective". *Cognition*, 3.

Brüner, J.S. (1984). "Language, mind and reading" in H. Goelman, A. Oberg and F. Smith (eds.). *Awakening to Literacy. The University of Victoria Symposium on Children's Responses to a Literate Environment: Literacy before Schooling*. London: Heinemann Education Books

Brüner, J.S., Jolley, A. & Sylva, K. (eds.) (1976). *Play: Its Role and Development in Evolution*. New York: Penguin.

Cazden, C.B. (1976). "Play with language and meta-linguistic awareness: one dimension of language experience" in J.S. Brüner et al, *Play: Its Role in Development and Evolution*. New York: Penguin.

Curaclam na Bunscoile (1971) (Primary School Curriculum). An Roinn Oideachas. Parts 1 and 2. Dublin: Stationery Office.

Dahlberg, G. & Åsén, E. (1994). "Evaluation and Regulation: A Question of Empowerment", in P. Moss and A. Pence (eds.), op.cit., pp.157-171.

Department of Education Statistics (1997). Tuarascáil Staitistiúil (Statistical Report). Dublin: Stationery Office.

Donaldson, M. (1978). *Children's Minds*. Glasgow: Fontana/Collins.

Douglas, F.G. (1993). "A Study of Preschool Education in the Republic of Ireland with Particular Reference to those Preschools which are listed by the Irish Preschools Playgroups Association in Cork City and County". Unpublished Ph.D. Dissertation, University of Hull.

Dunlea, C.P. (1990). "The Relevance of Montessori Education: A Study of Montessori Schools in the Cork Area". Unpublished M.Ed. Thesis, University College Cork.

Dwane, C.E.C. (1998). "A Study of the Linguistic and Cognitive Development of Children in Naíonraí in Cork City and County." Unpublished M.Ed. Thesis, University College Cork.

Ewert, O.M. & Braun, M. (1978). "Ergebnnisse und Probleme vorschulischer Foerderung", in Struktu foerderung im Bildungswesen des Landes Nordrhein-Westfalen. Eine Schriften-reibe des Kultusministers, vol. 34: Modellversuch Vorklasse in NW-Abschlussbericht. Koeln: Greven.

Horgan, M.A. (1987). "A Study of the Importance of Play in the Education of Junior Infant Class Children in Cork City and County". Unpublished M.Ed. thesis, University College Cork.

Horgan, M.A. (1995). "Management of the Junior Infant Curriculum in Irish Primary Schools — Rhetoric versus Reality." *Compare* 25(3), pp. 253-261.

Horgan, M.A. & Douglas, F.G. (1998). "Where Angels Fear to Tread", *Irish Journal of Applied Social Studies*, 1(1), pp. 13-36.

Horgan, S. (1995). "A Study of the Linguistic and Cognitive Development of Junior Infant Class Children in Gaelscoileanna in Cork City and County". M.Ed. Dissertation, University College Cork.

Hutt, C. (1979). "Exploration and Play" in B. Sutton-Smith (ed.) *Play and Learning*. New York: Gardner Press.

INTO (1995). "Early Childhood Education: Issues and Concerns". Dublin: Author.

IPPA (1996). Statistics Central Office.

Jensen, C. (1994). "Fragments for a Discussion about Quality", in P. Moss and A. Pence (eds.), op.cit., pp.142-256.

Johnson, J.E. (1976). "Relations of divergent thinking and intelligent test scores with social and non-social make-believe play of preschool children." *Child Development*, 47, 1976.

Johnson, J.E., Ershler, J., & Lawton, J. (1982). "Intelligence correlates of preschoolers' spontaneous play." *Journal of Genetic Psychology*, 106, pp. 115-22.

Jowett, S. (1981). "The effects of preschool education on the behaviour of working class children in the reception class". Unpublished M.Litt. Dissertation, Oxford University.

Kärrby, G. (1990). De Aldre Förskolebarnen-Inlärning och Utveckling (The Older Preschoolers — Learning and Development). Stockholm: Utbildningsförlaget.

Katz, L.G. (1987). "What Should Young Children Be Learning?" *ERIC Digest*.

Kellmer-Pringle, M. (1975). *The Needs of Children*. London: Hutchinson.

Kelly, A.V. (1994). "A High-Quality Curriculum for the Early Years — Some Conceptual Issues." *Early Years*, 15(1), pp. 6-12.

Luria, A.R. (1963). "The role of speech in the formation of temporary connections and the regulation of behaviour in the normal and oligophrenic child" in B. Simon and J. Simon, (eds) *Educational Psychology in the U.S.S.R.* London: Routledge and Kegan Paul.

Moore, N.V., Evertson, C.M. & Brophy, J.E. (1974). "Solitary Play: some functional reconsiderations." *Developmental Psychology*, 10, pp. 830-34.

Moss, P. and Pence, A. (eds) (1994) *Valuing Quality in Early Childhood Services*, London: Paul Chapman

Murphy, B. (2000). "Support for the Educationally and Socially Disadvantaged — An Introductory Guide to Government Funded Initiatives in Ireland", Education Department, University College, Cork.

Nabuco, M. & Sylva, K. (1995). "Comparisons between ECERS ratings of individual preschool centres and the results of target child observations: do they match or do they differ?" Paper presented to the Fifth European Conference on Quality in Education, Paris.

Nunes, T. (1994). "The Environment of the Child". Occasional Paper No. 5. The Hague: Bernard van Leer Foundation.

Osborn, A.F. & Milbank, J.E. (1987). *The Effects of Early Education: A Report from the Child Health and Education Study*. Oxford: Clarendon.

Piaget, J. (1962). *Comments on Vygotsky's Critical Remarks*. Cambridge, MA: MIT Press.

Roper, R. & Hinde, R.A. (1978). "Social behaviour in playgroups: consistency and complexity." *Child Development*, 49, pp. 570-79.

Rutter, M. (1985). "Family and School Influences on Cognitive Development." *Journal of Child Psychology*, 26(5), pp. 683-704.

Schweinhart, L. & Weikart, D. (1993). *A Summary of Significant Benefits: The High/Scope Perry Preschool Study Through Age 27*. Ypsilanti: MI: High/Scope Press.

Schweinhart, L. & Weikart, D. (1997). *Lasting Differences: The High/Scope Preschool Curriculum Comparison Study Through Age 23*. Ypsilanti, MI: The High/Scope Press.

Sutton-Smith, B. (1967). "The role of play in cognitive development." *Young Children*. 22, pp. 361-70.

Sutton-Smith, B. (ed.) (1979). *Play and Learning*. New York: Gardiner Press.

Sylva, K. (1996). "Research on Quality in the Curriculum." *International Journal of Early Childhood*, 28(2), pp. 1-6.

Sylva, K., Roy, C. & Painter, M. (1980). *Child Watching at Playgroup and Nursery School*. London: Grant McIntyre. The "Target Child Schedule" was designed in 1977 (see Sylva, K. (1977), "Play and Learning" in B. Tizard and D. Harvey (eds.) *Biology of Play*. London: Heinemann, SIMP 1977.)

Tietze, W. (1987). "A structural model for the evaluation of preschool effects." *Early Childhood Research Quarterly*, 2(2), pp. 133-159.

UN Committee on the Rights of the Child (1998) (concluding observations) published in *Children's Rights: Our Responsibilities*, The Children's Rights Alliance, 4 Christchurch Square, Dublin 8.

Vygotsky, L.S. (1962). *Thought and Language*. Cambridge, MA: MIT Press.

Vygotsky, L.S. (1978). *Mind in Society: The development of higher mental processes*. Cambridge, MA: Harvard University Press.

Wells, G. (1987). *The Meaning Makers: Children Learning Language and Using Language to Learn*. London: Hodder and Stoughton.

Winkelmann, W., Jollaender, A., Schmerkotte, H. & Schmalohr, E. (1979). Kognitive Entwicklung und Foerderung von Kindergarten und

Vorklassenkindern. Bericht uber eine laengsschnittliche Ver-
gleischsuntersuchung zum Modellversuch des Landes Nordrhein-
Westfalen, vol. 2. Kronberg, Ger.: Sciptor.

Woodhead, M. (1996). *In search of the rainbow (pathways to quality in
large-scale programmes for young disadvantaged children).* The
Hague: Bernard van Leer Foundation.

Woodhead, M. (1998). "Quality in Early Childhood Programmes — A
Contextually Appropriate Approach", *International Journal of Early
Years Education*, 6(1), pp. 5-17.

Notes

[1] For a discussion of high/scope curriculum see O'Flaherty, J. (1995), *Intervention in the Early Years: An Evaluation of the High/Scope Curriculum,* London:
National Children's Bureau

Chapter 7

Locating the Child's Voice in Irish Primary Education

Dympna Devine

INTRODUCTION

Children in Irish society have traditionally held a contradictory position with respect to adults, valued within the private sphere of family life, as they fulfilled both emotional and functional roles (Arensberg and Kimball, 1968; Curtin, 1984) with little regard shown at a public level for their position and status within the society as a whole (Benson, 1991; Constitution Review Group, 1996). Adult discourse on children in Ireland, then, has traditionally precluded consideration of rights and status issues, centring primarily on the socialisation of children in line with future adult-defined needs and_ expectations (Devine, 1999). Throughout the history of Irish primary education, such discourse is prevalent, reflected in the establishment of the state school system in 1831 for the purposes of "civilising" the population (Inglis, 1998), to the adoption of a rigid, nationalistic ideology at the foundation of the new Republic, in which children were to be the mechanism through which a new Gaelic and Catholic order was to be achieved (Devine, 1999). Child-centred policies, introduced via the new primary school curriculum of 1971, while advocating a more sensitive and interactive approach in adult/child relations, did little to challenge the underlying discourse, framed as it was in terms of the maximisation of individual talent in line with economic ideals. Difficulties in relation to the implementation of the ideals of this curriculum have been noted, centred on the reluctance of teachers to relinquish control over the learning process (O'Sullivan, 1980) coupled with the reluctance of the state to invest substantially in primary education (INTO, 1985), difficulties in themselves which are indicative of the absence of a "rights" discourse in relation to the education of children in Irish society (Devine, 2000).

Rights and status issues are interwoven with the capacity to have one's voice acknowledged, respected and heard. In the past ten years, significant steps have been taken to incorporate previously hidden voices into educational policy making, reflected in particular in the holding of the National Education Convention in 1994 (Coolahan, 1994). Such "partnership" in education, however, has been defined primarily in adult-centred terms, with the main users of the education system, children, excluded from the process of consultation. More recently, the Revised Primary Curriculum (Department of Education and Science, 1999), devised on the basis of extensive consultation with such "partners", makes welcome reference to the need to consider children as "active agents", yet the process of consultation leading to its formulation did not at any stage include the voices of children. This contradictory position is indicative of a particular power relation between adults and children, itself governed by discourses relating to the nature of children and childhood (Devine, 2000). Drawing on the work of Foucault (1979) and Giddens (1984), this chapter seeks to explore such issues, locating the absence of children's voices in terms of the exercise of power between adults and children generally, and more specifically in the primary school. How children experience this power relation is then outlined with specific reference to research detailing their voices in relation to their experiences of social relations, the curriculum and the pedagogical and evaluative practices in use in a sample of primary schools. The paper concludes by stressing the need to consider children as central actors within the school system, having the right as young citizens, to be incorporated as co-participants in decision-making structures in Irish primary schools.

SCHOOLING AND THE EXERCISE OF POWER BETWEEN ADULTS AND CHILDREN

Foucault (1979), in his analysis of the exercise of power in modern society, draws attention to the important role of institutions in promoting, reproducing and disseminating particular discourses, which both govern and regulate our identities and behaviour. This process of "subjectification" occurs through the implementation of a range of "disciplinary technologies" which divide and classify the population, defining them according to their perceived "normality" or "otherness". Institutions such as prisons, mental hospitals and schools may be considered in this light, their establishment giving rise to a whole series of discourses related to criminality, insanity and, the specific focus of this paper, childhood. By segregating children from the adult population through the establishment of state-wide school systems, a new form of power was exercised between adults and children, with children en masse compulsorily confined to an institutional setting which sought to discipline, control and regulate their behaviour in line with adult-defined needs and expectations. A process of individuation ensued, through the physical partitioning of the child population from the adult population, an architectural composition of space which allowed for the further subdivision of the targeted group based on age, gender and ability, and the induction of normalising tendencies through a system of surveillance based on strict adherence to a timetable and completion of examinations on a regular basis. Such practice both derived from and gave rise to particular discourses centred on the nature and needs of children and childhood (Devine, 1998). Grouped together in a manner previously unknown, children became increasingly subjected to intervention by "experts" (teachers, psychologists) who in turn appropriated more and more knowledge about the school-aged child. This "individualisation" of children is personified in recent times not only in the growth in child-care manuals for each distinct period of childhood, but more generally by child-centred discourse, with its specific focus on catering to the "needs" of each individual child. In terms of the exercise of power, it is significant that this process of individualisation in modern society extends to those groups which are perceived to be in need of normalising, with Foucault (1979) stating:

> In a system of discipline, the child is more individualised than the adult, the patient more than the healthy man, the madman and the delinquent more than the normal and the non-delinquent. In each case it is towards the first of these pairs that all the individualising mechanisms are turned in our civilisation — and when one wishes to individualise the healthy, normal, law abiding adult, it is always by asking how much of the child he has in him (Ibid, 193).

Schools, then, are fundamentally intertwined with the exercise of power between adults and children, promulgated by a discourse which defines the child as "other" in need of being normalised into an adult "end-state". However, while Foucault highlights the role of the school in the creation of "docile bodies", this does not presuppose that children conform totally to adult norms. Power is never exclusively in the hands of one group to be exercised over another but:

> . . . individuals are also in the position of simultaneously undergoing and exercising this power. They are not only its inert or consenting target, they are also the elements of its articulation. In other words, individuals are the vehicles of power, not its points of application (Foucault, 1980, p. 96)

Adult definitions of appropriate norms for children are mediated by children themselves as they adapt, accommodate and interpret their experience, giving rise to behaviours, beliefs etc. which may or may not correspond to the norms of adult discourse. Giddens (1984), in his analysis of the dialectic of control, substantiates this conception of power as something which circulates between people in the course of social interaction. As active agents, children will reflexively monitor their behaviour, positioning themselves in the light of the expectations and evaluations of significant others (parents, teachers, peers).

In spite of their capacity as active agents, however, children's voices have been absent from recent debates in Irish education. The breadth of consultation in relation to proposed changes, as reflected in both the National Education Convention (Coolahan, 1994) and the Revised Primary Curriculum (Department of Education and Science, 1999), as already noted, did not include children. The related absence of any consideration of the issues and concerns which children may have to offer on their educational experience in the White Paper in Education (Department of Education, 1995), suggests that they are not considered as partners in the educative process, with whom one negotiates and dialogues. Further, the conditionality attached to legislative changes in relation to children's rights in schools, as outlined in the Education Act (Government of Ireland, 1998), indicates that children's rights remain closeted within boundaries set by adults, encouraging them to assert themselves in relation to bullying (among peers) and child abuse, but failing to allow them make a meaningful and relevant contribution to the organisation of school life. Thus, the education system which judges, monitors and evaluates children on a daily basis, is not itself open to scrutiny and evaluation by children. Highlighting children's experience of this power relation is important, not only in furthering our understanding of the dynamics of adult/child and teacher/pupil relations, but also in validating the perspectives and views of children themselves — in so doing enabling them to exercise their voice in education.

CHILDREN'S PERSPECTIVE ON SCHOOL — HEARING THEIR VOICE IN EDUCATION

With this in mind, research was conducted into the views and perspectives of a sample of primary school children on their experience of school (Devine, 1998). In total, three primary schools were involved, all co-educational with contrasting socio-economic intakes: "Churchfield" which was predominantly middle/upper middle class, "Hillview" which served a lower middle class population and "Parkway" which was a designated disadvantaged school. A mixed methodological approach was utilised, consisting of qualitative fieldwork over a period of one school year, continuous observations of classroom practice, open-ended questionnaires and semi-structured interviews with 133 pupils in first/second and fifth class. Questionnaires consisted of open and closed questions, and covered aspects of school practice in terms of social relations, pedagogy, curriculum and evaluative systems in use in school. Class teachers were not present when the questionnaires were being completed. To facilitate younger children, the questionnaires were administered in small groups, each question was read aloud, and each child was given sufficient time to complete their response. Interviews were conducted in friendship groups of three and four, the children free to select with whom they wished to be interviewed. This reduced the formality of the interview context and gave rise to a greater sense of ease on the part of the children in discussing issues of interest to them. The older children in the study were also asked to complete diaries, noting incidences or events which they personally viewed as being important in their school lives. Drawings of an ideal yard/classroom were also used to elicit information from the children, providing a useful context within which to identify children's sense of the use of space within the school. Semi-structured interviews with the teachers of these pupils (five in total) as well as their school principals (three) were also conducted. Such interviews, beyond the scope of this paper, focused in particular on their perceptions of children and childhood in modern Ireland, their attitudes toward education, the curriculum, pedagogy and evaluation as well as the moral and social education of children in their care.

For the purposes of this paper, the analysis of the children's perspectives will focus on the following areas:

1. Social relations and children's experience of school

2. Children's attitudes toward and experience of the curriculum

3. Children's perspectives on pedagogical practices

4. The experience of evaluation systems in school.

Social Relations and Children's Experience of School

The school environment is a highly social one in which both teacher's and children's identities are simultaneously challenged and affirmed. The analysis of children's experience of social relations is broken into two distinct, but interrelated areas: (a) the experience of teacher/pupil relations and (b) perceptions of relations with peers.

The Experience of Teacher/Pupil Relations

Teacher/pupil relations are governed in large part by the role expectations each group has for the other, the latter determined by the discourses governing adult/child relations in society in general and specifically between teachers and pupils in schools. Findings of the study indicated that children have clear perceptions of what it is to be a teacher: as one who is grown up, knowledgeable, bossy and free, reflecting their superior power, hence status in school:

> . . . the children have the least power cos they're not allowed do anythin . . . say what they want . . . do what they want . . . the principal has the most power . . . and the teachers . . . they're grown ups so they're meant to be the bosses (5th class boy, Parkway).

From the children's perspective, the greater power of teachers is reflected not only in their greater access to facilities within the school, as well as in their apparent freedom of rules (as previously highlighted), but also in the sensitivity children felt they must display to teacher mood:

> Sometimes you can ask her a question but you never know when she is going to jump on you . . . like you are just talking to her and she could jump on you and give out to you no matter what you say . . . especially if she has a bad day . . . she takes it out on us (5th class girl, Hillview).

The extent of children's sensitivity to teacher power was also reflected in their constant references to the level of surveillance they experienced in school, with younger children in particular convinced of the magical powers of detection of some of their teachers!

> I think the teacher has eyes in the back of her head, cos when she's out of the room she knows stuff that happened and even when she's at her desk she is looking at the side of her eye to see who is even whispering (2nd class girl, Churchfield).

The lack of reciprocity in teacher/pupil relations was also referred to by older children, indicating for them the greater power of teachers, as adults, in the school:

> In the classroom the teachers and the principal have more power cos we can't give out to them like they give out to us . . . we can't tell them to be quiet or send them up to the office . . . they are adults and they think they have more power, but kids have rights as well (5th class boy, Hillview).

In typifying teachers in these terms, it is clear that children perceive themselves in opposite terms, as having subordinate status within the school. This is reflected not only in the fact that just 1 per cent of children felt the school belonged to them but also in their comments listing the most to least important people in the school:

> Mr _____ (Principal) is the most important cos he runs the school, then Mr_____ (Vice Principal), the teachers, and the children are the last . . . we are important to our mams . . . you don't see the children bossing others . . . children don't boss adults (5th class boy, Hillview).

> . . . the children are the least important cos we are just children (5th class girl, Hillview).

Not being taken seriously as children is a prime indicator of their subordinate status and emerged in their accounts of not being listened to, being unfairly treated and not being given a voice in school. Their views are reflected in the following comments:

> . . . when adults are treated unfairly they stand up and object to it . . . but they don't kinda take children seriously . . . they think they are just messin or lookin for attention (5th class girl, Churchfield).

> Sometimes children should have a say . . . if something is really hard for children and they might feel scared . . . if they have a say the teacher might understand more . . . but you need to know they won't say oh listen to this and listen to that . . . that's what they do sometimes at staff meetings with the black book (2nd class girl, Churchfield).

However, not all children subscribed to these views, and factors such as social class and age level mediated the level of dissatisfaction expressed. This was particularly the case in relation to children's desire to exercise a greater voice in school, with fifth class children and those of middle class origin most likely to assert their right to be respected and to voice an opinion on matters which concerned them in school. Familiar with the changing discourses governing adult/child relations in the wider sphere (typified by a breakdown in traditional authority relations between adults and children), such children question the traditional structures of domination in school, suggesting alternatives which would radically alter the nature of teacher/pupil interaction:

> I think there should be a vote over rules . . . cos we live in a democracy . . . if we could have different lunch times that would be brilliant . . . we should be allowed vote about whether or not we want to go to the choir (5th class boy, Churchfield).

> I think the children should get a say in deciding rules . . . well there are votes for Presidents or whatever so we could put our vote in the box . . . she'd have her rules and then we'd vote for them (5th class girl, Churchfield).

While children, particularly older middle class children, were clearly dissatisfied with aspects of their social interaction with their teachers, the study also indicated that most children were positively disposed to the socio-emotional climate in their classrooms. In the busy and often pressured environment of the classroom, children in general perceived their teachers to be kind and caring and wanted to have a positive relationship with them. Children were particularly sensitive to teacher praise and the care and attention received when required:

> I feel happy when I get everything right and the teacher says good boy (2nd class boy, Churchfield).

> I feel good about myself in school knowing the someone cares enough to teach you stuff and give you a good education (5th class girl, Parkway).

However, the increasing workload on older children toward the end of primary school results in a more instrumental and disciplined approach by teachers in working with them. This gives rise to a more qualified perspective by such children on their relations with teachers:

> The teachers are much nicer to the younger children but as they get older they expect you to be more responsible . . . they give us loads of work and expect us to do it on our own (5th class boy, Hillview).

Perceptions of Relations with Peers

As with teacher/pupil relations, much of children's interaction with one another was shown to be governed by particular discourses and norms. Children identified four main traits which gave rise to dominance in their world: strength, size/age, cleverness and sporting ability, such dominance reflected in terms of popularity and status among peers along with the accompanying capacity to influence and exercise authority over them:

> We're the most popular people in the class . . . cos everyone knows us . . . they think we're mad an we're the best footballers . . . if there was a fight between our class and a different class, we'd be the ringleaders (5th class boy, Parkway).

> Tina's very good at her Irish and Art and everybody really likes her (2nd class girl, Churchfield).

Observational data, as well as children's ratings of their own popularity, indicated that gender was also a factor influencing power dynamics among peers, with boys typically more dominant than girls. At its most sinister level, dominance was reflected in the practice of bullying with children reluctant to report such incidences in fear of the consequences of "telling" for their own status and popularity within the peer group:

> . . . if ye get called names in the classroom yer always afraid to tell the teacher in case ye get called a rat (5th class girl, Hillview).

The importance of peer relations to children in their experience of school was evident from the extent to which they mentioned support as being the trait most valued in their friends. Through such support, children are empowered to deal with challenges which arise in the academic and social spheres of school life. Children's friendships, however, are governed by a series of norms which both define and set limits to their behaviour. Strict rules were evident for example related to "not telling" and being seen not to be a goody-goody, indicating that part of the process of bonding between children involves transcending adult norms and expectations:

> . . . you have to keep up your reputation . . . you can't be goody two shoes either . . . like always telling and always getting your work right, asking questions and not breaking the rules (5th class boy, Churchfield).

> I'd love to have the brains and all the knowledge but you wouldn't want to be a loner with no friends or anything . . . if Mick was a loner we'd bring him back in and make him popular by not letting him get too much into his work . . . cos then people would call him a swot (5th class boy, Hillview).

Friendship bonds differ, however, with a clear distinction drawn between children who are "best friends" and "friends". Within this social hierarchy, best friends are those who display loyalty, trust and total support and with whom one can entrust one's most personal secrets:

> Patricia and myself are not best friends . . . we are good
> friends . . . best friends are loyal to each other . . . you can
> tell secrets to them . . . other friends if you tell them secrets
> they go around blabbing (5th class girl, Hillview).

Through their friendships, children are also enabled to mediate
adult domination and control and this is particularly evident in
the school yard. Here backstage behaviour abounds (Giddens,
1984; Goffman, 1971), affording children the opportunity to regain a sense of control and dignity in the face of persistent adult
surveillance in school. Children's sense of liberation during
yard time was evident not only from the screeches and rush to
get to the yard first, but also their awareness that teachers find
it impossible to keep an eye on all that happens there:

> Sometimes there does be a big crowd and everyone gath-
> ers around and the teacher does be saying get away get
> away   . . . and the teacher is trying to find out who did it
> and doesn't unless someone tells . . . mostly children say,
> Oh I didn't see it (5th class boy, Hillview).

In spite of teachers' best attempts at keeping order over yard
activities (circling the yards, taking names in notebooks) children's behaviour went mostly unchecked — the yard was their
space and they interacted freely within it. Free from the glare of
adult eyes a world of backstage behaviour prevailed that consisted of fights, "rude" rhymes and the use of "bad language".
While beyond the scope of this paper, data highlighted the
manner in which friendships are forged and lost, identities
formed and confirmed as children also played a host of games
differentiated in terms of gender and age.

In terms of the exercise of power the data indicates children's awareness of and sensitivity to power differentials in the
school, with such power exercised along two distinct yet interrelated dimensions, between teachers and pupils and pupils
with one another. While peer relations provide an important
forum within which children explore and establish boundaries
for social interaction, the importance of such interaction in mediating children's relations with adults must also be considered. This is particularly the case given the status and power

differentials between teachers and children in schools. Tensions, anxieties and concerns which arise in the course of classroom life are suspended or worked through, as children immerse themselves in their own world of games and disputes — a world that is relatively free from adult interference. In this process, children regain some measure of autonomy within the school, enabling them to cope with the restrictions of classroom life. The facilitation of child culture through the provision of yard-time is an example of the negotiated character of social relations in the school. While teachers have greater access to authoritative resources by virtue of their adult status, such authority is not complete and can only be exercised when children are afforded some opportunity to be free. In this freedom they exercise power with one another, exploring and negotiating their own position within the boundaries of child culture.

Children's Attitudes Toward and Experience of the Curriculum

The primary school curriculum is devised and implemented by adults, and as such reflects their concerns and priorities in the education of children. It provides a framework in which the time-space paths (Giddens, 1984) of children are organised in school. Findings of this study were analysed in terms of children's attitudes toward and perception of school subjects as well as how they experience the curriculum in practice. Interview data with teachers was used to supplement the analysis.

A consistent pattern emerged in relation to children's preferences and dislike of subjects with Art and Physical Education favoured by most, while Irish, Mathematics and English were the most disliked. In terms of dominant discourses influencing children's perceptions the data highlighted aspects of both child culture and adult norms. As this relates to children's preferences for particular subjects, it is evident that what children want most from their learning is to enjoy it, to be stimulated by it and to be able to tackle it with some measure of ease:

> I like doin Art and PE cos in PE ye can run around the halla
> an play an in Art ye can slap around the paint on pictures
> (2nd class girl, Parkway).

> I don't like Irish cos it's a different language and I don't
> know how to do it and I have to work really hard at it . . .
> every time she says take out your Irish book we all say ahh.
> (2nd class boy, Churchfield).

Perceptions of the relevancy or otherwise of aspects of the
school curriculum, however, drew on a more adult-oriented
discourse which perceives education, and specifically schooling, in highly instrumental terms. This was particularly evident
in relation to the subjects which children perceived as being
the most and least important, with clear distinctions drawn between what constitutes "real learning" that is needed for
work/life (Mathematics, English and Irish) and what constitutes
learning which is not really work and can be done outside of
the school environment (Art, Physical Education and Music):

> PE, Art and Music are least important because they are fun
> and school is not meant to be fun (5th class girl, Hillview).

> I think she wants us to work our hardest at Maths, cos you
> wouldn't get into third level without them (2nd class girl,
> Churchfield).

In considering children's perception of the curriculum, attention must also be given to the way they actually experience it
on a daily basis. While children have specific likes and dislikes,
as well as a clear understanding of what is important and what
is not, interview data also highlighted the pressure which children experienced in working through particular aspects of the
curriculum. This pressure arises not only from the quantity of
work done but also by the time in which work must be done.
Such pressure was particularly felt by older children in the
study:

> Children aren't allowed to sit together cos they talk and
> they have a lot of work to do . . . but twenty minutes to do
> fifty sums . . . I don't think that's fair . . . she gives us too little
> time and then we have to do it for homework (5th class girl,
> Churchfield).

> . . . always after a holiday, say at Easter . . . and we are
> meant to do Art or something she says no we can't cos we
> have to catch up on our work . . . she makes you make up for
> the time you had off . . . so it isn't fair . . . we might as well
> work through Easter (5th class boy, Churchfield).

Their views in many ways parallel those of teachers in the study who also complained about the heavily loaded nature of the primary curriculum. A further source of pressure related to the assignment of homework which children viewed as an unfair intrusion into their private lives, and one over which they had little control. Indeed, for many children, homework epitomised the powerful position of the teacher, in terms of using it as a form of punishment, as well as extending control beyond the school:

> Homework is bad cos we work hard every day . . . and then
> you are sent home to do more . . . teachers give children
> homework to keep them occupied . . . after school you are
> supposed to go home and relax . . . not do more homework
> . . . it's like the teacher is still there watching you even
> though you are at home . . . the only way you get out of it is if
> you are sick (5th class boy, Hillview).

Aspects of child culture also mediate children's experience of the curriculum, as in, for example, the extent to which children race against one another in an attempt to be finished first:

> There is competition between the children in the class . . .
> one girl always rushes her work and tries to get up to the
> teacher first and says I'm finished . . . it's stupid . . . and she
> copies . . . that's why she gets full marks . . . last year I was
> quite fast at my work but now I don't mind . . . I just try and
> get through it (5th class girl, Churchfield).

While teachers may use such competition to motivate children towards the completion of greater amounts of work, it highlights how children's jostling for status and position within the peer group can exacerbate the pressure they already feel in completing school work. Social class, however, was an important mediating variable here, with middle class children more likely to compete on these terms than their working class counterparts.

Taking Foucault's assertion regarding the circular nature of power, dominant discourses in education (which define success in highly instrumental and academic terms) become ingrained in educational practice through the definition and implementation of the primary school curriculum. Such discourses, transmitted by adults in their interaction with children both at home and in school, become internalised into children's own perceptions of what is valued and relevant in their education. The organisation of the school timetable, with its division of subjects in time and space is central to the implementation of these discourses in practice, with the curriculum shaping experience, identity and relations in a predominantly instrumental and narrowly focused manner.

Children's Experience of Pedagogy in School

While the school curriculum provides the framework within which children's time and space in school is organised, pedagogy is concerned with the manner in which such organisation takes place. Foucault (1979) highlights how schools are used to discipline the child population through the adoption of an "analytical pedagogy" characterised by regularity and rhythm as well as the standardisation of all procedures in the school day, and the specification of children's behaviour to the minutist detail. Giddens (1984) speaks of the importance of authoritative resources in the mapping of the time-space paths of individuals, establishing boundaries on the nature and extent of their activity. As this applies to schools, teachers with their superior access to authoritative resources by virtue of their adult status, classify children's activity into work and play time, control their interaction and influence their life chances through the pedagogical practices they adopt. Pedagogy, then, is fundamentally concerned with the exercise of power between teachers and pupils, and by extension adults and children.

Children's experience of pedagogical practices in school focused on three main areas: the control and use of time and space within the school, children's experience of school rules and finally, perceptions of teaching style and practice. Differences were evident in the data with respect to children's perspectives on the amount of control exercised by teachers over their time and space in school. Thus girls and younger children were found to be more accepting of such control:

> I think the teacher should choose all the time cos then there would be no arguments . . . some of the class likes some things that half the class doesn't (5th class girl, Parkway).

In contrast, boys and older children were more negative in their responses, critical of the imbalance between work and play time in school and the organisation of classroom space around the surveillance of children:

> We should be allowed choose about PE more or going out to the yard . . . we'd mix work and play more . . . .like at the beginning of the year we could decide the timetable and have an hour of work and an hour break (5th class boy, Churchfield).

> I'd put the teacher's desk as far away as possible . . . outside the classroom door . . . cos she's watchin yer every move . . . every time you even look in yer bag she's watchin over ye . . . an if ye want to get a headstart in yer homework she sees you (5th class girl, Hillview).

Understood in the context of the exercise of power between adults and children, what these children sought was a marrying of both the adult and child worlds where the priorities of each group are given equal weight during the school day.

While most children in the study were favourably disposed to the manner in which their classroom space was organised, space as a form of symbolic power between adults and children emerged in their accounts of differences in access to resources and facilities between teachers and pupils in school. For the children, the superior status of teachers was confirmed in their access to a well equipped staffroom and furniture which was comfortable and relaxing:

> I wish we had more comfortable chairs . . . teachers have
> big comfortable chairs and they have drawers in their desks
> . . . the teachers have them cos they are grown ups . . .
> teachers are respected more by the principal and other
> teachers (5th class boy, Churchfield).

Recreation space also differed greatly between teachers and
children, with the barren appearance of the schoolyard in each
school visited, in sharp contrast to the more comfortable space
of the school staffroom. While all children valued their yard-
time, they were critical of the lack of space and facilities afforded them:

> I wouldn't call it a playground cos there is nothing to do ex-
> cept run around and we're not even allowed do that cos
> we're so squashed up (5th class girl, Churchfield).

The control of children's time and space in school takes place
within a disciplinary framework in which they are required to
monitor their behaviour in line with a series of rules and regulations. Conformity to these rules is part and parcel of the process of normalisation and is tied to the exercise of power between adults and children. Interview data indicated that rules
related to movement, social interaction and control of speech
were foremost in children's minds, with teachers by and large
taking the decision as to what the rules should be. Children's
perceptions of the fairness/legitimacy of school rules drew on
two contrasting discourses: one which defined children in a
paternalistic light and therefore in need of containment and
guidance, and another which seeks a greater voice for children
in the making of rules:

> If there were no rules in school children would be fightin all
> the time (2nd class girl, Churchfield).

> It would be better to share decisions about rules with chil-
> dren . . . at the start of the year he just comes in with a long
> list and says now abide by the rules . . . it's like being in
> boarding school (5th class boy, Parkway).

In general, girls, younger children and children from working class backgrounds subscribed to the former discourse, while boys, older children and those from middle class homes related to the latter viewpoint in their attitudes to school rules.

In discussion on rules, children most readily identified those related to the control and discipline of self in a crowded environment. However, observation data of classroom practice indicated that considerable emphasis was also placed on the normalisation of children in terms of the development of a positive work ethic. The internalisation of such norms was evident among most children in the study, and was reflected in their specification that doing work correctly, neatly and getting it finished was important in making them feel happy in school. The assumption that teachers liked children who behaved and worked well in school, further indicated the internalisation of norms related to both self control and productivity:

> A teacher likes a child when they do their work neatly or do their work right . . . when you work work work work and do more work work (5th class girl, Churchfield).

> When they are good at listening and not messin all the time (5th class girl, Parkway).

That girls and younger children were more likely to perceive themselves as being liked by the teacher suggests that they have internalised these values to a greater extent than either boys or older children.

While the data highlighted the extent to which children's behaviour in school is circumscribed by a range of adult defined rules, this is not to suggest that teacher control over children's behaviour is complete. Interviews and observational data also indicated the highly negotiated character of school discipline. Thus teachers sought to control children by setting one subject off another — attempting to steer the balance sought by children themselves between work time and playtime in school. Reduced homework or the threat of extra homework, the promise of doing/not doing Art and Physical Education, watching videos were all used as a means of inducing conformity and learning among the children. In Parkway, a working class school, a complex system of stars and points was utilised, with mixed views from the children themselves:

> I think the points are good cos they are takin us on a trip to Delphi in May . . . she does the points to see who is good enough to go (5th class girl, Parkway).

> I think the points are stupid . . . we had a rule last year that if ye fell below five points ye get suspended . . . well one boy is at four points now an he's not suspended (5th class boy, Parkway)

While the children generally felt their own behaviour in school was highly circumscribed by rules, their awareness of the existence of rules for teachers was significantly mediated by age level. In this regard, the data indicated that younger children were highly ambiguous about the concept of control over teacher's behaviour, suggesting a relatively unquestioned acceptance of the authority of adults in the school. Thus, in the words of one young boy, "the teachers are allowed to do everything they want" (2nd class boy, Parkway).

Older children, however, were more sensitive to the power context within pupil/teacher interactions, expressed in their desire to limit teacher control over them, as well as their resentment at the ability of teachers to circumvent school rules:

> The teachers are allowed smoke . . . they 're allowed walk around the classroom whenever they want . . . they're allowed talk whenever they want . . . they're allowed have cups of tea in the middle of school when we're not allowed even a drink of water . . . they should have to follow the rules they make . . . the same ones as us (5th class girl, Parkway).

For older children, the perception of double standards in teacher behaviour highlighted for them the unfairness of many rules and the uneven distribution of power between adults and children in school.

Older children's sensitivity to the power context in teacher/pupil relations was also evident in the views they expressed regarding their perceptions of teaching style and practice, with their typification of a good teacher as one who was strict and ensured adequate learning, but who exercised power in a fair manner:

> Sometimes be nice and sometimes be strict . . . you can't be nice all the time cos children will break the rules . . . a bad teacher is if they are nice all the time and don't give the children any discipline (5th class girl, Hillview).

In contrast, younger children were more likely to focus on the interpersonal dimension of teacher/pupil interactions:

> A good teacher is someone who likes you, who cares for you and who minds you if you fall (2nd class girl, Churchfield).

Overall the data highlights the centrality of pedagogical practices to the exercise of power in schools. To be a child in school is to have one's behaviour, thoughts and gestures controlled and defined in terms of adult norms and expectations. This is borne out, not only from observational data detailing the content and manner of teacher exchanges with pupils, but also from the extent of children's awareness of being monitored and restrained in school. School is a space where children are compulsorily confined and where they are subjected to a range of normalising practices, which both signify and legitimise their subordinate status relative to adults. That girls, younger children and those of working class origins are most accepting of these practices indicates the manner in which they have internalised dominant discourses governing school life, to a greater extent than either boys, older children or their middle class counterparts. The findings suggest, then, that the manner in which children exercise their agency differs in terms of the individual attributes of children themselves, with boys and older children in particular articulating their agency in a more overt and resistant manner. That teacher ideologies related to social class and gender are reflected in their pedagogical practices (epitomised in the organisation of space in schools as well as the differential treatment of boys and girls) highlights the significant impact of the authoritative resources of teachers on the life chances of girls and working class children in particular. Thus with respect to girls, the focus of teacher seating arrangements lay in utilising their acquiescence to induce "good behaviour" among boys (rather than, for example, encouraging girls to sit together where they could perhaps support and encourage one another). Similarly, disciplinary considerations were the main focus of seating arrangements for working class children, with the tendency for desks to be arranged in rows, thus limiting their opportunity for interaction with one another in the course of classroom learning. While younger children were equally acquiescent in their responses, this must be understood in terms of the differing orientation of education at the junior end of the primary school system, with teacher authority exercised in a more flexible and interpersonal manner than is evident in the senior end of the primary school.

Children's Experience of Evaluation in School

Evaluation involves the exercise of normative judgements on the behaviour and performance of children in schools. It is a fundamental part of the process of normalisation as, in the making of assessments, adults qualify, classify and punish children in terms of the values which are dominant in the particular society (Foucault, 1979). Through the administration of examinations/tests and the constant monitoring of their behaviour/performance, children become both objects of social control as well as subjects with particular identities, incorporating teacher typifications of their performance into their own self-evaluations. Power is exercised then through these processes of objectification and subjectification, controlling children's life chances, as they compete against one another and are compared to one another in an effort to find their place within an increasingly credentialised hierarchy (Giddens, 1984).

Data related to children's experience of being evaluated in school focused on four main areas: attitudes toward the teacher correcting work, tests, reports and parent/teacher meetings. Findings indicated that younger children hold the most positive attitudes toward teacher evaluation. This was expressed in feeling proud when the teacher looked at their work, wanting to please the teacher and feeling that, in general, the teacher was proud of their work. Girls, in general, were more positive than boys, with working class boys most likely to feign indifference or defiance in relation to negative teacher evaluations:

> Tests are good . . . I love them . . . it tests your brain and it proves that what you are told to do outside school you study yourself and she knows you did it (5th class girl, Churchfield).

> Tests wreck me fuckin head . . . I don't learn them cos they are a waste of time . . . they're not gettin ye anywhere . . . seriously you don't need them (5th class boy, Parkway).

While most children appeared positively disposed toward tests, attitudes were mediated in particular by class level, with fifth class children in general more nervous about them. This is undoubtedly related to the greater frequency of testing of such children (in Mathematics in particular) and the greater awareness of the importance of these tests for preparation for future examinations. While children felt in general that tests were there to help them learn, a substantial proportion of children also viewed them in disciplinary terms — to check who was listening and to keep children quiet. Teacher strategies of offering rewards or incentives for doing well in tests (stars, trips) was favourably commented on by all children, but particularly those in Parkway:

> If ye do yer work ye get points and that's good cos if ye get 15 points ye get a homework pass . . . that's deadly that is and sometimes ye might get to see a video or a trip (5th class boy, Parkway).

Most children were favourably disposed toward reports, and their importance was evident in the fact that many, particularly girls, could recite exactly what had been written about them in the report of the previous year:

> I love them . . . I got "Mary is an outstanding pupil who works to a very high standard" (5th class girl, Churchfield).

More ambiguous views were identified in the sample in relation to parent/teacher meetings, suggesting that as the domain of school and home meet, children's nervousness increases. Such nervousness arose from the fear of being punished/given out to in the event of a negative review being given:

> When I get a bad school report me da didn't touch me cos he didn't know about it . . . but when me ma came in she started yellin at me . . . anytime I get a bad report now I lock meself in the bedroom (5th class boy, Parkway).

A suspiciousness of adults was evident in the desire expressed by some children to be present at parent/teacher meetings to monitor the truth of what was being said. Most children, however, wished to be excluded, fearing that they would be hurt by comments made during the parent/teacher exchanges:

> I would like to be there to interrupt them to say if they were saying something wrong (5th class girl, Hillview).

> I do be shiverin for the meetins . . . we shouldn't be there cos the teacher wouldn't be able to say how bad you are . . . but I would like to see me ma's expression to see if she was happy or disappointed (5th class girl, Parkway).

In considering children's experience of evaluation in school it would be a mistake to focus only on the manner in which they are evaluated by adults. A consideration of the dynamics of child culture highlights the intense scrutiny which children make of one another, evident not only in their eagerness to find out how everyone did in a test or school report, but also in their tendency to slag and tease one another for their school performance:

> I hate when she opens up your copy and reads out the story . . . say it's an Irish story and you have something wrong like a sentence backwards . . . she'd read that in front of the class and everyone would go duuuuh and you'd be sitting there embarrassed (5th class boy, Hillview).

A related issue concerns the annoyance children felt at having to swap copies for corrections. Such annoyance arose from the uncertainty over other children being fair in their corrections, as well as the increased visibility of their performance among peers:

> What annoys me about tests is that for spellings say you have to swap them around to get them corrected but you are not allowed swap with your best friend . . . you usually have to swap with the person beside you and you might not trust them . . . I would trust my best friend (2nd class girl, Churchfield).

Children adopt different strategies to deal with the risk to self brought on by such exposure, ranging from feigning indifference at the whole experience (most notable among boys, particularly in Parkway), to seeking the answers from someone else. Bullying to obtain the answers is sometimes used, as well as the denigration of children who are consistently good in school:

> Anto and Grasser an all them . . . they're always askin me the answers . . . and they look as if they are gettin everythin right . . . I always tell them the answers just in case they slagged me or somethin an sometimes they say if I get this wrong I'll kill ye . . . (5th class boy, Parkway).

A number of central issues emerge in relation to this analysis. First, in terms of the exercise of power, the data highlights children's awareness of being judged and monitored in schools. This is not surprising given the range of evaluation strategies, both formal and informal, which teachers employ throughout the school day and year. That such evaluation takes place primarily within a public domain has significant implications for the control and socialisation of children. Second, the classification of children on the basis of their ability is another important element in their social control, influencing the way they perceive themselves in academic and social terms. Such classification was evident in the study in the ease with which children could recount teacher typifications of them, coupled with the significant correlation identified between teacher and student assessments of ability. The findings suggest that children per-

ceive evaluation as something which is done to them or about
them and which marks their ability/performance in a highly
definitive manner, influencing the identities which they form in
school. Finally, the data also indicates how children themselves
contribute to this process. In the competitive atmosphere of the
classroom, children jostle for status, exercising normative
judgements on one another in the course of the school day. As
active agents within the system children can both reinforce or
detract from dominant adult norms by slagging, bullying or
admiring children on the basis of their performance in school.
Their interaction with one another in evaluative terms is an important aspect of the cycle of power exercised in schools.

CONCLUSIONS

Children are central actors within schools, yet they are frequently presumed not to have the capacity to reflect critically
and constructively on their experience. The data in this study
suggests otherwise, with children, when given the opportunity
to do so, clearly able to document and reflect on all aspects of
their schooling. The strength of the analysis undertaken in this
research lies in locating their views within a framework which
considers the power dimension in adult/child relations, in so
doing challenging and deconstructing traditional concepts of
children as immature and irresponsible. Within an adult-
centred framework, the greater power which adults exercise
over children is interpreted in terms of equal exchange, of
benefit to teachers in terms of enabling them to carry on with
the business of teaching and learning, and of benefit to children
in terms of facilitating them in the promotion of their life
chances. When viewed through a child's eyes, however, the
paternalism inherent within such a perspective is open to question, given the sense of alienation older children, in particular,
reflected in recounting their experiences of school. This is of
concern, given the enthusiasm and commitment demonstrated
by younger children in the study, suggesting that as children's
experience of the system grows, so too does their level of alienation and disenchantment.

To exclude children from decision-making in matters of concern to them is not only to undermine their experience of school as an important part of their childhood, but it is also to detract from developing within them the critical skills with which all citizens living in a democratic pluralistic society should be equipped. Research conducted into the creation of more democratic forms of schooling highlights the benefits which evolve for all when students are allocated greater say in the organisation and structuring of their school experience (Bennathan, 1996; Ashworth, 1995). Citizenship and the practice of democracy does not occur automatically, however, but only through a process of training in the rudiments of argument, negotiation, planning and dealing with social realities (Fumat, 1999; Holden, 1999). Given the complexity of the school as an organisation (Weick, 1988), the implementation of any programme geared toward giving children a greater voice in school must focus on the "nested layers" that comprise the school community: at the school level, class level and at the level of each individual child (Daly, Devine and Swan, 1999). At the school and class levels, teachers must be given the time and space to reflect, debate and tease through their own constructs of children and childhood, to examine their definitions of their role within the classroom, and to facilitate the development of a school plan that aims to create a listening culture for children within the school. As the main mediators of educational policy in practice, they must be convinced as to the benefits which accrue for both themselves and the children in their care when children are given a greater voice in school (Davie and Galloway, 1996; Francis, 1993). The Revised Primary Curriculum (Department of Education and Science, 1999) provides a welcome opportunity and framework for doing so through the newly formulated Social, Personal and Health Education programme (SPHE), with the development of citizenship through shared participation and decision-making identified as a key strand. The formation of a student council (given legislative backing in the recent Education Act (1998) at second level, but surprisingly not at primary level) would give formal, institutional recognition to such an approach, providing pupils with the opportunity to represent their priorities and views in relation to school, developing the skills and aptitudes necessary to the functioning of a democratic system, within an environment which is meaningful and context specific. Such councils will only be effective, however, where clear guidelines are put in place, worked through between adults and children within the school community (Danielsen, 1989), and represented perhaps in a pupils' statute (Smit, 1989), outlining both the rights and responsibilities of pupils within the school. The induction into participation in such a council must be a gradual process, however, with pedagogical and social relational practices at class level from the point of entry into the primary school, geared toward the development of children's skills in democratic participation. Thus workshop education, circle time, co-operative learning projects, as well as children constructively evaluating their own and other's work, can all be used to create a more democratic culture for children in school. Such practices can also develop within children their capacity to be reflective, autonomous learners, able to articulate their voice in a clear and articulate manner, respectful of the views and perspectives of others. Given the socially constructed nature of personal identity (Burr, 1995), children who experience democracy in practice, in their relations with adults, will incorporate concepts of equality, difference and respect into their world view. The findings in this study suggest that children are interpreting much of their experience in terms of subservience and conformity — concepts alien to democracy and equality. This has implications for their lived present lives as children, as well as for their future lives as adults within the society.

References

Arensberg, C. and Kimball, S. (1968) *Family and Community in Ireland,* Cambridge, MA: Harvard University Press

Ashworth, L. (1995), *Children's Voices in School Matters:* A Report of an Advisory Centre for Education (ACE) Survey into School Democracy, LondonO Advisory Centre for Education

Bennathan, M. (1996), "Listening to Children in School — An Empirical Study", in Davie, R. and Galloway, D. (eds.) : *Listening to Children in Education,* London: David Fulton Publishers

Benson, C. (1991), "Play, Culture and Becoming a Child" in *The Rights of the Child — Irish Perspectives on the United Nations Convention.* Dublin: Council for Social Welfare

Burr, V. (1995), *An Introduction to Social Constructivism,* London: Routledge and Kegan Paul

Constitution Review Group (1996), *Report of the Constitution Review Group*, Dublin, Stationery Office

Coolahan, J. (1994), *Report of the National Education Convention*, Dublin

Curtin, C. and Varley, A. (1984), "Children and Childhood in Rural Ireland: A Consideration of Ethnographic Literature" in Curtin C. et al (eds.): *Culture and Ideology in Ireland*, Galway: Galway University Press

Daly, P. Devine, D. and Swan, T. (1999), "School Effectiveness and School Improvement in a Changing Ireland", in Townsend, T. et al. (eds.), *Third Millennium Schools: A World of Difference in School Effectiveness and Improvement,* Lisse, Netherlands and Exton, PA: Swets and Zeitlinger

Danielsen, N. (1989), "Helping Pupils to Help Themselves: Pupils' Councils and Participation" in Jensen, K. and Walker, S. (eds.): *Towards Democratic Schooling,* Milton Keynes: Open University Press

Davie, R. and Galloway, D. (eds.) (1996), *Listening to Children in Education,* London: David Fulton Publishers

Department of Education (1995), *Charting Our Education Future — White Paper on Education*, Dublin: Stationery Office

Department of Education and Science (1999), *Revised Primary Curriculum,* Dublin: Stationery Office

Devine, D. (2000), "Constructions of Childhood in School: Power, Policy and Practice in Irish Education", *International Studies in Sociology of Education*, Vol. 10, No 1, pp. 23-41

Devine, D. (1999), "Children: Rights and Status in Education — A Socio-Historical Perspective," *Irish Educational Studies,* Vol 18, pp.14-29

Devine, D. (1998), "Structure, Agency and the Exercise of Power in Children's Experience of School", Unpublished PhD Thesis, University College Dublin

Foucault, M. (1980), *Michel Foucault: Power Knowledge*, Hertfordshire: Harvester Wheatsheaf

Foucault, M. (1979), *Discipline and Punish: The Birth of the Prison*, New York: Random House

Francis, H. (1993), *Teachers Listening to Learner's Voices*, London: British Psychological Society

Fumat, Y. (1999), "School and Citizenship," in Ross, A. (ed.): *Young Citizens in Europe*, London: CICE

Giddens, A. (1984), *The Constitution of Society — Outline of the Theory of Structuration*, Los Angeles, CA: University of California Press

Goffman, E. (1971), *The Presentation of Self in Everyday Life*, London: Penguin

Government of Ireland Education Act, 1998

Holden, C. (1999), "Education for Citizenship: The contribution of social, moral and cultural education," in Ross, A. (ed.): *Young Citizens in Europe*, London: CICE

Inglis, T. (1998), *Moral Monopoly* (2nd ed.), Dublin: UCD Press

Irish National Teacher's Organisation (1985), *Primary School Curriculum — Report and Discussion Papers*, Dublin: INTO

O'Sullivan, D. (1980), "Teacher Socialisation and Teaching Style in an Irish Cultural Context", *European Journal of Education*, Vol. 15, No 4

Smit, F. (1989), "The Need for a Pupils' Statute in a Democratic School" in Jensen, K. and Walker, S. (eds.): *Towards Democratic Schooling,* Milton Keynes: Open University Press

Weick, K. (1988), "Educational Organisations as Loosely Coupled Systems" in Westoby, A. (ed.) *Culture and Power in Educational Organisations,* Milton Keynes: Open University Press

Chapter 8

Gender Identity in the Primary School Playground

Anne Lodge and Marie Flynn[1]

INTRODUCTION

Gender is a fundamental part of each person's identity and has a significant impact on life experiences. It is one means of differentiating between people in terms of access to power and privilege. Part of the debate about gender identity relates to how fixed or immutable femininity and masculinity are. The ability to assign identity by sex both to the self and to others is one of the first general categories learned by very young children (Lloyd & Duveen, 1992).

The child is born into a community that has pre-existing shared meanings, rituals and patterns of organisation. The child learns these shared meanings and rituals, and their own identity is constructed by the interplay of the individual with the social structure (Donehower, 1983). In learning the social norms of their community, the child creates and reproduces the same social meanings, rituals and structures. The relationship between the individual and social structures and meanings is a reflexive one. The social system which provides the shared rules and meanings of social interaction both enables people to act and interact, while also limiting the possibility of their actions (Giddens, 1984).

The playground is one of the sites within which children have the greatest autonomy from adults. It is the one place in school where the world of childhood is most significant and most visible. Studies of children in their playgrounds afford an opportunity to examine how the culture of childhood both enables and constrains individual children in their expression and exploration of gender identity. They also provide the opportunity to view children as agentic beings interacting with, and contributing to, the creation and reproduction of the social structures of the world of childhood. Through the observation of children interacting and operating within the culture of childhood, it is possible to examine the ways in which social and peer definitions and meanings of gender identity are created and reproduced. It allows the observer to consider how these definitions and meanings operated in enabling and constraining ways for different children, as they express themselves as gendered persons and explore their gender identities.

The playground is an area that has received relatively little attention in comparison to studies of other aspects of children's school lives, in part because play has been considered as "peripheral to the business of living" (Eifermann, 1978, p. 443). It is often overlooked by parents, teachers and those conducting research or developing policy who prioritise children's academic achievements in the classroom (Blatchford, 1994; Evans, 1989; Pellegrini, 1995). From an adult perspective, playtime could be regarded as the forgotten part of the school day (Blatchford et al, 1990). This is in spite of the fact that psychological theorists such as Bruner, Piaget, Vygotsky, Sylva and Donaldson have placed emphasis on the important contribution children's play makes to their social and cognitive development. Hart (1993) describes how, in recent times, many advances are being made in our understanding of child development by using the playground as a naturalistic setting for inquiry.

Playtime represents a unique part of the school day. It is one of the few times when children can interact with their peers on their own terms, with minimal adult intervention. When afforded this freedom, children reveal much about themselves and their social world — more, or at least, different things than are revealed in the more closely supervised world of the classroom (Blatchford and Sharp, 1994). In the classroom, an adult, in the role of teacher, has greater power to define the contents and rules of interaction than do children. The social world of childhood exists as a subversive, and often invisible, element of classroom culture rather than occupying a central role (Lodge, 1998).

For children (and certainly for those who participated in the two projects under discussion here) playtime and any play activities were afforded a central place in their school lives. As one boy in Flynn's (1996) study said of Physical Education (which is the only subject on the curriculum with a physical play element) "my favourite subject is PE so that I can get away from the awful books". The vivid and constant excitement of children's lives in the primary school playground is recalled very effectively by Byrne:

> The day that David Attenborough tires of swamps, jungles, poisonous frogs, and requires a new challenge, he could do a lot worse than make a series of documentaries about lunchtime in a boys' school. It would only be marginally less dangerous, but infinitely more fascinating (1998: 1).

The relative dearth of research on the playground may well be argued to result partly from the inherent difficulties involved in studying playgrounds full of apparently uncontrolled confusion (Opie, 1993). It could also be a consequence of the fact that the very presence of an adult researcher interferes with the culture of childhood (Smith, 1997). It may also be accounted for by the relatively low status, in society and correspondingly in the academy, of both children and their priorities (Lynch and Lodge, forthcoming). Much of the traditional research on children's play focused on adult-directed activities rather than those involving only the peer group (Finnan, 1982). However, it is play that takes place away from adult supervision and interference that is central to the culture of childhood and is of such significance and importance to children. It is within the culture of childhood that children are free to organise their own interactions and activities, where their games and activities are based on rules devised, adapted and understood by themselves (Piaget, 1978). The culture of childhood is constructed and reconstructed through the children's shared understandings of their interactions with the social group (their peers) and their shared activities (play) (Woods, 1983).

TWO PLAYGROUND STUDIES

Flynn's study focused on gendered aspects of the views, experiences and self-images of senior pupils (N=95) in fifth and sixth classes in three rural primary schools. These schools were selected due to their similarity of size and location, and the research focused on senior pupils because of their ability to complete individual questionnaires. Children filled out a questionnaire in which they were asked to discuss their playtime activities under four main headings: (a) views about playtime in general; (b) activity preferences; (c) children's perception of their own sporting ability and that of opposite-sex peers; and (d) social relations. In an effort to provide children with greater scope outside the parameters of the questionnaire, respondents were also afforded the opportunity to write a short account of their playtime experiences.

Prosser (1998) argues that much qualitative research is dominated by language, and that over the last three decades there has been a growing interest among researchers in the use of images (such as photographs, drawings, diagrams, cartoons, signs and symbols) as signifiers of culture. Evans (1989) claims that children often have vivid impressions of play that they can express through pictures of people and objects on the playground. In Flynn's study, further data was yielded through the use of photographs taken by the researcher during breaktimes in the participating schools, as well as by illustrations of playtime activities produced by the children themselves.

Lodge's study focused on a core group of 30 children[2] aged between six and nine years of age, over a two-year period while they were in first and second classes. During the course of this two-year study, the children moved from a coeducational environment to single-sex schools. This was because they were, in fact, attending a single-sex girls' school, but one which also catered for infant boys. Among the notable features of Irish education has been the high proportion of single-sex schools at both primary and second level. This is one of the consequences of the denominational nature of ownership and management of schools, and the preference by the Roman Catholic hierarchy for single-sex educational institutions (Akenson, 1975; Drudy and Lynch, 1993). An interesting by-product of the high proportion of single-sex educational institutions at primary level was the development of single-sex schools with mixed junior standards. The majority of these schools, which currently constitute 4.9 per cent of Irish primary schools and cater for 9.8 per cent of primary school children (Department of Education, 1996), are single-sex girls' schools, but also take boys from junior infants to first class. On reaching the end of first class, only girls may progress to second class in that school. Their male peers must move to local single-sex boys' schools offering classes from second to sixth (Lodge, 1998).

Lodge's study was not focused solely on the children's experiences of the playground, but was interested in all aspects of the children's school lives over the two-year period. Their playground, classroom and overall school experiences were each examined. While gender identity development, exploration and expression was the central focus of the study, other aspects of identity such as social class, ascribed academic ability level, and participation in the culture of childhood were also considered. The core group of 30 children at the centre of this ethnographic study was selected, in part, because of the willingness of the school they were attending to allow such relatively long-term research to take place involving one of their classes.

This study utilised a range of methodologies. Those which focused on the children's lives in the playground included participant and non-participant observation, taking place up to four times a week throughout the duration of the study. Children were twice interviewed individually during the course of the research (May, Year 1; January, Year 2) about various aspects of their school lives including their playground experiences. The 30 children filled out short questionnaires about playground activities on three separate occasions during the research (December, June, Year 1; December, Year 2). Similar questionnaires were also filled out by the classmates of the core group (now divided across five different classes) during the second year, and by the children from third to sixth classes in the single-sex girls' school and in one of the three single-sex boys' schools. For the purpose of this chapter, the main focus will be on the findings from the first year of the study, when the children were in a coeducational environment.

RESEARCH FINDINGS

Most of the literature on children's playgrounds (and, indeed, on children's games in general) reveals that children's play spaces have gendered turf (e.g. Blatchford, 1994; Brady, 1984; Opie, 1993; Thorne, 1993). This is evident in a number of ways which emerged significantly, although not always similarly, in both of the studies under discussion here. It is important to note that there were marked differences between the two studies in terms of methodology, duration and focus. Flynn's study, for example, did not involve the type of lengthy participant observation conducted by Lodge; thus it is impossible to find universal parallels between the findings of the two studies. There were important differences also in terms of the children's ages, the urban or rural location of the schools, the size of the schools, the communities that they served, as well as the types of playgrounds and their populations. As a consequence of these differences, it is not possible to attribute reasons for differences in our findings regarding playground culture to any particular variable, such as school location.

We propose to discuss the findings of both studies regarding gender identity in the playground in four main sections. The first of these examines gender differences in the ways in which girls and boys used playground space and environment. The second section looks at the clear gender preferences in types of activities, many of which were associated solely with one gender group or the other. Section three considers differences in observed behaviours and expressed attitudes which tended to be polarised by gender, although there were differences within, as well as between, the gender groups. Finally, cross-sex peer interaction is considered. This was quite limited in both studies, with many children of each sex expressing rather negative and exclusionary attitudes towards their opposite-sex peers.

Gender Differences in the Use of Playground Space and Environment

A playground environment can act as both a constraining and enabling influence on the children's behaviours and activities. The playground environment includes a number of factors, such as the amount of available space; the type of environmental "props"[3] present within that space; the changing seasons and the ways in which these impact on possible activities; and the level of adult surveillance in a particular play area. All of these factors influenced children's ability to play certain games, and impacted on peer relations.

In Flynn's study, children were asked to name the games they played most and least during their breaks and to explain their preferences. It was clear from their replies that boys and girls in this study used playground space in fundamentally different ways. The predominant activity reported by the boys was football, a game requiring a large number of players as well as central, open space, because the ball travels relatively long distances and players move swiftly in pursuit. The team game given preference by girls was basketball, a game which requires less space and in which the ball remains more in the control of players who bounce and throw over short distances. Girls also reported activities that involved a smaller number of participants and less space, such as talking or "messing" with friends. These social activities preferred by the girls could occur on the playground periphery. Girls in Flynn's study were particularly concerned about boys' monopolisation of space when bad weather made playing pitches unusable. They reported that when it rained boys invaded the peripheral spaces normally occupied by female students. Some boys' responses indicated that they considered girls to be invading their play space, e.g., "Boys should have a different court because girls keep getting in the way".

The type of colonisation of space by boys' games found by Flynn has been reported in many playground studies (e.g.

Grugeon, 1993; Holly, 1985; Shilling, 1985; Whyte, 1983). However, it was not found in Lodge's research. One reason for this
was that the children had a huge amount of available play space
shared with only one other class. Therefore, there was sufficient
space for all playground activities to operate within separate
spaces without any group needing to encroach on the territory
in use by other children. Furthermore, this large area included
a variety of environmental "props"; thus games, utilising or
based around these, were possible in different parts of the
playground without children needing to compete for limited
resources. Another important factor was a continuous adult
presence in this playground space. Unusually, this was not a
supervising teacher. The school operated a FAS scheme[4] em-
ploying a number of local people on a half-time basis over a
minimum period of one year. One of the male employees was
assigned to be present for all breaktimes in this particular yard.
He organised football games, and regarded ensuring that certain dominant boys did not take control of the playground as
one of his prime duties. In this particular study, boys (identified
in other studies as being more likely to colonise the largest and
most central sections of playground space) were subject to ongoing adult control. For these reasons, gender differences in
the use of space in this particular school playground were not a
contentious issue.

Gender Differences in Preferred Activities

Children's choice of games was influenced by a number of
factors listed in the above section, such as amount of space,
level of adult influence or interference, and environmental
"props". Semi-formal games such as Colours, and informal activities such as building grass nests,[5] both observed in Lodge's
study, were reliant on the presence of particular items in the
playground. Children's wish to play with others in their friendship group (most of which were single gender) were significant
influences on choice of activities (both reported and observed)
for the majority of children in both studies.

The games played by children on a consistent basis in both
studies under discussion here showed marked gender differ-

ences, mirroring the findings of many other studies (e.g. Barnett, 1988; Blatchford, 1989; Blatchford et al., 1990; Mahony,
1985; Roberts, 1980; Skelton, 1991; Thorne, 1993). There were
noticeable differences in preferred games and activities between the older girls in Flynn's (1996) study and the younger
ones in Lodge's (1998) research. Many of the older girls reported that they enjoyed talking in small friendship groups,
while others said that they played basketball, a formal team
game. The younger girls in Lodge's study reported preferences
for a wide variety of games. These included chasing (an informal game); a variety of traditional games (e.g. rhyming, skipping and clapping games); domestic or fantasy games (such as
"Mammies", which involved baby-minding and shopping); and
semi-formal games such as Red Rover and Snatch the Bacon.[6]
These semi-formal games have rules and involve teams of
players. However, unlike games such as basketball and football, they do not have formal adult sporting equivalents. Such
variations in reported preferences did not exist between the
older and younger boys, with football being indicated as favourite by both age groups. Other studies (e.g. Blatchford et
al., 1990) have also reported that females were involved in a
wider variety of games and other playground activities than
were their male peers.

There was little evidence emerging from either study of
widespread mixed-sex groups of playmates. Children's reported activities in Flynn's study mainly involved gender-
differentiated activities, taking place in single-sex groups. In the
case of females in particular, these were also friendship groups.
In Lodge's study many of the children were observed during
their coeducational year having either limited or no interaction
with opposite-sex peers, although, as will be examined in the
final section, there were a number of occasionally observed activities involving female and male participants. Not all of the
children in the study took part in these mixed activities.

A number of pieces of research examining the role of children's play in child development have made arguments about
the greater benefits for their participants of traditional boys'
games. It has been suggested that traditional boys' games (e.g.
football) provide their participants with enhanced life-skills

learning opportunities in comparison with the inferior experiences provided by girls' games (Lever, 1978). It has also been claimed that games typically played by girls concentrate on interpersonal relationships, while those preferred by boys are rule-bound (Gilligan, 1982), with the latter being considered to offer greater opportunity for the development of co-operative, competitive and leadership skills (Pitcher and Schultz, 1983). Furthermore, it has been argued that rule-based games such as football, played by boys, tend to be longer lasting and less likely to end in dispute (Lever, 1978).

The observations recorded throughout the coeducational year of Lodge's (1998) study were contrary to these arguments. The boys' football games (when played without adult supervision) tended to be short in duration, and to end in acrimonious disputes concerning different interpretations of rules. The variety of formal, semi-formal, fantasy and traditional games played by groups of girls often lasted for the full duration of a half-hour lunchbreak. Where disputes occurred, individual members of the group were observed either attempting to, or successfully, resolve them. Furthermore, many of these games involved a variety of roles including leadership and the emergence of negotiated rules. This included domestic and fantasy games, a finding supported by Goodwin (1988).

There are a number of possible reasons for the differences between arguments made by researchers on play such as Lever (1978) and those found in Lodge's study. In the first place, the children involved in the latter research were younger. Secondly, Lever's findings regarding the superiority of traditional boys' activities were disputed by Goodwin (1988) because of the fact that they were based solely on children's reports of their own activities and did not include an observation component. Males are more likely to report on their own abilities, characteristics and activities positively than are females (Flynn, 1996; Lundeberg, et al., 1994; Lynch and Lodge, 1999).

Behavioural and Attitudinal Gender Differences

When children's peer group and playtime behaviours and expressed attitudes in both studies were considered overall, there were two characteristics most likely to be gender-associated. Both adults and even very young children equate aggressive characteristics with males and nurture with females (Beall, 1993; Best et al., 1977; Evans, 1982; Herzeberger & Tennen, 1985; Lloyd & Duveen, 1992; Siann, 1985). Children are also more likely to associate themselves with gender-appropriate traits in self-report or description (Zammuner, 1987). This is in spite of the fact that some female and male children exhibit a range of behaviours and attitudes that can be categorised across both of these areas. Many of the games played by the children were gender-differentiated in terms of participation, and mirrored stereotypical femininity and masculinity (e.g. football, aggressive chasing games and play-fighting are associated with masculinity, while domestic fantasy/role-play and the contents of traditional rhyming or clapping games are linked with femininity).

Boys' aggressiveness as a gender group was visible in both of these studies in a number of ways. In the first place, their dominant use of space, as well as the physicality of their games in Flynn's study, was regarded as evidence of male aggressiveness by their female peers. Girls in this study complained about the way in which boys' football games invaded their peripheral spaces when the pitches were unplayable due to poor weather conditions, a complaint borne out by photographs taken by the researcher. Boys were more likely to perceive themselves in an aggressively dominant role (Davies, 1989; Pitcher & Schultz, 1983). One of the boys in Flynn's (1996) study described girls as "getting in the way" of the boys' games, implying that the playground space belonged first to the boys. Evidence of girls' more nurturing outlook could be found in some of the comments about playtime which they made, e.g. [Playtime could be improved] "if people shared more and didn't leave people out of their games". One girl wrote at the end of her description of her playtime activities, "You should always have your playtime and be good to each and one another". Boys' greater tendency to define themselves favourably in terms of sporting ability reflects the link between sporting prowess and institutionalised physical, aggressive masculinity (Connell, 1987).

There were also differences, which emerged in Lodge's study, in self-descriptions of playground attitudes and behaviour given by children regarding their own activities and those of their peers. Children's definition of nurture both as an abstract trait, and in their application of this to themselves, showed particularly stark gender differences.

All 30 children immediately involved in Lodge's (1998) central case-study were interviewed individually about their experiences of school, including their time in the playground. Each child was asked if any other individual in their class behaved aggressively. The majority of respondents named the two most dominant boys, one of whom was nominated by 19 of his peers, and the other by 12 of his classmates. Both of these boys also described themselves as being rough. Two girls were each selected by two of their classmates. Neither of these described themselves as rough. In terms of self-labelling as rough, almost half the boys (5 out of 12) regarded themselves as aggressive, while approximately one-fifth of the girls (4 out of 18) described themselves similarly.

Aggressive behaviour did not simply involve physical fighting. It also included verbal aggression, as well as participation in certain types of games and activities such as playfighting. A minority of the girls in Lodge's study involved themselves in playfighting during the coeducational year of the study. Real physical fights were much more rare than were playful chasing and wrestling games. Only one of the girls and two of the boys from the class were involved in any of the three actual physical fights observed over the course of the year. The female combatant took part in two of these frays. Interestingly, this girl did not define herself as an aggressive person, while both boys participating in these fights regarded themselves as "rough".

While female and male children were agreed on a broadly similar understanding of aggression and "rough or tough" behaviour, the definition of nurture showed noticeable gender differentiation. In the definitions they gave of "kind" or nurturing behaviour, a greater proportion of the girls in the class group focused on a description involving caring behaviour towards other people. Half of the 18 girls listed taking care of peers and allowing others to participate in games as nurturing traits. Of the 12 boys, only one referred to either of these other-oriented activities. Two-thirds of the boys focused on "not being in trouble" and "not fighting", both of which were characteristics first and foremost focused upon themselves, and defined as an absence of aggression and its potential consequences for themselves. Each of the girls in the coeducational class group described herself as "kind and caring", while three-quarters of the boys described themselves similarly. However, in defining themselves thus, children were noticeably gender-differentiated in their understanding of what being "kind and caring" actually meant.

Mixed-gender Peer Interaction

The senior primary school students taking part in Flynn's (1996) study were more likely to be observed, and to report themselves, playing in single-sex groups. The same was true of the younger children at the centre of Lodge's (1998) study.[7] The gender-segregated nature of groups of playmates had to do in part with the preferred activities of children which (as has already been outlined) tended to be gender differentiated. It also had to do with the fact that children often played within friendship groups, and these tended to be single-sex. Furthermore, there was some evidence of a respect and understanding differential between the two gender groups. Among the examples supporting this is the comment made by one boy in Flynn's study claiming that girls "get in the way" of the important business of boys' football games. In Lodge's study, individual boys occasionally disrupted girls' dancing and singing games by joining in and spoiling them through use of teasing and mockery. One girl confided to the researcher that she was looking forward to the boys departing for the single-sex school because they were all "too rough".

While the majority of games and playing groups were normally gender-segregated, or possibly involved a very small minority of serious participants of the opposite sex, there were particular medium or large-scale activities occasionally observed in Lodge's study which involved female and male chil-

dren. One of these was an aggressive chasing game, sometimes known as "Wolfs" and on other occasions as "Dragons".
This was a game in which boys yowling in a bloodcurdling
manner pursued and caught other players, mainly girls. This
was observed on a small number of occasions and did not involve more than ten female and male children in any one game.

A much more popular mixed-sex game, observed and reported mainly during the summer months, was "kiss chase".
These games (which were observed approximately half a
dozen times in total) appeared to erupt spontaneously. Sometimes, one child claimed to "like" a member of the opposite
sex, who then gave chase, the pursuit ending with the pair
wrestling on the grass. On one occasion, the game began because an individual child shouted "let's play kiss chase" and a
general pursuit of all in the vicinity took place. While a large
number of female and male children participated in these
games, and talked excitedly about them, there were children of
both sexes who never took part. These were children who
tended not to have any observed contact with their opposite-
sex peers, and whose range of behaviours and expressed attitudes remained within gender-traditional parameters.

Some of the children referred to this very popular game as
"playing girlfriends and boyfriends" and would indicate a
wrestling pair, saying "he's going in the bed with her". These
games were kept hidden from supervising teachers, who were
unaware that they took place. As Best (1983) points out, even
very young children quickly learn that physical contact games
with any kind of sexual overtones should be hidden from adults,
as such activities tend to meet with disapproval and possible
punishment. Such games were only accessible to the researcher because she had spent a long time establishing trust
with the children and developing her non-adult persona.

A common part of the acceptance of the idea of childhood
innocence is the notion of children as asexual beings, too
young for such knowledge; indeed, consideration of any sexual
element in children's nature may be seen as repulsive (Goldman & Goldman, 1982). Gittins (1998) argues that the creation
of the state of childhood as a time of innocence and difference
from adulthood over the last two centuries has been closely

connected with children's exclusion from knowledge of sexuality. This is one manifestation of the developmentalist, protectionist model of childhood, which not only dominates intellectual thought about children, but also informs our commonly held assumptions and beliefs about young people (Archard, 1993). Children's curiosity about matters pertaining to sexuality is well-documented (Adams & Walkerdine, 1985; Best, 1983; Gesell et al., 1977; Groos, 1978; Pollard, 1985; Sluckin, 1981; Thorne & Luria, 1986; Thorne, 1993). Much of this curiosity is given expression in the form of games involving "chasing, teasing, speculation and 'romance'" (Pollard, 1985, p. 80).

The children in Lodge's (1998) study demonstrated their awareness of the "taboo" nature of any displays of interest in matters pertaining to sexuality from the point of view of adults in school. They hid games and activities with any sexual dimension from adult surveillance. Kiss chase was only played when supervising adults were absent from their section of the playground. A game played by some of the girls on one occasion involving the birth of babies (substituted by the children's dolls) took place between alcoves at the back of the school facing the high park wall. Children shared information and stories with one another, and over a period of time with the researcher, regarding relationships, pregnancies and births of relatives and neighbours. At no time did the researcher observe, or hear reports of, such conversations taking place involving any of their teachers.

CONCLUDING DISCUSSION

The majority of children in both Flynn's and Lodge's studies tended to segregate themselves by gender in the playground, and to involve themselves in activities such as games which were gender-differentiated, and which reflected traditional play patterns and interests. Where resources (such as space) were limited, boys taking part in traditional masculine games, such as football, tended to invade space used by female peers whose activities and identities they regarded as inferior, thus giving a clear indication of the assumed relative value of female and male activities. When females and males did interact in their play, it often involved games and behaviours with romantic overtones that reinforced hierarchical, heterosexual relations.

Many of the children tended to define themselves and their peers in ways which reflected traditional gendered expectations of behaviour, attitudes and characteristics. These children operated within quite limited and stereotypical ranges of gendered behaviour. They included those who acted within stereotypical parameters (playing of gender-appropriate games; absence of contact with opposite-sex peers; exhibition and self-reporting of traditional gendered characteristics). Little challenge was presented to gender-differentiated social relations even where a small number of children operated as "boundary crossers". This term, coined by Thorne (1993), describes those children who, with greater or lesser degrees of success, participate on an ongoing basis in activities generally associated with the opposite sex. In fact, "boundary crossers" often served to reinforce gendered status differences rather than to present a challenge to them.

There were a number of children (female and male) in Lodge's study who operated as "boundary crossers". Girls made up a higher proportion of this minority group. Their presence was less potentially problematic, in terms of their relationships and status with their same-sex peers as well as their opposite-sex classmates, than was that of all but one of the smaller number of male "boundary crossers" in the same group. The exhibition by male children of characteristics associated with the feminine served to distance them from the masculine norm and bring them closer to the feminine "other". For girls, the display of masculine traits raised their status by bringing them closer to the masculine norm. The relative low status within the peer group of border crossing males, and corresponding high status of their border crossing female peers, served to consolidate and confirm the traditional gender hierarchy.

The children taking part in both studies reported here displayed an awareness of gender as a means of differentiation and segregation. They used it as a marker of status within their peer group. In so doing, they were making active use of a pre-existing biological and social marker of difference in adult society. The gender order that permeated their peer relationships and activities was not merely a significant element of childhood culture. Through their expressed attitudes, behaviours and peer-relations operating within the culture of childhood, they were active participants in the creation and reproduction of society's differentiated and unequal gender order (Corsaro, 1997). These children were not operating as passive recipients of adult socialisation in their playground world of childhood. Rather, they were, as Qvortrup (1993) argued, active co-constructors of society. Through the culture of childhood as played out in the school yard, they were actively involved in the reproduction of a society characterised by hierarchical gender relations.

References

Adams, C. and Walkerdine, V. (1985) *Investigating Gender in the Primary School*, London: INSET/ILEA

Akenson, D. H. (1975) *A Mirror to Kathleen's Face: Education in independent Ireland 1922-1960* Belfast: McGill/Queen's University Press

Archard, D. (1993) *Children: Rights and Childhood*. London: Routledge.

Barnett, Y. (1988) "'Miss, girls don't like playing big games; they only like playing little games': gender differences in the use of playground space" *Primary Teaching Studies* 4, 1 pp 42-52

Beall, A. E. (1993) "A Social Constructionist View of Gender" in *The Psychology of Gender* Beall, A. E.; Sternberg, R. J. (eds) New York: Guilford Press

Best, D. L., Williams, J. E., Cloud, J. M., Davis, S. W., Robertson, L. S., Edwards, J. R., Giles, H., Fowles, J. (1977) "Development of sextrait stereotypes among young children in the USA, England and Ireland" *Child Development* 48, 4, pp 1375-1384

Best, R. (1983) *We've All Got Scars: What Boys and Girls Learn in Elementary School* Bloomington and Indianapolis: Indiana University Press

Blatchford, P. (1989) *Playtime in the Primary School: Problems and Improvements*, Windsor: NFER.

Blatchford, P. (1994) "Introduction" in Blatchford, P. and Sharpe, S. (eds), *Breaktime and the School*, London: Routledge

Blatchford, P. and Sharp, S. (eds) (1994) *Breaktime and the School* London: Routledge

Blatchford, P., Creeser, R. and Mooney, A. (1990) "Playground games and playtime: the children's view" *Educational Research*, 32, 3 pp. 163-174

Brady, E. (1984) *"All in! All in!" A Selection of Dublin Children's Traditional Street Games with Rhymes and Music* Dublin: Comhairle Bhealoideas Eireann

Byrne, R. (1998) *"Lunchtime at the castle"*, Unpublished short story

Connell, R. W. (1987) *Gender and Power: Society, the Person and Sexual Politics*, Cambridge: Polity Press

Corsaro, W. A. (1997) *The Sociology of Childhood*, London: Pine Forge Press

Davies, B. (1989) *Frogs and Snails and Feminist Tales: Preschool Children and Gender,* Sydney: Allen & Unwin

Department of Education (1996) *Statistical Report 1994/95* Dublin: Stationery Office

Donehower, N. L. (1983) *Constructing Gender: a study of the development of gender concepts*, Unpublished Ph.D. thesis, University of Edinburgh

Drudy, S. and Lynch, K. (1993) *Schools and Society in Ireland*, Dublin: Gill and Macmillan

Eifermann, R. K. (1978) "It's Child's Play" in Bruner, J.S., Jolly, A. and Sylva, K. (eds) *Play: Its Role in Development and Evolution*, Harmondsworth: Penguin

Evans, J. (1989) *Children at Play: Life in the School Playground*, Geelong, Victoria, Australia: Deakin University Press

Evans, T.D. (1982) "Being and becoming: teachers' perceptions of sex-roles and actions towards their male and female pupils", *British Journal of Sociology of Education*, Vol. 3, No. 2, pp. 127-142.

Finnan, C. R. (1982) "The Ethnography of Children's Spontaneous Play" in Spinglder, G. (ed), *Doing the Ethnography of Schooling: Educational Anthropology in Action*, New York: Holt, Rinehart and Winston

Flynn, M. (1996) "Fair Play: A Study of Gender Differentiation in Primary School Playgrounds with Particular Reference to Children's Playtime Activities", Unpublished M.Ed. thesis, Education Department, University College Cork

Gesell, A., Iig, F. L., Ames, L. B. and Bullis, G. E. (1977) *The Child From 5 to 10 (Revised Edition)*, New York: Harper & Row

Giddens, A. (1984) *The Constitution of Society*, Cambridge: Polity Press

Gilligan, C. (1982) *In a Different Voice: Psychological Theory and Women's Development,* Cambridge, MA: Harvard University Press

Gittins, D. (1998) *The Child in Question,* London: Macmillan Press

Goldman, R.; Goldman, J. (1982) *Children's Sexual Thinking*, London: RKP

Goodwin, M. H. (1988) "Co-operation and Competition Across Girls' Play Activities" in Todd, A. D. and Fisher, S. (eds) *Gender and Discourse: The Power of Talk*, New Jersey: Ablex

Groos, K. (1978) "The play of man: teasing and love play" in Bruner, J. S.; Jolly, A. and Sylva, K. (eds) *Play: Its Role in Human Development and Evolution*, Harmondsworth: Penguin

Grugeon, E. (1993) "Gender and the Playground" in Woods, P. and Hammersley, M. (eds) *Gender and Ethnicity,* Buckingham: Open University Press

Hart, C. H. (1993) *Children on Playgrounds — Research Perspectives and Applications,* New York: State University of New York Press

Herzeberger, S. D. and Tennen, H. (1985) "'Snips and Snails and Puppydog Tails': Gender of Recipient, and Observer as Determinants of Perceptions of Discipline", *Sex Roles* 12, 7/8, pp 853-865

Holly, L. (1985) "Mary, Jane and Virginia Wolf: 10 year old girls talking" in Weiner, G. (ed), *Just a Bunch of Girls*, London: Virago

Lever, J. (1978) "Sex Differences in the Complexity of Children's Play and Games", *American Psychological Review* 43, 4, pp 471-483

Lloyd, B. and Duveen, G. (1992) *Gender Identities and Education: The Impact of Starting School*, New York: St. Martin's Press, Harvester Wheatsheaf

Lodge, A. (1998) "Gender Identity and Schooling: a two year ethnographic study of the expression, exploration and development of gender identity in seven to nine year old children in their school environment", Unpublished Ph.D. thesis, Education Department, NUI Maynooth

Lundeberg, M. A., Fox, P.W. and Puncohar, J. (1994) "Highly confident but wrong: gender differences and similarities in confidence judgements", *Journal of Educational Psychology*, 86, 1, pp 114-121

Lynch, K. and Lodge, A. (1999) "Power: A Central Educational Relationship" Paper presented to the Annual Conference of the Educational Studies Association of Ireland, University College Dublin, 25-27 March

Lynch, K. and Lodge, A. (forthcoming) *Equality and Power in Schools*, London: Routledge/Falmer

Mahony, P. (1985) *Schools for the Boys?* London: Hutchinson

Opie, I. (1993) *The People in the Playground*, Oxford: Oxford University Press

Pellegrini, A. D. (1995) *School Recess and Playground Behaviour: Educational and Developmental Roles*, New York: State University of New York Press

Piaget, J. (1978) "The Rules of the Game of Marbles" in Bruner, J. S., Jolly, A. and Sylva, K. (eds) *Play: Its Role in Development and Evolution*, Harmondsworth: Penguin

Pitcher, E. and Schultz, L. (1983) *Boys and Girls at Play: The Development of Sex Roles*, New York: Praegar

Pollard, A. (1985) *The Social World of the Primary School*, London: Cassell

Prosser, J. (1998) *Image-based Research: A Sourcebook for Qualitative Researchers*, London: Falmer Press

Qvortrup, J. (1993) "Nine theses about childhood as a social phenomenon" in Qvortrup, J. (ed.) *Childhood as a Social Phenomenon: Lessons from an international project Eurosocial Report No. 47*, Vienna: European Centre for Social Welfare Policy and Research, pp. 11-18

Roberts, A. (1980) *Out to Play: The Middle Years of Childhood*, Aberdeen: Aberdeen University Press

Shilling, C. (1985) "Social Space, Gender Inequalities in Education Differentiation", *British Journal of Sociology of Education*, 12, 1, pp 23-44

Siann, G. (1985) *Accounting for Aggression: Perspectives on Aggression and Violence*, London: Allen & Unwin

Skelton, C. (1991) "Demolishing 'The House That Jack Built': Anti-Sexist Initiatives in the Primary School" in Woodhead, G., Light, P. and Carr, R. (eds) *Growing up in a Changing Society*, London: Routledge/Open University Press

Sluckin, A. (1981) *Growing up in the Playground: The Social Development of Children*, London: Routledge Kegan Paul

Smith, S. J. (1997) "Observing Children on a School Playground: The Pedagogics of Child-watching" in Pollard, A., Thiessen, D. and Filer, A. (eds) *Children and Their Curriculum: The Perspectives of Primary and Elementary School Children* London: Falmer Press

Thorne, B. (1993) *Gender Play: Girls and Boys in School*, Buckingham: Open University Press

Thorne, B.and Luria, Z. (1986) "Sexuality and Gender in Children's Daily Worlds", *Social Problems*, 33, 3, pp 176-190

Whyte, J. (1983) *Beyond the Wendy House: Sex Role Stereotyping in Primary Schools*, London: Longman for Schools/Equal Opportunities Commission

Woods, P. (1983) *Sociology and the School: An Interactionist Viewpoint*, London: RKP

Zammuner, V. L. (1987) "Children's Sex Role Stereotypes: A Cross Cultural Analysis" in Shaver, P.and Hendrick, C. (eds) *Sex and Gender* California: Sage

Notes

[1] We would like to express our thanks to Kathleen Lynch, Equality Studies Centre, UCD, and Pat Naughton, Education Department, MIC, for their helpful suggestions and comments on an earlier draft of this paper.

[2] The study was also looked at a wider group of approximately 120 children, who were the classmates of members of the core group during Year 2 of the study, as well as at a further group of approximately 200 older children (from third to sixth classes) in two of the single-sex environments. In total, this study involved 350 children, including the primary core group of 30. The gender breakdown on the core group is as follows: 18 girls, 12 boys.

[3] Environmental "props" as defined here include any outbuildings or other structures in the playground space; steps, benches, other raised areas; painted or marked areas for formal (e.g. basketball, football) or informal (hopskotch, coloured circles) activities; grass as well as hard surface areas; flower beds, bushes, trees; hidden areas such as alcoves or doorways.

[4] FAS Community Employment schemes were set up in 1993, taking over from the already-existing Social Employment Schemes. People are employed on a half-time basis for a one-year period with the possibility of being "rolled over" (i.e.: kept on) for a maximum of two further years. To be eligible the person must be in receipt of unemployment assistance for at least six months.

Schools, voluntary and community groups are eligible to avail of such schemes.

[5] Colours was played by a team and a leader and used circles of different colours painted on the floor of a shelter. The leader called out a particular colour and team members raced one another to stand alone on a circle of that shade. Building grass nests was an informal activity taking place on sunny days when the grass in the large playground field had been cut. Children collected armfuls of grass (preferably damp and sticky) and built big nests which they then sat in.

[6] Red Rover involves two teams. The players on each team hold hands and form a line facing their opponents. One team "calls" a member of the opposition, who runs at them attempting to break the chain. If the player succeeds her team picks one of the opposition to join her line, if not, she must join the opposition.

Snatch the Bacon, documented by Brady (1984), involves two teams, facing each other across a square/rectangular area used as a court and divided in half. Each team controls its own half which represents its "safe" area where team members cannot be caught by members of the opposition. The object of the game is for one team to take an object (usually a jumper, called "the bacon") from the other team's area without being caught. It is very similar to an ancient Asian game, Kabadi.

[7] All of the children from second class upwards who had any involvement with this study were in single-sex settings because the selected schools were either single-sex intake only, or single-sex seniors with mixed infants.

Chapter 9

"Bluebells, Cockle Shells": Skipping Games and Rhymes in Ireland

Geraldine Lynch

INTRODUCTION

A study of the games which children play offers us an insight into the world of the child.[1] It is possible to discover how children function in a world which is, momentarily at least, adult-free. We learn how play groups are formed, leaders chosen, rules and regulations laid down, and which areas of life are of real concern to the child. In this paper I intend to examine these aspects of childhood in Ireland by investigating the various forms of skipping played and some of the numerous rhymes associated with them. Although it is likely that skipping, in some form or other, is an ancient game, there is little known of its early history. We know that, by the 19th century, English boys were competing at individual skipping (Strutt, 1845, p. 383). Skipping was also played by 19th century girls, both individually and in groups (Sutton-Smith, 1972, p. 100). Skipping rhymes were known in the 19th century but did not achieve popularity until the beginning of the 20th century (McCaughan, 1971-72).

The first serious attempt to collect children's lore in Ireland was made in the Schools' Scheme, 1937-38. This scheme was organised by the Irish Folklore Commission in co-operation with the Department of Education and national schools in the Republic of Ireland.[2] In the guideline booklets in Irish and Eng-

lish, prepared by the Commission's archivist, Seán Ó Súilleabháin (1937a, 1937b), for teachers and pupils involved in the
scheme, information about traditional games was sought under
the headings, *Cluichí* and Games I Play, with additional information about skipping ropes requested under *Bréagáin agus
Caitheamh Aimsire* and Home-Made Toys. The popularity of
skipping throughout Ireland in the 1930s is evident from the 446
references to the game in the Schools' Manuscripts.

Replies to a questionnaire in 1989 show that skipping remains a popular children's game in present-day Ireland. This
questionnaire was circulated by the Department of Irish Folklore, University College Dublin, and by the Ulster Folk and
Transport Museum to senior primary schoolchildren throughout
Ireland. A total of 206 schools replied to the questionnaire and
2,743 completed answer sheets were received. Every county in
Ireland, north and south, is represented in the material.[3]

INDIVIDUAL DIFFERENCES

In building up a picture of how the game of skipping is played
in Ireland, trends and distribution patterns in questionnaire replies and archival data have been examined.[4] It is important,
however, to be aware of the influence which the individual
characteristics of the children may have on this material. In
considering how individual differences affect the games children play, we must look at five main areas: physical differences, gender differences, intellectual differences, temperament and character differences and the differences in children's social backgrounds, home and school environments.

It is inevitable that physical differences, to some extent, affect children's participation in sports and playground activities.
In order to participate fully in playground games, such as skipping, a certain level of physical fitness is required. Recent research has shown that many young people take very little exercise. A third of British twelve-year-olds (Swinburne, 1994) show
two or more of the risk factors normally associated with coro-
nary disease. Differences in physical fitness and skill may also
determine the skipper's status within the peer group. The
poorer skippers are, in some instances, relegated to the posi-

tion of turners, particularly in those games in which a group of children skip simultaneously in a long rope turned by two children, for example, the game in which the rhyme "All in together girls this fine weather" (A 700) is used.[5] This may be done openly and formally, or it may be achieved more subtly — the weak skippers, aware of their limitations, may volunteer to turn the rope.

In regard to gender differences, it is generally assumed, even in this equality-conscious era, that certain games are played almost exclusively by boys, and others almost exclusively by girls, while a certain number enjoy popularity with both. Is this true, and if it is, has the gender equality movement had any perceivable effect on children's game preferences? In their study on historical change in game preferences, Sutton-Smith and Rosenberg (1961) concluded that the game preferences of girls have changed to become more like those of boys, while the game preferences of boys have remained fairly constant. Recent studies agree that the game preferences of boys have remained more static than those of girls. In 1992 Ann Henshaw, of the School of Health Sciences in Wolverhampton Polytechnic, published the results of a small-scale study of gender-stereotyping among primary schoolchildren. Two main conclusions were reached:

> First it was evident that the children clearly differentiated between toys, activities and occupations and colours that they saw as appropriate for males and females. Secondly, it was evident that the children viewed male gender roles and activities as being more rigidly proscribed than those of females (Henshaw et al., 1992, p. 229).

A report published by the Department of Education (Ó Láimhín, 1992, p. 24) also concluded that, by the age of four, boys were "more stereotyped than girls in their attitude towards play and leisure activities, and parents to be more stereotyped in their choice of toys for boys than for girls".

The child's character, personality and temperament all contribute to the position held by the child within the playground. Natural leaders and organisers emerge, and in many instances these playground leaders show aspects of their personality which may not have been evident within the confines of the classroom, or indeed in the home environment. Cosbey (1980), in his study of skipping songs from Regina, Saskatchewan, Canada, found that some of the play group leaders were described as "problem children" in the classroom by their teachers. In the playground environment, the skills and personality of the youngest and weakest members of the group are nurtured until they are able to participate fully in the chosen activities. Where group skipping is the preferred activity, ownership of the skipping rope brings with it automatic leadership status within the group, enabling children who are not natural leaders to dominate the game, thus strengthening their character and personality.[6]

Cosbey (1980) also discovered that the skipping rhyme repertoires of children who attended school in working class areas were larger than those of children from middle class districts. This, he surmised, was due to middle class children taking part in a greater number of adult-organised activities, such as extra-curricular lessons, than working class children, who would be free to provide their own amusements.

THE SKIPPING GAME

Spring and summer are the most popular seasons for playing skipping.[7] Sixty per cent of the skippers who replied to the questionnaire played skipping both at home and at school. The frequency with which skipping was played during school play times depended on school policy on the organisation and use of play facilities.[8] School-based skipping groups were the preserve of girls.[9] The question of the gender composition of home-based skipping groups remained unresolved however; 49 per cent maintained that such groups would be composed only of girls, while a close 47 per cent said that both boys and girls played skipping at home. It was found that the majority of skippers were in the 7 to 13-year-old age group.

Skipping Ropes

Unlike many other playground games, such as chasing games, which can be organised on the spur of the moment, a certain amount of preparation is required before skipping can begin. A rope is essential to the skipping game, and it is probably for this reason that the child who provides the rope for the group achieves leadership status for the duration of the game.

Children writing in 1937-38 preferred to use long ropes suitable for group skipping but which could be shortened, by wrapping them around their hands, for individual skipping. The ropes of this period could be home-made, using rushes, sally rods, and even scutch grass. Suitable rope, discovered in the farmyard or in the workplace, was requisitioned for skipping, and occasionally shop-bought ropes with wooden handles were used. In 1989, Irish shops stocked skipping ropes imported mainly from China and Pakistan. Banaghans of Nenagh, one of Ireland's leading toy importers, sold 250 dozen skipping ropes in April 1989 at the beginning of the skipping season.[10]

Almost half of the children said that skipping ropes were available for use in school. The majority, however, preferred to bring their own ropes to school. Leadership of the game was one of the reasons given by the children for bringing their own ropes. Forty-four per cent of questionnaire respondents used long ropes suitable for group skipping; only 16 per cent preferred to use short ropes. Eleven per cent of children liked to have handles on their skipping ropes. Short ropes for individual skipping were often bought in shops. Baling twine, clothes lines and towing rope were all used to make long skipping ropes.

Having chosen the most suitable skipping rope, the players are ready to begin organising the skipping game. Individual or group skipping may be played. If individual skipping is played, the skipper is free to determine the movement, method and whether or not rhymes are to be used. If group skipping is played, the skipping group must decide who will turn the rope, the order of skipping and whether or not rhymes should be used. In order to facilitate this process, a leader organises the skipping group, in many instances this is the owner of the rope, or the person given the responsibility for a school rope by the teachers.

Turning the Rope

Although, at times, there are willing turners for the game, often nobody wants to be first "on rope". Counting-out rhymes are the most popular means of selecting the turners.[11] Another popular technique is the use of "loops": "We put the rope around one person's arm and each person picks a loop so the nearest to the end of the rope is 'on rope'" (Wexford B 10).[12]

In group skipping the people who turn the rope are given special names, particularly in the north and east of the country. These children may be known as "turners", "twisters", "swingers", "endeys", "whirlers", "winders", "twinders", and "twiners".[13] A child who makes a mistake, causing the rope to stop, was said to "break" in counties Wicklow and Kilkenny. "Tailsies" and "tailies" were the terms used in Belfast and Dublin respectively, when a skipper's clothes or footwear became entangled in the rope; in Co. Tipperary the term used was "tiptail".

Skipping Order

Popular methods of determining the order of skippers in a long rope game include using a counting-out rhyme (10 per cent), lining up (10 per cent), and shouting "first", "second", and so on (11 per cent). The owner of the rope often skips first and may decide the order in which the other children skip (7 per cent). The youngest child may skip first (4 per cent), or the oldest (4 per cent); children may pick a number to determine the skipping order (4 per cent), toss a coin (3 per cent), or run a race (1 per cent).

Individual and Group Skipping

A solitary skipper using a short rope makes their own decisions about the form of the game to be played. They may skip forwards, backwards or cross hands; while skipping they may jump with both feet together, perform a skipping action, hop or run. The individual skipper may also participate in various skipping competitions such as races, relay races, competitions to see who can skip for the longest period of time, or achieve the highest number of skips. The child skipping with a short rope may invite another child to join the game. Although this form of skipping sometimes occurs without the introduction of a rhyme, the skipper may invite another child into the rope by saying: "I like coffee, I like tea, I like (X) in with me." (I 1 400) In the second verse the invitation is withdrawn and the second skipper must leave the rope: "I hate coffee, I hate tea, I hate (X) in with me."

The vast majority of children reported taking part in both individual and group skipping. Many rhymes are suitable for any form of skipping, others are attached to a certain skipping method. "Keep the kettle boiling" (K 100) is suitable for a line of skippers who enter and leave the rope one at a time: "Keep the kettle boiling, If you miss a loop you're out." One child runs into the rope and skips through the verse; as the first skipper runs out of the rope, a second skipper runs in. In this way there is always a skipper in the rope and the kettle is kept boiling. As the children leave the rope they rejoin the skipping queue. "All in together girls this fine weather" (A 700) is used when all the skippers start together in the rope. Children run out of the rope when their month of birth is called out:

> All in together girls this fine weather
> When it's your birthday
> Please jump out
> January, February, March, . . ,

Although children were not asked specifically about skipping or skipping rhymes when they were told to write a school essay entitled "Games I Play" in 1937-38, 37 distinct and separate rhymes were reported by them. That children are conservative and traditionalist in their lore is witnessed by the fact that over 60 years later 23 of these rhymes, that is 62 per cent, appear in the questionnaire responses. The 196 skipping rhymes which feature in the questionnaire replies vary in frequency and geographical distribution. Some appear only once, while others occur hundreds of times. It is likely that the rhymes written out in full were personal favourites and/or the most popular ones in the locality at the time, since it is unlikely that the informants would have written down all the skipping rhymes they knew. Some of the rhymes are widespread in Ireland, and many of them are also found in other countries. Others would appear, at present at least, to have a rather limited geographical distribution.

Identifying international rhymes in local and national collections is not always an easy task, especially when a rhyme is reported only once in the collection, or is reported only by a particular school. Girls from St. Joseph's GNS, Rathnew, Co. Wicklow, reported skipping to the following rhyme (L 500):

Long nose, ugly face,
Sitting in the glass case.
If you want to know
Her name is (X).
Oh (X) turn away from me,
I don't want to speak to you,
Nor you to speak to me.
I thought you were my friend,
But now I see you're not,
So get out (X)
And leave the rope to me.

The rhyme was not reported from any other school in Ireland and was unknown in neighbouring schools. Furthermore, the rhyme was not mentioned in any of the pre-1989 Irish archival material, nor in the replies to a questionnaire circulated to adults in 1989. In September 1991, the Folklore Society in Britain published part of a collection by Alan Smith of games and rhymes from the 1950s in their Children's Folklore Newsletter. It included the following rhyme, recorded in Marner Primary School, London, in May 1956:

I know a little girl, sly and deceitful,
Every bit of tittle tattle,
She goes and tells the people.
Long nose, ugly face, fit to put in a glass case,
And if you want to know her name,
Her name is (X).

The introductory lines of Alan Smith's London version led to a version in Iona and Peter Opie's (1977, p. 195) compilation. The

Opies had collected versions from 15 schools throughout Britain and they stated that this rhyme was used as a skipping rhyme.

Although many versions of skipping rhymes used by Irish primary schoolchildren in 1989 have been listed in well-known international collections and articles, it is difficult to assess the popularity of these rhymes in a given time and place. A collection of rhymes from Regina, Canada, in the 1970s (Cosbey, 1980, p. 96) however, includes a table giving the 25 most popular — most frequently observed — skipping rhymes in the region. On comparing these rhymes with the 25 most popular — most frequently reported — Irish rhymes, it emerged that 13 of the most popular Irish rhymes featured among the top 25 Canadian rhymes.

The most popular skipping rhyme in the Irish 1989 collection is the calling-in rhyme "I like coffee" (I 1 400), mentioned above in relation to short rope skipping. A total of 471 children from 31 counties reported skipping to this rhyme.[14] The popularity of "I like coffee" in 1989 is not reflected in earlier archival material or Irish printed sources. There are no versions of this rhyme in the Schools' Manuscripts and it is not recorded in Eilís Brady's "All in! All in!" (1975). It was recorded in Co. Wicklow, however, in the 1970s and 1980s.[15] In 1948 Margaret Ann Bailey from Newcastle, Co. Down, then aged 57, told folklore collector Liam Mac Reachtáin that she had skipped to "I love coffee" as a child. Her version is as follows:

I love coffee,
I love tea,
I love the boys
And the boys love me.
I wish my mother
Would hold her tongue,
For she had a boy
When she was young (IFC 1036, p. 169-170).

No account is given of how the game was played, and no provision is made in this version for calling in another skipper.

"I like coffee" is an international rhyme, and is included by Abrahams (1969) in his dictionary of skipping rhymes (Rhyme no. 24). Here references are given to versions collected in the United States, Great Britain and New Zealand. The earliest version noted by Roger Abrahams dates from pre-1920 and was collected in Arkansas.

"Cinderella dressed in yellow" (C 600) is the second most popular rhyme in the 1989 collection.[16] A total of 325 complete versions of this rhyme from 23 counties were included in the questionnaire replies. Fifty-three per cent of these came from Ulster. Despite the large number of versions there is remarkably little variation. Cinderella is the main character in all versions, and in all but nine she is dressed in yellow. In 77 per cent of versions, Cinderella is said to have gone upstairs (downstairs) to kiss (see, meet, find) her fellow. In other versions she went to the ball to kiss (meet) her fellow (7 per cent); or she went to fetch an umbrella (3 per cent). We are told that Cinderella kissed a snake in 28 per cent of versions; in seven per cent "on the way her knickers (girdles) bursted". Ninety-seven per cent of versions of "Cinderella dressed in yellow" are counting rhymes. Sixty-one per cent of children count to determine how many kisses Cinderella gave or got; 26 per cent to find out how many doctors, pills or stitches she needed; and seven per cent to discover the number of people who were disgusted. Children may count in ones, twos, fives or tens.

"Cinderella dressed in yellow" is included in Roger Abrahams' dictionary (1969, Rhyme no. 80), in which American and Australian versions are given. This rhyme is not mentioned by the Opies (1977). A very short version, however, was collected by Alan Smith in Marner Primary School, London, in 1956. Canadian versions have been collected by Edith Fowke (1969) and Robert C. Cosbey (1980, Rhyme no. 22). This rhyme is placed third in Cosbey's table of the top 25 Canadian skipping rhymes. It is not found in the Schools' Manuscripts and is not featured in Brady (1975). It was, however, recorded in Ireland in the early 1980s.[17]

WORLD OF THE CHILD

In order for a rhyme to be suitable for skipping, its rhythm must reflect the beat of the rope. The rhyme also fulfils a variety of other functions: divination rhymes allow the children the chance to influence their future through skill at skipping; action rhymes allow the members of the skipping group to demonstrate and develop their skill at performing actions while skipping; and counting rhymes demand stamina of the skippers.

The content of the rhymes must be of interest to the skipping group. The subject matter usually concerns the everyday world of the child — home, school, family relationships, and the personal growth and development of the child. In the skipping group the children are able, in a non-threatening environment, to explore subjects of immediate personal concern. With the support of other group members, the children can cope with the demands made upon them by adult authority figures. In this way they can overcome fear of illness and hospitalisation, for example, or fear of rejection by the mother, which may be linked to the arrival in the household of a new-born baby.

Through the skipping rhymes children can also enter into a fantasy world, in which they can eat their favourite foods, drive cars recklessly, or become a girl guide, a Spanish lady, an exotic dancer, or an American beauty. It is possible to ask a pop star for a date, learn dancing from Charlie Chaplin and enter the world of other film stars. In their preadolescent years children become more aware of their own sexuality, and consequently many rhymes explore the themes of boyfriends, girlfriends, kissing, love, marriage, and having children. In rhymes which address these topics, a progression from love to marriage and to childbirth is usually to be observed.

ADULT AUTHORITY FIGURES

Adults are mentioned in 24 rhymes. These are the adults who play an important role in children's lives — mothers, fathers, grandmothers, teachers, doctors and policemen. Robert C. Cosbey's study (1980) showed that mothers, teachers, doctors and policemen are the adults most often mentioned in the rhymes he collected in Regina, Canada. Fathers were rarely mentioned in his collection in contrast to the 1989 Irish collection in which they appear to play a more prominent role. Grandmothers are also occasionally mentioned in the Irish collection.

. In the rhyme which begins "Mother, mother, tell me true/Who shall I get married to?" (M 900) the child seeks her mother's advice about her marriage prospects. In "Hop, hop, hop" (H 700) however, the girl is in a hurry home for fear of what her mother will say. Other children threaten to tell the skipper's mother, or father, that she has been kissing her boyfriend. This threat is made in over a quarter of the versions of "On a mountain stands a lady" (O 300). Leinster children threaten to tell the skipper's father, whereas children from Munster and Ulster threaten to tell the skipper's mother. There are no Connaught versions of this rhyme in the 1989 collection.

In a number of rhymes the mother's family duties are mentioned; she is pictured minding a new-born baby (R 700), or placing the baby in the high-chair for his meal (B 300). Other household duties mentioned are mending or stitching clothes. In "Granny in the kitchen" (G 600) the grandmother is usually found in the kitchen, stitching or knitting. A robber or a bogeyman comes in and frightens her away.

The teacher is perceived as an authoritarian and threatening figure who carries a stick in the Westmeath versions of "Bluebells, cockle shells" (B 700) and in "Here comes the teacher" (H 300). The policeman is usually depicted as either attempting to arrest, or actually arresting, the skippers, and putting them in jail for a number of years. In "I am a little bumper car" (I 200) the skipper is sent to jail:

> I had a little bumper car, number 48,
> I drove it around the corner
> And I put on my brakes.
> A policeman caught me and put me into jail.
> How many years was I there?
> 1, 2, 3, ...

In "Policeman, policeman" (P 800) the person about to be arrested pleads for leniency with the policeman:

Policeman, policeman, don't take me,
For I've got a wife and a family!
How many children have you got?
Twenty-four and that's the lot.
1, 2, 3, ... 24.

This verse is also included in two versions of "Sitting in the classroom" (S 700). The doctor is portrayed as a helpful adult figure (R 700, C 600).

CHILDREN'S FEARS

In their skipping rhymes children can explore common childhood fears and find solutions to those fears in the secure, non-threatening environment of the skipping group. The child may be afraid of the dark, and of creatures imagined to lurk in the darkness, as portrayed in the rhyme "Someone under the bed" (S 1 200).[18] In this rhyme the child solves the problem by calling on a friend to bring a light, indicating that there is nothing to be frightened of in the darkness after all:

There's somebody under the bed,
I wonder who it could be,
I feel so very nervous,
I call (X) in with me,
(X) lights a candle,
There's nobody there,
With you e, i, diddley-i,
And out goes (X).

The Australian version given by Durkin and Ferguson (1990, p. 86) has a humorous ending which diffuses the fearful situation:

Someone's under the bed
Whoever can it be?
Getting on my nerves, so Suzy comes to me.
Suzy lights a candle, under the bed she goes,
Get out Mary, get out Mary,
Before I light your nose.

In eleven versions of "I'm a little girl guide" (I 300) the child is rejected by her mother.[19] In "Rock, rock, call the doc" (R 700) the new-born baby is rejected by the older child, and in the following version a method of disposal, applicable to a high-rise building, is suggested:

> Rock, rock, call the doc,
> Mama's got a new-born baby.
> Wrap it up in tissue paper,
> Send it down the elevator:
> First floor stop,
> Second floor splits,
> Third floor turn around,
> Fourth floor tip the ground,
> Fifth floor get out of town,
> Sixth floor shut the door,
> Seventh floor scram.[20]

In the rhyme "Baby on the high chair" (B 300) the baby is also wrapped in tissue and is sent to the "operator". In a Donegal version the baby, wrapped in tissue paper, is sent to the "alligator". Fear of hospitalisation is discussed in the rhyme "I got the German measles" (I 1 100).

PARTNERS, LOVE, AND MARRIAGE

Girls' attitudes to boys are outlined in a number of rhymes. Although in general the boys in school may be considered nice, or unbearable, as the case may be, there is usually one boy who is thought to be special:

> All the boys in our school are really great
> Especially (X) he's the best.
> He took me to the pictures, he sat me on his knee,
> And he said, "dear (Y) will you marry me?
> Yes, no, yes, ... (A 800)

Cinderella goes upstairs in search of her fellow (C 600), while others are content to sit on the sofa (A 100). Partners may go to the cinema (A 800), spend time together in the countryside, or even seek privacy in a tree (A 1 100). Kissing is depicted as a secret activity in the rhymes, one which takes place out of sight — up a tree (A 1 100), behind the kitchen door (O 1 600), or around the corner (O 300) — and unknown to one's parents. Once a partner is found and it is agreed that they are in love, the wedding may be organised. The children skip through lists to determine details such as where the wedding will take place, the transport to the wedding venue, the type of wedding ring used, the wedding clothes and shoes, where the honeymoon will be spent, the night clothes of the newly married couple, and the place in which they will live.

FOOD AND DRINK

Food and drink are mentioned in almost a third of the rhymes in the 1989 collection. Tea is the most popular drink and is mentioned in nine rhymes, reflecting its dominant role as an everyday beverage in Irish society (Lysaght, 1987, p. 44-71). References to coffee are much less frequent. Other children's and adults' beverages mentioned in the skipping rhymes are milk, cocoa, Pepsi, ginger-ale and stout.

Fruit is frequently mentioned in the rhymes. Fourteen kinds of fruit are referred to: apple, banana, blackcurrant, cherry, gooseberry, lemon, lime, melon, orange, pear, plum, raspberry, redcurrant and strawberry. Fruit may be made into jams, jellies, pies, tarts, custards and shortcake. As might be expected, confectionery features rather prominently in these children's rhymes and, in addition to items mentioned, includes biscuits, cakes, barm brack, sweets, chocolates, candy and buns with sugar on top. Other foods mentioned in the rhymes such as sausages, chips and bread are also popular among children. Ice cream is mentioned in six rhymes, and sugar is referred to in four. The only vegetables mentioned are peas, beans and potatoes.

FILM

At least one rhyme in the 1989 collection has entered children's folk literature through the medium of film:

> One, two; Freddy's comin' for you
> Three, four; better lock your door
> Five, six; grab your crucifix
> Seven, eight; gonna stay up late
> Nine, ten; never sleep again. (O 1 300)

The film *A Nightmare on Elm Street* opens and closes with this rhyme. The Freddy of the rhyme is Freddy Krueger, "the horribly scarred man with the ragged slouch hat, dirty red-and-green striped sweater, and metal gloves with knives at the tips" (Virgin, 1992, p. 632). Six children reported using this rhyme as a skipping rhyme in 1989. They were from Westmeath, Wicklow and Tyrone. No appreciable change had taken place in the content of the rhyme. It will be interesting to discover if this rhyme continues to survive. The format of the rhyme is based on the traditional nursery counting rhyme, "One, two, buckle my shoe". The version reported by the Opies (1951, p. 333) goes up to 20. They mention a version quoted by Bolton, which he believed originally went up to 30, and was used in Wrentham, Massachusetts, as early as 1780. They also remark that a form of the rhyme was common in Germany, France, Holland and Turkey.

Divination

The simplest method of marriage divination involves skipping through the alphabet to discover a present or a future partner's name. This may be proceeded by a rhyme and eleven marriage divination rhymes were popular in Ireland in the late 1980s. In "Apple Jelly" (A 1 200) the skipper skips through the alphabet, whatever letter she "breaks" on is the initial of her "sweetheart", her "young man", or her "lucky love". "Apple Jelly" has been used for skipping in Ireland since at least the beginning of the 20th century and was already popular here in the 1930s.

The rhyme "Tinker, tailor" (T 900) is known to have been used as a divination rhyme by schoolchildren in Britain as early as the 1770s (Opies, 1977, p. 363). It was popular as a skipping rhyme in Ireland in the 1930s, and there are versions from 20 counties in the 1989 collection. Children skip to the rhyme, which consists of a list of eight or more occupations, to determine the kind of person they will marry. This rhyme may also be used to determine the skipper's future occupation.

Only one rhyme in the 1989 collection deals with death divination. Four children from Moneystown, Co. Wicklow, reported skipping to

> Apple tree, plum tree, pear tree, pie
> How many children die before I?
> 1, 2, 3,... (A 1 300).

This rhyme has also been collected in Britain and in the United States (Abrahams, 1969, Rhyme no. 20).

ACTION RHYMES

Over a quarter of the rhymes in the 1989 collection may be described as action rhymes. The most popular of these is "Teddy Bear, Teddy Bear". Versions of this rhyme were received from 26 counties and from 186 children. Each version follows a similar pattern. All lines begin with the words "Teddy Bear, Teddy Bear", and the skipper is required to perform some actions while continuing to skip. The most popular variant is:

> Teddy Bear, Teddy Bear, turn around;
> Teddy Bear, Teddy Bear, touch the ground;
> Teddy bear, Teddy Bear, run up the stairs;
> Teddy Bear, Teddy Bear, say your prayers;
> Teddy Bear, Teddy Bear, turn off your light;
> Teddy Bear, Teddy Bear, say goodnight;
> Goodnight!

Abrahams (1969, Rhyme no. 545) refers to versions of this rhyme published in Canada, Britain and the United States. It has been collected by Virtanen (1978, p. 41-42) in north Finland and is also popular in Norway (Enerstvedt, 1971, p. 108). An Australian version beginning "Koala bear, Koala bear, touch the ground" was published in a collection of Australian games entitled "Far out, Brussel Sprout" in 1983 (Factor, p. 90). Although the Teddy Bear versions of the rhyme can be dated to post-1903,[21] children in Ireland were skipping to a version called "Lady fair, Lady fair" towards the end of the nineteenth century.[22] "Teddy Bear, Teddy Bear" is now an accepted part of nursery lore and can be found in contemporary collections of nursery rhymes published for young children, such as Prue Theobalds' *For Teddy and Me* (1992).[23] A number of other rhymes, for example "Lady, Lady" and "Scout girl", are similar in format to "Teddy Bear, Teddy Bear". "Lady, Lady" often forms part of "On a mountain stands a lady" (O 300) and both of these are found in "I went down town" (I 2 400). The verse "Spanish Lady" is incorporated into the rhyme "Not last night but the night before" (N 300).

The first Dublin company of girl guides was formed at Harold's Cross in 1911. By 1920 there are records of guiding in Carlow, Cork, Kerry, Waterford, Wicklow, Limerick, Kildare, Westmeath, and Donegal.[24] By the 1930s children from at least three counties — Dublin, Monaghan and Wexford — were skipping to "I'm a little girl guide" (I 300). Eighty-six versions of this rhyme were included in the 1989 questionnaire returns:

> I am a little girl guide,
> All dressed in blue,
> These are the actions I must do:
> Salute to the Captain, bow to the Queen,
> Run around the corner and buy an ice-cream.

Sixty-five per cent of 1989 versions were reported from Leinster. Over half begin with the two lines above, while in some other versions a brownie or a Dutch girl is dressed in blue. Actions include saluting the captain or master and bowing to the queen. In counties Carlow, Dublin, Longford, Offaly, Wicklow, Clare, Cork and Limerick the skipper then has to "run around the corner to buy an ice-cream", and in Waterford and Kildare versions the skipper has to count to 16 when she has gone around the corner. Some children from Tipperary and Antrim have to "Show my knickers to the football team", an ending also found in a published Australian version (Factor, 1983, p. 86). A schoolgirl from Dunlavin, Co. Wicklow, finished her rhyme with "And turn my back on the old submarine". This line is also contained in the version given by Roger Abrahams (1969, Rhyme no. 206).

CONCLUSION

Although the information received about skipping in the Schools' Scheme of 1937-38 formed only a small part of a large-scale project, 37 skipping rhymes were reported. Of these 23 continued to be popular in 1989, having been passed on by many generations of young active tradition bearers. The large skipping rhyme repertoire — 196 rhymes in all — reported by Irish schoolchildren in 1989 includes divination rhymes, action rhymes, calling-in and counting rhymes. These rhymes explore a variety of topics of immediate concern to the children, such as how to interact with adult authority figures; overcoming common childhood fears; love and marriage, food and drink; and film. While some rhymes, such as "Tinker, tailor", can be traced back to a different kind of divination game played in the 18th century, others, popular with Irish schoolchildren, can also be found in other countries around the world. In addition, the range of terminology and ritual associated with organising a group skipping game which was recorded by questionnaire respondents is testimony to a vibrant living playground tradition.

References

Abrahams, R. (1969), *Jump Rope Rhymes: A Dictionary*, Austin: University of Texas Press

Brady, E. (1975), "All in! All in!" Dublin: Comhairle Bhéaloideas Éireann

Cosbey, R.C. (1980), "All in Together Girls: Skipping Songs from Regina, Saskatchewan", occasional paper 2, Canadian Plains Research Center

Danaher, K. (1979), "The "Schools' Collection"", *Ros*, Vol. 9, No. 1, pp. 2-3

Durkin, P. and Ferguson, V. (1990), *You Beaut, Juicy Fruit*, Melbourne: Oxford University Press

Enerstvedt, Å. (1971), Kongen Over Gata, Oslo: Universitetsforlaget

Factor, J. (1983), *Far Out, Brussel Sprout*, Melbourne: Oxford University Press

Fowke, E. (1969), *Sally Go Round the Sun*, Toronto: McLelland and Stewart

Henshaw, A., Kelly, J. and Gratton, C. (1992), "Skipping's for girls: children's perception of gender role and gender preferences", *Educational Research*, Vol. 34, No. 3, pp. 229-235

Lysaght, P. (1987), "'When I makes Tea, I makes Tea . . ': Innovation in Food — The Case of Tea in Ireland", *Ulster Folklife*, 33, pp. 44-71

McCaughan, M. (1971-72), "Cinderella dressed in yella: Some Belfast Skipping Rhymes", *Ulster Folk and Transport Museum Year Book*, pp. 20-33

Ó Catháin, S. (1988), "Súil Siar ar Scéim na Scol 1937-1938", *Sinsear* 5, pp. 19-30

Ó Catháin, S., agus Uí Sheighin, C. (1987), A Mhuintir Dhú Chaocháin, Labhraigí Feasta!, Indreabhán: Cló Iar-Chonnachta

Ó Láimhín, P. (1992), "Towards Improved Access to the Whole Spectrum of the Primary Curriculum for Girls and Boys", Dublin: Department of Education

Opie, I. and P. (1951), *The Oxford Dictionary of Nursery Rhymes*, Oxford: Oxford University Press

Opie, I. and P. (1977 ed.), *The Lore and Language of Schoolchildren*, St. Albans: Paladin

Ó Súilleabháin, S. (1937a), Béaloideas Éireann, Dublin: Department of Education

Ó Súilleabháin, S. (1937b), *Irish Folklore and Tradition*, Dublin: Department of Education

Smith, A.W. (1991), "Children's Games and Rhymes Collected by Alan Smith in East London/Essex in the 1950s", *FLS Children's Folklore Newsletter,* No. 5, pp. 21-31

Strutt, J. (1845), *The Sports and Pastimes of the People of England*, London: Thomas Tegg

Sutton-Smith, B. (1952), "The fate of English traditional games in New Zealand", *Western Folklore*, Vol. 11, pp. 250-253

Sutton-Smith, B. (1972), *The Folkgames of Children*, Austin, TX: University of Texas Press

Sutton-Smith B. and Rosenberg, B.G. (1961), "Sixty Years of Historical Change in the Game Preferences of American Children", *Journal of American Folklore*, Vol. 71, pp. 17-46

Swinburne, C. (1994), "Fit For Nothing", *Junior Education*, February 1994, pp. 22-23

Theobalds, P. (1992), *For Teddy and Me*, London: Blackie

Virgin (1992), *The Virgin Film Guide*, London: Virgin Books

Virtanen, L. (1978), "Children's Lore", *Studia Fennica*, Vol. 22, Helsinki

Appendix

C 600
Cinderella dressed in yellow
Cinderella dressed in yellow,
Went upstairs to kiss her fellow.
By mistake she kissed a snake
How many doctors will it take?
1, 2, 3, ...

M 900
Mother, mother
Mother, mother, tell me true,
Who shall I get married to?
A tinker, tailor, soldier, sailor,
Rich man, poor man, beggar man, thief,
A doctor, a lawyer, an Indian chief.

H 700
Hop, hop, hop
Hop, hop, hop, to the butcher's shop,
I dare not stay any longer,
For if I do my mother will say
I was playing with the boys in the corner.

O 300
On a mountain stands a lady
On the mountain stands a lady,
Who she is I do not know,

All she wants is gold and silver,
All she wants is a fine young man.
All right (X) I'll tell your mother,
You kissed (Y) around the corner,
How many kisses did you give him?
1, 2, 3, ...

B 300
Baby on the high chair
Baby on the high chair,
Who put you there?
My Ma, my Da,
Whoopsee ah.
Wrapped him up in tissue paper,
And sent him to the operator.
How many hours did the baby sleep?
1, 2, 3, ...

B 700
Bluebells, cockle shells
Bluebells, cockle shells, ide, idy, over,
Granny in the kitchen,
Doing a bit of stitching,
How many stitches does she do?
5, 10, 15, ...

G 600
Granny in the kitchen
Granny in the kitchen
Doing a bit of stitching,
When in comes the robber
And pushes granny out.
Oh, says granny, that's not fair,
Oh, says the robber, I don't care.

B 700
Bluebell, cockle shells (Westmeath)
Bluebells, cockle shells,
Evey, ivy, over.
Here comes teacher
With a big fat stick,

Now it's time for spellings:
Cat c-a-t, rat r-a-t, mat m-a-t, sat s-a-t,
Now it's time for sums:
2+2=4, 4+4=8, 8+8=16 and 16+16=32
Now it's time for history:
George Washington never told a lie,
So he went around the cor-ner
And stole a penny pie.
For his punishment his father said,
Tip the wall before I count to ten.
1, 2, 3, ... 10.

H 300
Here comes the teacher
Here comes the teacher
With the big black stick,
Now it's time for arithmetic:
1+1=2, 2+2=4, 3+3=6, 4+4=8.
Now it's time for spelling:
Spell rat, cat, bat, mat.
Now it's time for exercise:
Put your hands in the air,
Put them down by your side,
Beurl around and touch the ground,
Now your lessons are over.

S 700
Sitting in the classroom
Sitting in the classroom
Eating bubble gum,
In comes the teacher
And out goes the gum.
Policeman, policeman, don't take me,
For I have a wife and family,
How many children have you got?
24 and that's the lot.

I 1 100
I got the german measles
I got the german measles,
I got them very bad,

They wrapped me in a blanket,
And put me in a van.
The van was very shaky,
I nearly tumbled out,
And when I got to the hospital,
I heard a baby shout:
Ah! Mammy, Daddy, take me home,
Take me from this mental home,
One year, two year is enough,
Mammy, Daddy, do your stuff.

A 100
A, B, C, ... on the sofa
A, B, C, ...
(X) on the sofa with (Y) on his knee,
(X) says, will you marry me?
Yes, no, yes, ...

A 1 100
(X) and (Y) up a tree
(X) and (Y) up a tree
K-I-S-S-I-N-G.
First comes love, then comes marriage,
Then comes a baby in a golden carriage.

O 1 600
1, 2, 3, I call in my best friend
I call in my best friend (X).
Is she in? yes, no, certainly so, ...
Can she wash the dishes?
Can she wash the floor?
Can she kiss her boyfriend behind the kitchen door?

A 1 200
Apple jelly
Apple jelly, my jam tart,
Tell me the name of your sweetheart.
A, B, C, ...

T 900

Tinker, tailor

Tinker, tailor, soldier, sailor,
Rich man, poor man, beggar man, thief.

I 2 400

I went down town

I went down town, I met Mrs. Brown,
She gave me a nickel,
So I bought a pickle,
The pickle was sour,
So I bought a flower,
The flower wouldn't smell,
So I bought a bell,
The bell wouldn't ring,
So I began to sing:
On the hillside stands a lady,
Who she is I do not know,
All she wants is gold and silver,
All she wants is a nice young man.
Lady, Lady, touch the ground,
Lady, Lady, birl right around.
Lady, Lady, show your shoes,
Lady. Lady, run right through.

N 300

Not last night but the night before

Not last night but the night before,
24 robbers came knocking at my door,
As I went down to let them in,
This is what they said to me:
Spanish lady turn all around,
Spanish lady touch the ground.
Spanish lady do the high kicks,
Spanish lady do the splits.

Notes

---

[1] This paper is based on research conducted as part of the requirements for a PhD thesis: Lynch, G. (1994), "'Miss a loop you're out': A study of skipping in 1989", unpublished PhD thesis, 2 volumes, National University of Ireland.

[2] For a full account of the background to this scheme and an outline of its success see: Danaher, K. (1979), "The 'Schools' Collection'", Ros, vol. 9, no. 1, pp. 2-3; Ó Catháin, S. (1988), 'Súil Siar ar Scéim na Scol 1937-1938', Sinsear, vol. 5, pp. 19-30; Ó Catháin, S. agus Uí Sheighin, C. (1987), A Mhuintir Dhú Chaocháin, Labhraigí Feasta!, Indreabhán. The Irish Folklore Commission became the Department of Irish Folklore, University College Dublin in 1972.

[3] Schools received the questionnaire as follows: a) all national schools in Co. Wicklow with the exception of special schools; b) a further 200 schools or so, selected at random from a list supplied by the Department of Education; c) twenty-five per cent of the schools listed as Gaeltacht schools. These are schools in areas recognized by the Irish Government as Gaeltacht areas, that is, areas in which Irish is the first language of the majority of the population; d) all Gaelscoileanna — schools not situated in Gaeltacht areas in which Irish is the medium of instruction; and e) all schools in four of the five Education and Library Board areas in Northern Ireland. The North Eastern Education and Library Board was unable to participate in this project.

[4] In addition to the Schools' Manuscript Collection (IFC S) the following archival sources in the Department of Irish Folklore, University College Dublin, were used: 1. In November 1932 'Roddy the Rover' in the Irish Press newspaper invited children to write to him describing the games they played. There are five references to skipping in this collection; all from male informants. The entries are in box 71 in the Department's archive. 2. The Main Manuscript Collection (IFC) contains some material on children's games collected by fulltime, part-time, and occasional folklore collectors. In addition this collection contains information on games received as a result of various competitions and projects outlined below: a) In 1969 the sound archivist of the Irish Folklore Commission, Leo Corduff, and the full-time collector, James G. Delaney, recorded five audio-tapes on a variety of topics from the Sisters of Mercy N.S., St. John's Road, Wexford (IFC T 471-475). b) The Irish Life Assurance Company sponsored schools' folklore competitions in 1976 and 1978. Children's Games was one of the project topics. c) The Urban Folklore Project, 1979-1980, was organized by the Department of Irish Folklore and sponsored by the Department of Education. As part of this project children's lore and games were collected in 33 primary schools in counties Dublin and Wicklow. d) In 1985 as part of its Newspaper in the Classroom series the Irish Times, in co-operation with the Department of Irish Folklore, organized a schools' folklore project based on the Schools' Scheme of 1937-38.

[5] The rhyme numbers refer to Appendix D, Vol. 2 of Lynch, G. (1994), "'Miss a loop you're out': A study of skipping in 1989", unpublished PhD thesis, National University of Ireland.

[6] An excellent example of a playground leader may be seen in IFC V 6, a video made in Ringsend N.S., Co. Dublin, as part of the Urban Folklore Project.

[7] In 1989, 1,079 children reported playing skipping only, or mostly, in summer. A further 528 said that they play mainly in spring and summer.

[8] In some schools skipping is banned, due perhaps to a lack of space, while in others it is actively encouraged, with the schools supplying skipping ropes for use at play times.

[9] Sixty-two per cent replied that the participants in school-based games were girls only.

[10] I am grateful to Joe Banaghan for this information.

[11] The term most widely used throughout Ireland to refer to counting-out is "dip"; this was used in counties Galway, Mayo, Roscommon, Sligo, Cork, Kerry, Limerick, Dublin, Kildare, Louth, Wicklow, and Armagh. The term "give it out" was found mainly in the east and north — counties Carlow, Kildare, Wexford, Armagh, Derry, Donegal, Monaghan, and Tyrone. This term was also used in Co. Clare. "Give out tig" was used in Co. Fermanagh. In counties Cork and Waterford the children are said to "spell"; in Co. Westmeath they "ink"; they "abble" in Co. Offaly and in Co. Tipperary where they also "aben" or "abain". In Co. Kilkenny children "ible" or ebbil" and in counties Kildare and Offaly they "ittle". Children from Co. Donegal may "put out the tig" and in counties Antrim, Down and Fermanagh they "put their feet in".

[12] The questionnaire answer sheets were sorted according to county. 'B' refers to a reply to the children's questionnaire. Each answer sheet within a county was also given a number.

[13] The term "turners" was reported from eighteen counties. The names "twinders" and "twinners" are only recorded in the north of Ireland — counties Donegal, Derry, Down, Armagh and Tyrone. Another predominantly northern term is "endeys" and its variants.

[14] Co. Leitrim being the exception.

[15] IFC 1920: 15, IFC 2011: 29.

[16] Rhymes referred to, but not written out in full, in the text, are given in the appendix.

[17] IFC 2007: 95, 285; IFC 2011: 5; IFC 2119: 151; IFC 2125: 191.

[18] There are seven versions of this rhyme in the 1989 collection. Four are from Co. Wicklow, two from Co. Dublin, and one from Co. Kildare. The two Dublin informants were male, the others female. Abrahams (1969) states that this rhyme has been collected in Great Britain (Rhyme no. 551).

[19] These versions come from counties Kildare (1), Wicklow (1), Antrim (8), and Donegal (1).

[20] All four versions of this rhyme in the 1989 collection were reported from Milford Grange N.S., Co. Limerick. It has also been collected in the United States and in Great Britain (Abrahams, 1969, Rhyme no. 148).

[21] The year the first teddy bear was manufactured.

[22] P.J. Gaynor collected a version of this from Julia Gargan, then aged 74, from Co. Meath in 1949. IFC 1161:475-6.

[23] This book contains a collection of 30 nursery rhymes.

[24] Lady Powerscourt was appointed the first Chief Commissioner of "The Irish Free State Girl Guides" in 1929. By 1938 the movement had become known as "The Irish Girl Guides". The trefoil badge with the Celtic knot in the centre was adopted and some changes were made in the wording of the girl guide promise. Membership is open to all girls and young women irrespective of creed, race and nationality. There are four branches in the organisation — Ladybirds, Brownies, Guides and Rangers. Girl guides wear a blue uniform. At the time of the skipping questionnaire one could find girl guides in 112 countries around the world. (From a leaflet issued by Guiding — the Irish Girl Guides, entitled, A Little Bit About Us). I am grateful to Vivian Pigott of the Irish Girl Guides for this information.

Chapter 10

In the Land of Youth? Children's Literature in a Changing Ireland

Pat Donlon

The last 30 years has seen dramatic changes in Irish society. The advent of television and video together with multiplex cinemas, video and computer games has meant that our children have available to them a dazzling range of entertainment options. Time too has kaleidoscoped with activity-packed days now the norm. It is nothing short of a miracle that Irish children can still find a space for the solitary act of reading. But then children's literature in Ireland over the last three decades has witnessed something little short of a miraculous revival — from near extinction in the 1960s to a thriving industry in the late 1990s. We had been slow to provide a home-grown, home-produced literature for Irish children and for decades bookshops and libraries were stocked with foreign-produced English language authors.

Something happened in the 1960s and 1970s which, with the pace of change and the advent of television into all our lives, somehow meant that we lost sight of the need for a home-grown literature specifically for our children. Few of the Irish children's classics remained in print and little or no fresh writing for children was happening. There were notable exceptions — in the 1960s Patricia Lynch and Sinéad de Valera kept the beacon alight whilst Eilís Dillon was a solo voice for many years. It is difficult to arrive at precise statistics — no history of Irish children's literature has been written to date; there are few easy ways of extracting Irish titles from the bulk of publications in England.[1] In Ireland the annual volume *The Irish Publishing Record*, though not infallible, does give a good guideline for publishing figures and trends.[2] An analysis of the records supplied indicates an interesting and remarkable trend. Taking just three years at random over the decades 1970s to 1990s shows that in 1973 the *Irish Publishing Record* noted two children's titles; by 1983 the figure had risen to just 15 and a decade later in 1993 to 53 titles. These figures are exclusive of the textbook market because, as the trade magazine *Publisher's Weekly* commented, in 1981 the youth textbook market was vibrant.[3] At that stage 50 per cent of the population was under the age of 25. The text book market was and continues to be healthy, because Irish parents and not the State purchase the books. The long queues of parents and children snaking out into the streets from bookshops in the annual school book purchasing bonanza is a scene as familiar as falling leaves and darkening days. The educational market aside, publishing in Ireland has always been a knife-edge occupation — the population base is small and has remained constant, therefore the unit cost per book is high and profit margins for all concerned are minuscule. Small wonder then that, despite the long queues to purchase school books, there were no parallel queues of writers eager to enter the children's book market. Jeremy Addis, the founder and editor of *Books Ireland*, who single-handedly has done more for Irish books over the past three decades, writes with hindsight:

> In 1960 I had taken on the management of the general list (religion, history, biography) of a similar old, established printer-publisher, Browne & Nolan, and a lot of my time in the following eight years was taken up with rejecting unsolicited children's stories which came to us because our list included one or two of the books of Patricia Lynch, almost the only author who wrote specifically for Irish children. I always lived in hopes of finding a new Patricia Lynch, and once or twice thought I had found it. One of these finds was Tom McCaughren, but he had to wait another fifteen years before his talents were finally seen in print (and in translations all over the world), for always the Boardroom would

shoot me down. Surely I had learned by now that Irish publishers couldn't compete with the big London imprints for that market? *They* were printing in tens of thousands, and we would be lucky to sell more than a few hundred. But abroad? Couldn't we find a market in Britain? The answer was always the same: children's books were too high a risk, and Irish houses could never compete. "Never", I obediently told the hopeful authors, and learned to spell out the commercial realities in a regretful but final standard paragraph of my rejection letters. [4]

It is difficult to find a logical explanation why a country with such an imposing literary history as Ireland should have had such a pitiful output in publishing for children. The *UNESCO Handbook* of 1974 gives the number of children's books produced in England and the United States at 2,500 each, but only one for Ireland — a figure which was matched by Tanzania. No culture produces literature in isolation; each generation draws inexorably on the past whilst creating new and fresh works. In Ireland in the early 1980s there did not exist a corpus of books which could be classified as children's literature. Whilst the creative arts flourished through the works of poets, dramatists, novelists and artists, this flowering was not reflected in the children's book market. Apart from the lack of financial incentives, competition was stiff from the volume and quality of books imported from England. Nevertheless, between 1981 and 1991 something happened to alter the face of publishing for children in Ireland, and the period which has been lauded as the "golden age" of Irish children's literature dawned. There were several, it appears, almost spontaneous initiatives which now can be viewed as milestones on the road from virtual non-existence to "golden age".

1981 — The 14th Loughborough Conference on children's literature is held in Dublin

— The Children's Press imprint is launched

1982 — RTÉ Radio Programme *Children Reading* is broadcast

1982 — First Children's Book Week Festival is held

1985 — Reading Association of Ireland Book Award

1986 — Children's Literature Association of Ireland (CLAI) founded

— Children's Books of the Celtic World Exhibition Munich

1989 — Irish Children's Books Trust (ICBT) established

— Children's Books Ireland published

1990 — Bisto Book Awards

1991 — First Summer School on Children's Literature

1996 — Illustrator P.J. Lynch wins prestigious Kate Greenaway Medal

1997 — CLAI and ICBT merge to form Children's Books Ireland

1998 — IBBY Ireland (International Board on Books for Young People) is launched

1999 — Siobhán Parkinson is appointed Writer in Residence at the Irish Writer's Center

The Loughborough Conference brought together over one hundred delegates and speakers, many from Europe and America, whose sole focus was children's literature.[5] *The Irish Times* reporting on the event comments:

> A glance at the Irish names on the delegate list, however, suggests that the subject holds little or no interest for many of the people in this country charged with encouraging the cultural tastes and experiences of Irish children.[6]

That said, several of the speakers raised the issue of an Irish literature for Irish children, most notably Eilís Dillon and Tony Hickey. The latter argued most forcibly speaking from his childhood recollections of the impact on him of a book thrust into the hands of the then nine-year-old reader by the local librarian:

> Two miles down the road was the bog of Allen. On that bog were the cottages and the turf cutters and children just like Eileen and Seamus. There were local stories of the Fianna

and the association with the Hill of Allen. That book by Patricia Lynch showed me that the world that I lived in was as exciting as anything anywhere. Patricia Lynch was the writer for my generation of childhood. . . . But where are the Irish writers for this generation? Ireland has changed so much in the past twenty years. It is no longer predominantly rural. Most children live in towns and cities. I find it very hard to believe that there is not the need and the urge in people to write for children about such things. Yet where is the resulting prose?[7]

The debate had begun. Some years later the Arts Council published a booklet, and although not accredited it is clearly the work of the then Literature Officer Lar Cassidy. Acknowledging that for many years there had been available a range of children's books published in the Irish language, he comments:

> In 1981, the first grants were made to works of children's literature. The Children's Press, an imprint of Anvil Books, was initiated and a range of other publishers began to bring out titles. Thus, we have seen a new flowering in our children's publishing in the English language take place in the 1980s. The Council is convinced of the great need to have modern works, set in Ireland, in contemporary situations, made abundantly available for our children.[8]

Tony Hickey, who had worked scripting and directing the successful BBC children's programme *Jackanory*, sent a manuscript to Rena Dardis of Anvil Press who, contrary to all the canons of publishing at the time, decided to publish it. *The Matchless Mice* with illustrations by Pauline Bewick was a success and encouraged by this Dardis decided to establish a children's imprint and The Children's Press was born.

Simultaneously, the first of the emerging support groups was established. The Youth Libraries Group of the Library Association of Ireland set about actively involving librarians, teachers and parents in the whole area of provision of books for children. Less than one year later, in March of 1982, the Youth Libraries Group was working closely with John Quinn, an award-winning highly respected broadcaster, on a series of Saturday morning broadcasts under the title *Children Reading*.[9]

A series of annotated reading lists were produced and RTÉ printed a run of 4,000. Such was the response to the programme and the demand for the reading lists that the series went into several reprintings. Clearly, somebody out there cared about what children were reading. Encouraged, the Youth Libraries Group went on to organise the first Children's Book Week Festival which has been running successfully ever since, some years stretching from the original one-week-long event to one month and accompanied by the by now mandatory booklists, either in pamphlet or book format. In 1984 the Children's Book Week committee was in the unusual position to be able to issue alongside its standard lists one entitled *Children's Books of Irish Interest* and contained in it annotations of 100 books currently in print.

Between that 1984 Irish-interest booklist and 1991 two significant organisations entered the field, a specialist journal was issued, an annual conference and summer school were instigated and a lively book award scheme was in operation. The Children's Literature Association of Ireland (CLAI) was established in 1986 with very clear-cut aims:

- To encourage children and teenagers to read worthwhile books

- To provide information for parents, teachers, librarians and all those interested in children's literature

- To provide a forum for discussion of children's literature

- To organise seminars, lectures and an annual conference

- To promote the study of and research into children's literature at all levels

- To promote the writing of children's literature in all its forms.

Three years later it launched the first and to date only specialist children's literature journal in Ireland — *Children's Books in Ireland*.[10] The then President of CLAI Robert Dunbar in the editorial restates those objectives and aims and *inter alia* gives us a state of the art synopsis of some of the issues at that time:

The past few years have seen a number of exciting developments in Irish writing, illustrating and publishing for the young. Standards of production and illustration have improved to such an extent that we can now fairly claim to have some Irish children's books which will match those produced anywhere. . . . But there remains an "unevenness" in many of our publishing lists. This is most visible in a tendency to concentrate on a limited number of themes and genres — animal saga and fantasies involving allegorical battles between good and evil are prime examples — and, especially where the teenage reader is concerned, an almost complete absence of that brand of contemporary fiction which might throw some light on what growing up in Ireland today is about. On a different level, there is frequently a disturbing lack of attention to detail: an Irish children's book without spelling, punctuation or typographical error is a rare phenomenon . . . there is no need to add another "layer of piety" to the topic of children's reading by promoting the notion that what is available to them locally is unquestionably excellent.[11]

The Irish Children's Book Trust (ICBT) was established in 1989 with its primary aims being to encourage and facilitate Irish writing for children and to improve the status of children's literature in Ireland by creating an awareness among children and their parents of a shared cultural heritage. The ICBT sought also to establish a centre of excellence bringing together Irish-published children's books together with related reference materials. It published two guides — *The Irish Guide to Children's Books: Decade 1980-1990* and *The Irish Guide to Children's Books 1991*.[12] By now Irish children's writing had a visibility hitherto undreamed of, and what is more it was not just a cultural success but also an economic one. Not only were Irish children's books reaching the bestseller lists at home, they were also reaching more and more international markets, through co-productions with English and American publishing houses and through translation into other languages. This was a profile and level of penetration into foreign markets experienced only once before when the prolific Patricia Lynch was writing and publishing. There was one major area of difference

— then English and America publishers published Lynch, now these were from the presses of small Irish firms whose authors and illustrators were making it onto the larger world stage. There were other factors at play — factors neatly observed by Eilís Dillon:

> Perhaps because the whole nation has become more confident, Irish parents are no longer afraid that they are accepting something inferior when they buy a book with an Irish background, published in Ireland. This in spite of the fact that the books are sometimes priced higher than their foreign counterparts. . . . For the children the relief is immense. They need no longer struggle with names and places and attitudes that they don't understand. Inevitably they get new insights on their own world, and the writer can develop humorous situations which the children will recognise in the life around them.[13]

She fires a warning shot across the bows of the tight-fisted:

> Some parents who will spend money on books for themselves are unwilling to supply their children with the same luxury. . . . A child who has set up a library for himself when he was small will make a thinking adult.[14]

The two organisations CLAI and ICBT came together in 1997 in a merger unusual in the Irish climate more accustomed to splits. The new body adopted the name Children's Books Ireland (CBI) and pledged to serve its joint membership better through this consolidation and maximisation of resources. Before the merger ICBT published one more guide and its most significant publication to date. *The Big Guide to Irish Children's Books* has become a landmark publication and an invaluable reference book. Thirteen experts provided the introductory essay preceding each section of annotated books and there is an insightful introduction from its editors, Valerie Coughlan and Celia Keenan.[15] The book was published to coincide with the opening of Ireland's themed pavilion at the annual Frankfurt Book Fair in 1996.

This was not the first time that Irish children's books had been given a shop window in Germany. In 1986 a major international exhibition of children's books was held in Schloss Blutenburg, a medieval castle and home of the International Youth Library under the title "Kinderliteratur der Keltischen Welt". In this first ever exhibition of pan-Celtic children's books to be held at the Library, children's books from Ireland, Wales, Scotland, Cornwall, Isle of Man and Brittany were on display. The aims of the exhibition were to present children's literature as a vehicle for the revitalisation of Celtic culture, to give the general public and especially German children some insight into Celtic culture with its strong tradition in myth and fairy tale, and to introduce German publishers to current trends in children's writing and illustration. A poster and catalogue were produced to accompany the exhibition and the illustration chosen to adorn both was by Brian Bourke from the story in translation from Irish of the well-loved Jimeen.[16] The exhibition gave rise to much discussion with various articles appearing in the German national press. The exhibition went on tour in Germany to universities such as Munich and Freiburg and from there to Brittany and the Edinburgh Festival.[17] Jeffrey Garrett, who curated the exhibition, later wrote of his experience and understanding of Irish children's literature:

> When the dust has settled, or — to choose a more appropriate metaphor — when the mist has cleared, we shall probably find Irish Gaelic children's books co-existing peacefully with English-language ones, each language nuancing in a different way aspects of Irish life and culture. . . . Our hope is, of course, that children's literature will make its own gentle contribution to the preservation of Irish bilingualism, enabling future generations in Ireland to "face both inward and outward".[18]

Elsewhere Valerie Coghlan voices that same concept of looking both inward and outward. The occasion is the launch to mark Ireland's membership of IBBY, the International Board on Books for Young People, and to celebrate our entry into this international community of the children's book world — the last country in western Europe to do so.[19] IBBY was founded in 1953 as Europe was picking up the pieces after the end of World War II, and its mission is to promote international understanding through children's books.

> Becoming part of IBBY will also provide the Irish section with opportunities to avail of travelling exhibitions of chidrens [sic] books and illustration and to become more involved in both an inward and an outward direction with the promotion of books for young people.[20]

Whilst most commentators rejoice at the extraordinary flourishing of publishing for children in Ireland, from the outset warning notes have been sounded in relation to quality and to the provision, or lack of it, of constructive critical assessment of the authors' outpourings in print. Writing in 1985, this author signaled her misgivings:

> Such children's books as are published have to survive on a word-of-mouth recommendation. Nothing remotely approaching the seriousness with which we take other art forms has been bestowed on children's books. Ireland, for so long politically neutral, is also critically neutral with regard to books for the young. Garner together the "critical" reviews of books written by Irish authors, or published by Irish publishing houses over the last decade, and the resulting harvest would make the 1985 disaster-stricken field look like the promised land. Bland, cheerful, four-line reviews constitute the standard response in the national press.[21]

Not much has changed in the intervening years. *Books Ireland* and *Children's Books in Ireland* apart, the column inches allocated to reviews of children's books in the national newspapers restricts discussion. In a conversation with Shirley Kelly of *Books Ireland*, Dunbar cogitates on the realities facing him in his task as reviewer:

> We have, predictably, been accused of being too kind to Irish children's books, but this may be partly due to my reviewing practice. If I receive six books for review and I feel that three of them are rubbish, then I'll use the limited wordage available to me to enthuse about the good books

rather than to slate the bad ones. But there are aspects of the world of children's books in this country of which I am openly critical. I do detect a little parochialism, for instance, which I find a wee bit numbing . . . we now have far too many children's books coming from Irish publishers and in this respect I think it's time for publishers to think about re-trenching.[22]

Children's literature is seen as an applied art, as literature applied to children rather than as a literature in its own right. This has always been so and children's authors have long railed against the pigeonholing which accompanies this perception. C.S. Lewis, scholar, medievalist and author of the Narnia stories puts it like this:

I am almost inclined to set it up as a canon that a children's story which is enjoyed only by children is a bad children's story. The good ones last.[23]

Attitudes to children's books have resulted in a ghettoisation — with book shops usually locating their children's section to the back of the store, thereby ensuring that the majority of the adult population are never exposed to the beauty, imagination, inventiveness, humour and sheer quality of much of the writing, illustration and production of children's books today. Book selection for the children's sections is frequently relegated to the most junior member of staff with little or no training being provided in what is a critical function. The child readers of today may become the adult readers of tomorrow; the non-readers are unlikely to become so. This patronising attitude is not confined to those in the children's book world but extends across the board to all who work with children — nurses, nannies, junior teachers, child care workers, librarians and of course the authors who write for children. A librarian colleague of mine, a long-time professional whose work for children in Cork is legendary, confessed to me that when she started working in the children's section of the County Library, her mother enquired anxiously of her, "When you get better at it, will they let you work with adult books?"

Reviews in the media tend to be regarded as seasonal or special features, at Christmas and Halloween, or to coincide with Children's Book Week. In a civilised country every week should be children's book week. Children's books are part of the publishing output of the country just as children are citizens with equal rights. Siobhán Parkinson, a prize-winning children's author and the first children's writer to be awarded a Writer in Residency at the Irish Writer's Centre, has very definite views on how we treat children and their books:

> . . . our whole view of childhood is often sentimental and patronising. And this rather precious view of childhood — apart from being reprehensible in itself — at once lays unsustainable burdens on the children's writer and excludes him or her from serious consideration as a professional and a literary craftsperson.
>
> On the one hand, children's writers are expected to evince a saintly devotion to education and "reading" — which by the way, is generally viewed not as a tool that it is essential to acquire in order to live and succeed in our literate, logocentric world, but as some sort of moral good that it is the writer's duty to nurture in the young. On the other hand, we are expected to live in a literary vacuum where our work is seldom reviewed or even discussed. . . . We have a powerful sense of ourselves as a child-loving people. We are not. We have, in truth, scant regard for our children.[24]

That honest, deeply felt frustration epitomises the concern and exasperation of the majority of professionals working in this sector. The status of children's literature within the education sector is consistent with this marginalisation. No department of children's literature exists in any of our universities, and where it is taught it is as an addendum to professional courses for teachers or librarians. Some encouraging signs are emerging within English Departments where increasingly Master's and Doctoral theses are being presented on children's literature topics.

One interesting feature since the 1970s is the increase in publishing of anthologies of young people's writings, mainly though not exclusively as a result of awards' schemes or community initiatives and usually reflecting the concerns of the time. In the 1980s the Women's Community Press published several volumes of non-sexist stories and poems written and illustrated by young Irish people. Yet another scheme — the Irish Schools Creative Writing Award — was launched in 1982 and received over 1,000 entries. By the end of the decade the entries had swollen to over 7,000 and the winners were published under the editorial directions of the chair of the judging panel, inevitably a distinguished poet or novelist. In the 1990s the McDonald's Young Writers award was established and a series of imaginatively titled anthologies were published.[25] Special events, commemorations and celebrations have all been echoed in the writings of Irish children. *A Child's Famine*, published by the Cork Women's Poetry Circle, is one community's response to the traumas of its predecessors of 150 years ago, whilst *I Have a Dream* was one of RTÉ's more inspired ways of celebrating the Millennium. In its introduction Gabriel Fitzmaurice comments on the children's ability to articulate the timeless concerns of humankind. He concludes:

> In this book we have a fine representation of the children of this country. Facing into a new millennium, they are not paralysed by fear; rather they look into the future full of hopeful joy.[26]

It remains to be seen if these budding writers sustain the passion and talent to become authors in later life. Someone who did not emerge via the competition route, but who is now a fully established author of several successful books, is Aislinn O'Loughlin. Her first stories, pacy reworkings of famous fairytales like *Cinderella's Fella* and *A Right Royal Pain: The True Story of Rumpelstiltskin*, were written when she was just 14. The latter had the distinction of winning an International Youth Library White Raven Award from entries from some 43 countries. She has maintained this output with titles such as *The Emperor's Birthday Suit, Shak & the Beanstalk* and *Fionn the Cool.*

The importance accorded to children's literature can be ascertained by examining the attitudes and level of commitment of the Government, publishers, writers, educators and parents.

The Government receives few bouquets for its funding of public libraries and its lack of policy and funding on the impoverished and virtually non-existent school library system in this country over the past three decades. Under the editorial banner "Sad and Disgraceful" in *Children's Books in Ireland* in 1990, Valerie Coughlan states the bald reality:

> Education is no longer about knowing the answers but about learning how and where to find them. It is often said that we live in an "information age"; but can we claim to do so, when libraries, a major source of information, receive so little support?[27]

Some hopeful signs have emerged over the last two years, with injections of funding to public libraries to help them boost their book stocks. In November 1998 the then Minister for Education and Science, Micheál Martin, announced that primary and post-primary schools would receive funding for resources for the school library. It is to be hoped that the day will dawn when a school library is no longer seen as a luxury but as an integral part of the educational infrastructure. In one area, however, the Government has had considerable success. It has helped through subventions to bring Irish language children's books from their impoverished, dull, school-book state of the 1940s, 1950s and 1960s, to the glossy, polished, assured picture books which are the stock in trade of An Gúm. During the 1970s Clódhanna Teoranta arranged with Russian publishers to translate illustrated children's books from Russian to Irish and had them printed in the then USSR. This project was taken up by An Gúm in the 1970s and 1980s and many of their books were co-productions with the text set in Ireland and published abroad with the best of European illustrators. Today most of An Gúm's children's books are entirely home-produced, both written and illustrated by the emerging coterie of talented authors and illustrators living and working in Ireland. Some of the Irish language books which have challenged their English language counterparts in the book award stakes have been Marie-Louise Fitzpatrick's *An Chanáil*, Máirín Uí Chomáin's *Tamall Sa Chistin*, Ní Nuadháin's *Cois Tra*, Mary Arrigan's *Lá Le Mamo,* Ré Ó

Laighléis, *Ecstasy agus Scéalta Eile,* Gabriel Rosenstock's *Pádraig agus Crom Dubh* and *An Rógaire agus a Scáil.* And the themes? Urban life by the canal, eccentric grannies, drug abuse — all of human life is there!

One of the curious anomalies in this bilingual culture is the reality that there is little or no interchange between the two languages. In the realms of children's literature both exist in parallel isolation. Most children's authors writing in Irish will not have their books translated into English and *vice versa.* An interesting exception to this was the translation of Ó Siochfhradha's *Jimeen,* when it was translated into English some 60 years after its first publication in 1921.

Inevitably the books that constitute the flowering of children's literature in English have been Irish-based and with Irish themes — a degree of self-absorption which is beginning to lessen and broaden into a newfound internationalism. Certain themes have been common — an interest in wildlife as exemplified by Tom McCaughren's *Run Wild* books, Eugene McCabe's *Cyril* and Don Conroy's books being ever popular. Carolyn Swift was one of the first authors published by The Children's Press and one who made a conscious decision that her young readers would have "no need to look to England or America or elsewhere for excitement" in her urban-based adventure stories.[28] Historical fiction, time-slip stories and fantasy are popular genres with both writers and readers — together with some finely written teenage books. It is estimated that anything up to a quarter of all books published for Irish children are historical novels, and this, one expert argues, is because the historical novel has a particular importance in colonial and post-colonial cultures.[29] As the literature develops, the genres widen out to include the beginner reader and very young children. It is at last a case that within the canon of Irish children's literature, you can find "all kinds of everything".

But what are the children *really* reading and how do they react to all these outpourings? *Children's Books Ireland* took a straw poll in 1998 by asking three fifth and sixth classes from very different schools to reveal what, if anything, they were reading — the classes were questioned without the teacher's intervention and it is believed answered honestly. The pupils were all Dublin-based, from schools in Terenure, Coolock and Shankill.[30] The survey revealed that 14 per cent of the books read were Irish, a surprising 19 per cent were classics, with science fiction totaling 16 per cent, and the ever-popular horror series Goosebumps 11 per cent. That left 16 per cent reading magazines and 19 per cent declaring themselves non-readers. The survey suggested something that educators have always suspected — that children's interest in books reflects the importance placed on literature by their parents and teachers. And Irish authors, what of them? They fare rather well, with Margrit Cruickshank's *SKUNK* series, Maeve Friel's *Lantern Moon* and Siobhán Parkinson's *Amelia* books all getting rave notices. But the author that is a perennial favorite is Marita Conlon-McKenna with children saying that they read "everything" by this author of *Under the Hawthorn Tree, Wildflower Girl, The Blue Horse* and many, many more. The types of books that are popular now bear little resemblance to those that would have been read by their parents 30 years ago — but then society in Ireland bears no resemblance to what it was 30 years ago. Books really are a reflection of society with reading patterns and tastes mirroring the trends that are taking place in society as a whole.

Notes

---

[1] This author has been researching and is currently writing such a history which will be published by Institute of Irish Studies, Queen's University Belfast.

[2] *The Irish Publishing Record* has been in existence since 1967 and is an annual record of books, pamphlets and serials published in Ireland in a given year.

[3] Special Report on publishing in Ireland in *Publisher's Weekly,* January 23, 1981, pp. 63-102.

[4] Coughlan, Valerie and Keenan, Celia (1996) *The Big Guide to Irish Children's Books.* Dublin: The Irish Children's Book Trust, p. 17

[5] So called because University of Loughborough first hosted it.

[6] Leland, Mary (1981) "Writing for Children", *The Irish Times*, Saturday August 8, p. 8

[7] *Proceedings of the 14ᵗʰ Loughborough International Conference on Children's Literature*. Dublin, 1982.

[8] *Services in Literature*(1985). Dublin: The Arts Council, p. 12.

[9] Quinn has made a significant contribution to raising awareness of children's books, both through the above mentioned series and a later series for teenagers *The Growing Years*. He regularly includes children's authors or educationists in the weekly *The Open Mind* programme. Not surprisingly Quinn subsequently published several children's and teenage books and was awarded the *Bisto Book of the Year* award in 1991/1992 for his first novel *The Summer of Lily and Esmé* published by Poolbeg.

[10] It later changed its title to *Children's Books Ireland*.

[11] Dunbar, Robert (1989) "CLAI: Who, what and why" *Children's Books in Ireland*, No. 1, December, p. 1.

[12] Reece, Lesley and Rosenstock, Gabriel (1990) *The Irish Guide to Children's Books: The Decade 1980-1900*, Dublin: Irish Children's Book Foundation, Reece, Lesley, et al. (1991), *The Irish Guide to Children's Books 1991*, Dublin: The Irish Children's Book Foundation.

[13] Dillon, Eilís (1991) "The unclouded vision", *Books Ireland*, No. 149, April, p. 65.

[14] Ibid. p. 66.

[15] Coughlan, Valerie and Keenan, Celia (1996),*The Big Guide to Irish Children's Books*. Dublin: The Irish Children's Book Trust.

[16] Pádraig O Siochfhradha (1984) *Jimeen*. Illus. By Brian Bourke. Dublin: Lucky Tree Books. The translation was by Patricia Egan and Peter Fallon.

[17] See Donlon, Pat (1986, new edition 1988) "Publishing in Ireland" *Children's Books of the Celtic World*. Munich: Erasmus Grasser Verlag, pp. 20-27..

[18] Garrett, Jeffrey (1986), *Publishing for Children in the Celtic World*. Munich: The International Youth Library, p. 17.

[19] Coghlan, Valerie (1998), "The Launch of IBBY Ireland", *Children's Books Ireland*, No. 20, Winter, p. 7.

[20] Ibid.

[21] Donlon, Pat (1985), "Irish Children's Fiction" *The Linen Hall Review*, Vol. 2, No. 3, p. 13.

[22] Kelly, Shirley (1997), "The Children's Guru" *Books Ireland,* No. 208, November, p. 282.

[23] Lewis, C.S. (1980) "On Three Ways of Writing for Children", *Only Connect: Readings on Children's Literature.* Toronto: Oxford University Press, p. 210.

[24] Parkinson, Siobhán (1999) "Show some respect", *The Irish Times,* October 5.

[25] *The Cat's Pyjamas* (1992), Dublin: O'Brien Press, *The Bee's Knees* (1994), Dublin: O'Brien; *The Top Dog* (1996) Dublin: O'Brien Press; and *The Whole Shebang* (1998) Dublin: O'Brien Press.

[26] *I Have a Dream: Irish Children Writing for RTÉ's Millennium Eve* (1999), Dublin: Marino & RTÉ, , p. 7

[27] Coghlan, Valerie (1990), "Sad and Disgraceful", *Children's Books in Ireland,* December, p. 1.

[28] Reece, Lesley. op.cit.

[29] See Keenan, Celia, "Irish Historical Fiction" *The Big Guide to Irish Children's Books.*

[30] Morris, Liz (1998), "What are children *really* reading?", *Children's Books Ireland*, No. 18, pp. 8-10.

Part 3:
Children and the Economy

Chapter 11

Child Poverty in Ireland

Brian Nolan

INTRODUCTION

In Ireland, relative income poverty for households with children has grown rapidly over the past 25 years and now affects a particularly high proportion of children. Figures for European Union member states produced by Eurostat, the Statistical Office of the European Communities, show Ireland with the highest percentage of children living in poor households (using half average income in each country as the poverty standard). National studies have shown a marked divergence in trends in poverty over time between Irish households with and without children (Nolan and Farrell, 1990; Callan et al., 1996), so that poverty rates for children are substantially higher than for adults.

In this chapter we assess the level of child poverty in Ireland, put this in comparative perspective, examine the way it has been changing and explore the key factors at work. In assessing poverty and living standards, we make use both of income and of non-monetary indicators of deprivation to provide a rounded picture of child poverty in a booming economy. We draw on results from a study carried out for Ireland's Combat Poverty Agency, which has adopted the reduction of child poverty as one of its key strategic aims.

We begin with a brief discussion of the macroeconomic and policy context. We then present relative income poverty rates from the early 1970s up to 1997, for children and for all persons. We then try to get behind these trends by looking at the types of low-income household in which children live. Non-monetary indicators of deprivation are then used to give a more comprehensive picture of trends in child poverty in a time of rapid economic growth. Finally, some pressing issues for policy are discussed.

THE MACROECONOMIC AND POLICY CONTEXT

The central feature of the Irish economy from the 1970s has been exceptionally pronounced fluctuations in economic growth. Following a misplaced fiscal pump-priming in the late 1970s, there was little or no economic growth from 1980 to 1987 as the government struggled to bring the public finances under control. In each of the years from 1987 to 1994, on the other hand, growth in real Gross Domestic Product exceeded both the European Union and OECD average. Economic growth has been even more rapid since then, with GDP increasing by 7-8 per cent per annum — the "Celtic Tiger" phenomenon. Over the 1990s as a whole, Ireland has been one of the fastest growing economies in the OECD. The factors producing this growth are many and the balance between them debated; for an overview and interpretation of recent Irish growth experience, see, for example, Bradley et al. (1997), Barry (1999), Duffy et al. (1999).

The absence of growth meant that unemployment rose very rapidly during the 1980s, reaching 18 per cent of the labour force by 1987 (as measured in the Labour Force Survey rather than by numbers "signing on" for social welfare). The extent of long-term unemployment was of particular concern, with those unemployed for a year or more accounting for a particularly high proportion of total unemployment in the Irish case. Unemployment proved initially resistant to the renewal of economic growth, still remaining as high as 16 per cent by 1994, but subsequently fell rapidly, down to 11 per cent by 1997 and has fallen a good deal further since then. Again, with something of a lag, long-term unemployment has also now fallen very considerably.

Tax and social security policies can also be a key determinant of the welfare of families and children, and during the 1970s and 1980s these policies tended to disadvantage families with children. From a social welfare perspective, increases in social welfare pensions were seen as providing a way of targeting resources to a needy group without distorting financial incentives to work. As a result, at one point rates of payment for many of the unemployed were close to 40 per cent of average household income (adjusted for household size), while those on social insurance pensions received close to 60 per cent of that mean. Since then, following the recommendations of the government-appointed Commission on Social Welfare, the rates of support for different contingencies have been brought much closer together, with what had been the lowest rates of support receiving above-average increases. Welfare rates have generally increased significantly faster than prices in the 1990s, but during the years of very rapid economic growth since 1994 they have not kept pace with average incomes from employment.

On the tax side, erosion of the real value of allowances and bands has pulled an ever-increasing proportion of the population into the tax net. From the mid-1980s no account was taken of the presence of children in determining the amount of tax paid by those in the tax net, as support was concentrated in the universal (and untaxed) Child Benefit, paid monthly in respect of all children. Tax exemption limits were raised, however, for those with children from the late 1980s, and the Family Income Supplement cash support for low-income working families has been expanded over time in terms of coverage and support rates.

CHILD INCOME POVERTY IN IRELAND

Child poverty, like poverty more broadly, is usually measured using the results of household surveys seeking to represent the situation of the population as a whole. (Certain small groups with very high poverty rates, such as the homeless or Travellers, will generally be missed by such surveys, as will those living in institutions.) Here we draw on data from household surveys carried out by the Central Statistics Office in 1973 and

1980 (the Household Budget Surveys), and by the Economic and Social Research Institute in 1987, 1994 and 1997.[1] The overall representativeness of these data has been validated by comparison with information from external sources. As well as income, the ESRI surveys included a range of questions about a range of non-monetary indicators of life-style and deprivation, which are also particularly useful in assessing living standards.

A relative standard for measuring poverty in developed countries is by now widely though not universally accepted. The definition of poverty employed in the National Anti-Poverty Strategy recently adopted by the Irish government is fairly typical:

> People are living in poverty if their income and resources (material, cultural and social) are so inadequate as to preclude them from having a standard of living which is regarded as acceptable by Irish society generally. As a result of inadequate income and resources people may be excluded and marginalised from participating in activities which are considered the norm for other people in society. (NAPS, 1997, p. 3).

In actually implementing such a definition to measure the extent of poverty, the most common approach has been to define a poverty line in terms of income, and regard those with incomes below the line as poor.[2] One way to set that income poverty line is then to take it as a proportion of average income, adjusted for the greater needs of larger families, and this is the general approach widely adopted in comparative studies of poverty across industrialised countries.[3] Various cut-offs can then be derived and the sensitivity of conclusions to the precise location of the poverty line tested, and here we use 50 and 60 per cent of mean income.

Table 11.1 shows the percentage of children (aged under 14) and adults living in households below each of the relative income lines in each of the years for which we have such data. We see that at the start of the period, in 1973, the poverty rates for children and adults were similar to each other for both cut-offs. Between 1973 and 1987, the risk of relative income poverty for children increased (as examined in depth in Nolan and Farrell, 1990), whereas the poverty rates for adults were broadly unchanged. As a result, by the late 1980s the poverty rate for children was up to 50 per cent higher than that for adults.

Table 11.1: *Risks of Relative Income Poverty for Adults and Children, Ireland 1973-97*

	1973	1980	1987	1994	1997
	% children below relative income line				
50% line	16.2	18.5	25.5	29.6	26.0
60% line	27.5	29.5	37.8	40.6	37.2
	% adults below relative income line				
50% line	15.1	15.2	16.1	18.0	20.5
60% line	24.4	25.4	26.5	32.0	34.4

From 1987 to 1994, the poverty risk increased again for children at both lines. It also now increased for adults, though, so the gap between children and adults was more stable. Between 1994 and 1997, the trends for children and adults diverged sharply again. The risk for children fell, back to 1987 levels, while relative income poverty rates for adults continued to creep up, so the gap between children and adults narrowed significantly. The most recent information we now have available, for 1997, thus shows children with higher poverty rates than adults, but this is no longer nearly as pronounced as it was ten years before.

How does child poverty, measured in this way, compare with other industrialised countries? Eurostat, the Statistical Office of the European Community, has recently produced figures for 1994 from the European Community Household Panel Survey for most of the EU member states which allow such a comparison to be made. These relate to the percentage below half the average income in the country in question, and are shown in Table 11.2. We see that at 30 per cent Ireland in fact has the highest rate of child poverty, measured in this way, of any of the member states included in the survey. Only Portugal and the UK have a child poverty rate nearly as high, and in many of the countries the rate is half Ireland's or below.

***Table 11.2: Percentage of Children Below 50 per cent
Relative Income Poverty Line in European Union Countries,
1994***

	Children (under 16) below Poverty Line (%)
Belgium	15
Denmark	5
Germany	18
Greece	14
Spain	22
France	15
Ireland	30
Italy	20
Luxembourg	19
Netherlands	10
Austria	18
Portugal	27
UK	28
Average	19

These results relate to income poverty lines tied to the average income. In the Irish case, adopting a poverty line set in terms of fixed purchasing power, similar to the official poverty line employed in the US, for example, would give a totally different picture of trends over time. For much of the 1980s, with the economy stagnating, average household income did not in fact increase in real terms so relative and "real" income lines would have shown a similar picture. For the 1990s, though, and particularly since 1994, average incomes have been growing rapidly in real terms and so fixed "real" lines would show sharp declines in poverty. Rapidly increasing average income also explains why relative income poverty rates for children did not fall by more from 1994 to 1997. Mean equivalised household income rose by about 22 per cent over those three years, which outpaced social welfare support rates, though these did rise well ahead of prices. This counter-balanced somewhat the impact of falling unemployment: the numbers relying on social welfare fell, but their relative income poverty rates rose.

LOW-INCOME IRISH HOUSEHOLDS WITH CHILDREN

To understand why so many Irish children find themselves in households below the relative income lines, and why this has been changing over time, we can look at the characteristics of these households across a number of dimensions. Focusing on the period to 1987, Callan et al. (1989) showed that the dominant factor increasing income poverty rates for families with children was unemployment. Almost all the dramatic increased risk in relative income poverty for families with children over that period was attributable to the increase in numbers unemployed.

From 1987 to 1994, while economic growth was healthier the percentage of households headed by an unemployed person fell only marginally. As a result, unemployment continued to be the dominant factor underlying income poverty for families with children. Over the 1994 to 1997 period, however, as growth accelerated unemployment fell markedly and a different pattern emerged. Table 11.3 shows that considerable changes took place over this short period in the composition of the low-income households in which children live. We see that in 1994, almost half of all children in households below half average income lived in households headed by an unemployed person. By 1997, this had fallen to 40 per cent. This was balanced by an increase in the proportion in households headed by someone at work, or by an ill or disabled person.

Table 11.3: Breakdown of Children Below 50 per cent Relative Income Poverty Line by Labour Force Status of Household Head, 1994 and 1997

	1994	1997
	%	%
Employee	10.4	17.7
Self-employed	7.1	8.5
Farmer	8.3	3.9
Unemployed	47.8	39.7
Ill/disabled	5.6	12.3
Retired	0.9	0.9
Home duties	19.8	17.0
All	100	100

A key factor in narrowing the gap in relative income poverty rates between adults and children over the 1994-1997 period thus appears to have been the decline in unemployment. As in the 1980-1987 period, the risk of the household falling below half average income if the head was unemployed was both high and quite stable. Just as the dramatic rise in unemployment between 1980 and 1987 pushed many households with children into relative income poverty, the fall in unemployment between 1994 and 1997 has pulled them over the relative income lines. Those continuing to be dependent on social welfare, on the other hand, have lagged behind since 1987, so the position of families with children on average has improved relative to, for example, pensioners. This is reflected in a significant increase in relative income poverty rates for households headed by someone aged 65 or over, documented in Callan et al. (1999).

Turning to household size and composition, Table 11.4 shows the type of household in which children below the 50 per cent relative income line lived in 1994 and 1997. We see that in 1994, about 46 per cent of these children lived in households comprising three or more adults with children,[4] while a further 18 per cent were in households of two adults plus four or more children. By 1997, a considerably higher proportion of the children below this line lived in households comprising two adults with one to three children.

Table 11.4: *Breakdown of Children in Households Below 50 per cent Relative Income Poverty Line by Household Composition, 1994 and 1997*

	1994	1997
	%	%
2 adults 1 child	3.2	6.2
2 adults 2 children	8.2	11.8
2 adults 3 children	13.8	24.3
2 adults 4+ children	17.5	13.4
1 adult + children	11.8	9.0
3+ adults + child(ren)	45.5	35.3
All	100	100

It is worth noting that, despite Ireland's rapidly-increasing lone parenthood rate, only about one in ten of the children in households below half average income were in single-adult households, and this did not increase between 1994 and 1997. Children below the income poverty lines do tend to be in larger families. Those below half average income in 1994 had, on average, about 3 children compared with 2.4 for the rest of the sample. By 1997 the average number of children had fallen, both for those above and below the relative income lines, but the gap between them remained.

NON-MONETARY INDICATORS AND CHILD POVERTY

So far we have focused on household incomes, but we now wish to broaden that focus. Poverty is conventionally defined in terms of exclusion due to lack of resources, but low income on its own may not be an entirely satisfactory measure of such exclusion. This is not primarily because of the (real) difficulties in measuring income accurately, but more because a household's command over resources is affected by much more than its current income. Long-term factors, relating most importantly to the way resources have been accumulated or eroded over time, as well as current income, play a crucial role in influencing the likelihood of current deprivation and exclusion.

It is therefore useful to complement income by measuring various aspects of living standards and deprivation directly through non-monetary indicators. The use of such indicators in poverty research was pioneered by Townsend (1979), and since then they have been studied in, for example, Mack and Lansley (1985), Mayer and Jencks (1988), Mayer (1993), Muffels (1993), Callan, Nolan and Whelan (1993), Hallerod (1995) and Nolan and Whelan (1996). All these studies face hard questions such as how the most satisfactory indicators for the purpose are to be selected, whether they are to be combined into a summary deprivation measure and if so how, and how they are then to be employed in exploring poverty.

In seeking to identify those excluded due to a lack of resources, research at the ESRI has focused on what we have called basic deprivation indicators. On the basis of survey results for 1987, 1994 and 1997, these are items which clearly represent socially perceived necessities, are possessed by most people, and reflect rather basic aspects of current material deprivation. They also cluster together, which lends support to the notion that they are useful as indicators of the underlying generalised deprivation we are trying to measure. Focusing on households that are both at relatively low income levels and experiencing basic deprivation should then give a better indication of the scale of generalised deprivation or exclusion due to lack of resources than those below income lines alone.

This way of identifying those most in need has, in fact, been incorporated in the global poverty reduction target adopted in the Irish National Anti-Poverty Strategy, which forms the benchmark against which progress in combating poverty is to be assessed (NAPS, 1997). Between 1987 and 1994 there was little change in the extent of poverty overall shown by these combined income and deprivation measures. Between 1994 and 1997, however, the percentage below the relative income lines and experiencing basic deprivation fell markedly. Thus, combining relative income poverty lines with a deprivation criterion gives a very different picture for all persons over that period to relative income lines alone.

What about children? Table 11.5 shows the percentage of children and adults in households below the relative income lines and experiencing basic deprivation in both 1994 and 1997. We see first that the poverty rates on this basis are a good deal higher for children than for adults. For example, 17 per cent of all adults but 24 per cent of all children were in households below the 60 per cent relative income line and experiencing basic deprivation in 1994. These are, in fact, rather wider gaps between children and adults than those shown by the relative income lines in that year.

Table 11.5: Percentage of Children and Adults Below Relative Income Thresholds and Experiencing Basic Deprivation, 1987 and 1994

Relative Income Line	% in Households Below Line and Experiencing Enforced Basic Deprivation	
	1994	*1997*
% of children		
50% line	17.9	14.9
60% line	23.5	16.9
% of adults		
50% line	9.0	6.8
60% line	14.8	9.4

From 1994 to 1997, the percentage of children and adults below the income lines and experiencing basic deprivation fell quite significantly. This is similar to the direction of change shown for children by the corresponding income lines alone, but very different to that for adults. This pronounced fall in deprivation, at a time when relative income poverty was rising for adults, is attributable to the very rapid rates of income growth experienced over the period. As explored in detail in Callan et al. (1999), the contrast brings out that, in a period of such rapid growth, relative income lines on their own may miss out on an important part of the story.

The issue of most relevance here, though, is the position of children versus adults. While the position of children on this poverty measure improved between 1994 and 1997, the pronounced gap between them and adults did not narrow in the same way as with relative income lines alone. Poverty rates for children in 1997 are about twice as high as the rates for adults on this measure. Examination of the households involved shows unemployment to be even more important than when relative income lines alone are used.

CONCLUSIONS AND POLICY IMPLICATIONS

We have seen in this chapter that, by the late 1980s, child poverty, measured by relative income poverty lines, had risen substantially in Ireland and a substantial gap had opened up between poverty rates for children and for adults. This reflected a combination of the effects of rapidly rising unemployment and improved pensions for the elderly. The gap between relative income poverty rates for children and adults was fairly stable between 1987 and 1994, as the rates for each group rose. With Ireland's recent exceptional rates of economic growth from 1994, unemployment had declined significantly by 1997 and relative income poverty rates for children declined. Those rates for adults increased, primarily because social welfare lagged behind average incomes, leading to a significant narrowing in the gap between children and adults.

A range of non-monetary indicators was also employed, together with income, to characterise more comprehensively the evolution of child poverty. Like relative income poverty lines, measures combining those lines with experience of basic deprivation showed children at a substantial disadvantage vis-à-vis adults in 1994. Unlike those relative lines, however, these combined income and deprivation measures showed no narrowing in that gap between 1994 and 1997, with deprivation levels for adults declining more rapidly than children on average.

As a result of the declines in the combined income/ deprivation poverty measures now shown by the 1997 data, the National Anti-Poverty Strategy global target has recently been rebased to aim at a greater fall than initially envisaged (see

NAPS, 1999). Here is not the place to explore the best way to frame such targets — we argue in Callan et al. (1999) for a tiered set of targets encompassing real income levels, deprivation indicators that adjust over time to enhanced expectations, and relative income levels. What is directly relevant is whether an overall target is likely to be adequate from the perspective of children. Given the significantly higher poverty risk faced by children, a strong case can be made for a distinct NAPS target focusing on child poverty. Indeed, the Combat Poverty Agency joined with a number of other organisations concerned with child welfare to call for the adoption of such a target. They also called for development of a National Children's Strategy including a programme for the advancement of the economic, social, civil and political rights of children. These concerns were addressed in the National Childhood Strategy *Our Children — Their Lives* announced by the Government in November 2000. It remains to be seen how this may be translated into policy.

While it would encompass many other areas, an important element in developing such a strategy would be an urgent assessment of the extent and nature of child income support offered by the Irish State. Substantial increases in universal Child Benefit would serve to improve the situation of children without adversely affecting work incentives (see, for example, Callan et al., 1995). The best way of assisting families with the costs of child-care has been the focus of particularly heated debate, with the range of options discussed in the report by the expert Commission on the Family (1998) set up to advise the government. Once again, the priority should be to develop support mechanisms assisting all those with children, rather than only those in the tax net, without distorting choices about caring for children in or outside the home. The benign economic environment projected for the next decade offers a unique opportunity to seriously tackle child poverty, and the success of some of our European partners shows what can be achieved.

References

Barry, F. (ed). (1999). *Understanding Ireland's Economic Growth*, London: Macmillan.

Bradley, J., FitzGerald, J., Honohan, P. and Kearney, I. (1997). "Interpreting the Recent Irish Growth Experience", in Duffy, D., FitzGerald, J., Kearney, I. and Shortall, F. (eds.), *Medium-Term Review: 1997-2003*, Dublin: The Economic and Social Research Institute.

Callan, T., Nolan, B. and Whelan, B.J, Hannan, D.F. with Creighton, S. (1989). *Poverty, Income and Welfare in Ireland*, General Research Series, No. 146, Dublin: The Economic and Social Research Institute.

Callan, T., Nolan, B. and Whelan, C.T. (1993). "Resources, Deprivation and the Measurement of Poverty", *Journal of Social Policy*, 22 (2), 141-172.

Callan, T., O'Neill, C. and O'Donoghue, C. (1995). *Supplementing Family Incomes*, Policy Research Series Paper No. 23, Dublin: The Economic and Social Research Institute.

Callan, T., Nolan, B., Whelan, B.J., Whelan, C.T. and Williams, J. (1996). *Poverty in the 1990s: Evidence from the Living in Ireland Survey*, General Research Series Paper 170, Dublin: Oak Tree Press.

Callan, T., Layte, R, Nolan, B., Watson, D., Whelan, C.T., Williams, J. and Maitre, B. (1999). *Monitoring Poverty Trends*, Stationery Office/CPA: Dublin.

Cantillon, S. and Nolan, B. (1998) "Are Married Women More Deprived than their Husbands?", *Journal of Social Policy*, 27 (2), 151-171.

Cantillon, S. and Nolan, B. (2001) "Poverty Within Households: Measuring Gender Differences Using Non-Monetary Indicators", *Feminist Economics*, forthcoming.

Central Statistics Office (1984). *Household Budget Survey 1980: Detailed Results*, Dublin : Stationery Office.

Commission on the Family (1998). *Strengthening Families for Life, Final Report*, Dublin: Stationery Office.

Duffy, D., Fitzgerald, J., Kearney, I., Smyth, D. (1999) *Medium-Term Review 1999-2005*, The Economic and Social Research Institute: Dublin.

Hallerod, B. (1995). "The Truly Poor: Direct and Indirect Measurement of Consensual Poverty in Sweden", *European Journal of Social Policy*, 5 (2), 111-29.

Mack, J. and Lansley, S. (1985). *Poor Britain*, London: Allen and Unwin.

Mayer, S. (1993). "Living Conditions among the Poor in Four Rich Countries", *Journal of Population Economics*, 6, 261-286.

Mayer, S. and Jencks, C. (1988). "Poverty and the Distribution of Material Hardship", *Journal of Human Resources*, 24 (1), 88-114.

Muffels, R. (1993) "Deprivation standards and style of living indices", in Berghman, J. and Cantillon, B. (eds) *The European Face of Social Security*, Aldershot: Avebury.

National Anti-Poverty Strategy (1997). *Sharing in Progress: National Anti-Poverty Strategy*, Dublin: Stationery Office.

National Anti-Poverty Strategy (1999). *Social Inclusion Strategy: 1998/99 Annual Report of the Inter-Departmental Policy Committee of the National Anti-Poverty Strategy*, Dublin: Stationery Office.

Nolan, B. (2000). *Child Poverty in Ireland*, Dublin: Oak Tree Press/ Combat Poverty Agency

Nolan, B. and Farrell, B. (1990). *Child Poverty in Ireland*, Dublin: Combat Poverty Agency.

Nolan, B. and Callan, T., (eds.), (1994). *Poverty and Policy in Ireland*, Dublin: Gill and Macmillan.

Nolan, B. and Whelan, C. (1996). *Resources, Deprivation and Poverty*, Oxford: Clarendon Press.

Rottman, D. (1994). *Income Distribution Within Irish Housdholds: Allocating Resources Within Families*, Dublin: Combat Poverty Agency.

Townsend, P. (1979). *Poverty in the United Kingdom*, Harmondsworth: Penguin.

Notes

[1] Detailed descriptions of these surveys can be found in Callan et al. (1989) and CSO (1984) respectively. These three years are the only years before 1994 for which such household surveys, gathering detailed income data on a large representative national sample, were carried out in Ireland. Our analysis of the micro-data from the budget surveys was kindly facilitated by the CSO.

[2] Conventional poverty measurement practice takes the household as the income sharing unit, so all members of a particular household have the same standard of living. For analysis of the situation of individuals within households using ESRI survey data see Rottman (1994) and Cantillon and Nolan (1998, 2001).

[3] The adjustment for household size is done using what are called equivalence scales. The equivalence scale underlying the results described here allows 1 for the "needs" of the first adult in the household, 0.66 for each other adult, and 0.33 for each child.

[4] Recalling that the definition of child being employed is under 14 years of age, many of these are households including two parents and children aged 14 or over.

Chapter 12

Children as Workers: A Case Study of Child Employment in Belfast

Madeleine Leonard

INTRODUCTION

In modern Irish society, children are to a great extent defined in terms of economic dependency. The focus has been on the effects parenthood has on adults in terms of mobility and access to the labour market. Children are often seen as presenting obstacles to the participation of women in the labour force because of the expectation that it is women who should care for children within the household. As children approach the minimum school leaving age, the focus shifts to the difficulties associated with making the transition from school to employment. The notion that children might combine school attendance with paid employment receives little attention in this debate. Yet a range of recent empirical studies (Hobbs et al., 1996; Lavalette et al., 1995; Morrow, 1994) indicate that children's participation in paid employment prior to leaving school is a *normal* experience for many school children. However, much of this empirical data refers to child employment in Britain. In the north of Ireland, "there is a pronounced absence of the primary data necessary to enable us to accurately assess the number of working children in our society and the range of jobs in which they are engaged" (McCloskey, 1997, p. 7). The aim of this chapter is to respond to this neglect by examining the participation of children in paid employment in Belfast.

BACKGROUND TO THE DATA

The chapter is based on a survey of 545 school pupils drawn from twelve schools in Belfast.[1] A total of 317 boys (58 per cent) and 228 girls (42 per cent) took part in the survey. All the pupils were aged 15 when the survey was carried out in 1998.[2] This age group was deliberately selected as empirical studies from various parts of Britain indicated that this age group is the one most likely to be involved in term-time employment. The main aim of the survey was to document the numbers of pupils involved in term-time employment, the types of work undertaken, hours worked and hourly rates of pay. The extent to which participation in term-time employment is influenced by gender was also addressed in the survey. The survey was complemented by classroom discussions with 56 boys and 38 girls and tape recorded interviews with 15 pupils who held term time jobs.

The issue of children working is complex and raises questions about children's role in society. The fact that children work challenges our conceptions of childhood as a period characterised by economic inactivity. It is common to think that working children are part of the distant past. Child labour is often considered to be a product of the industrial revolution. But while some of the worst examples of child labour may be attributed to this era, it is important to emphasise that children have always worked. Prior to the industrial revolution, children worked within the family and on farms and such work was often onerous (Thompson, 1968). Nonetheless, during the industrial revolution, children were involved in new forms of work such as working in factories, mills and mines. Their working conditions were so harsh that a number of prominent philanthropists campaigned on behalf of working children to get the State to restrict the employment of child workers. The introduction of compulsory education and a number of Factory Acts banning or restricting the use of child labour had the effect of removing large numbers of children from the labour market. However, it would be a fallacy to suggest that children disappeared from the labour market and that the employment of children has only recently increased in prevalence. Children have worked in varying numbers throughout the 20th century. Indeed, the practice of delivering milk and papers to doorsteps encouraged the development of new and specific forms of child employment. Compulsory schooling, rather than displacing child employment, merely facilitated the introduction of types of work that could be combined with school attendance. As this chapter will show, substantial numbers of children have experience of the labour market prior to leaving school. The first part of the chapter will outline the types of jobs that children do and present a descriptive account of some of the main facets of this employment. The second part of the chapter presents children's own perceptions of the costs and benefits of the work that they do. This reflects new thinking around children and childhood whereby children are acknowledged as active, creative, social agents worthy of study in their own right (Prout and James, 1997).

DEFINING CHILD WORK

Any exploration of children and work involves defining at the outset what is meant by the term "work". The survey was limited to the paid work of children but it is important to acknowledge the many other ways in which children may work in unpaid activities. Children may make a significant contribution to housework and in some cases release parents from household duties, thus enabling them to participate more effectively in the labour market (Mayall, 1994). When a parent or household member is sick or disabled, children may contribute to the care of that individual and hence reduce state responsibility (Aldridge and Becker, 1993). Children may also be involved in the care of younger siblings. In a Northern Ireland study on the use and demand for childcare services among the parents of children under eight years, it was noted that in some cases it was older siblings who provided childcare (Policy Planning and Research Unit, 1994).

Of course, this latter activity functions as one of the most common types of child employment once it is removed from the household. Babysitting for others outside the immediate household provides many children with extra income. While the survey focused on the paid activities of children, babysitting was considered as a problematic category. This is because the legislation on child employment does not take into account children's work as babysitters. The law is concerned only with children of compulsory school age (up to 16 years of age) who "assist in a trade or occupation carried on for profit" (Whitney, 1998, p. 137). For this reason, babysitting was treated as a separate type of child employment. As a result, the numbers of children working in Belfast cannot be compared to other British studies which included babysitting as a form of child employment (Hobbs et al., 1993; McKechnie et al., 1993; McKechnie et al., 1994; Lavalette et al., 1995). These studies indicate that between 35 per cent to 49 per cent of children between the ages of 14 and 16 are involved in term-time employment. However, when babysitting is removed, the numbers are substantially reduced.

The survey in Belfast found that overall 22 per cent of the sample held a term-time job. However, if babysitting is included in this definition, the numbers increase significantly to 63 per cent of the sample. The remainder of the chapter will concentrate on types of employment excluding babysitting that pupils engage in. It is argued that these types of employment are qualitatively different from babysitting in that they are regulated (albeit ineffectively) by legislation and they take place under different circumstances. The relationship between employer and worker is distinct from the relationship between babysitter and adult in that the former is structured by a profit motive while the latter represents a drain on adults' income through paying for a personal service.

EXTENT AND NATURE OF CHILD EMPLOYMENT IN BELFAST

There is a common sense assumption that when children do work, they do so in a narrow range of activities. This viewpoint is often put forward by government ministers and policymakers to justify their lack of intervention into this area of children's lives. Child employment is presented as harmless and performed merely to obtain a little extra pocket money. Paper rounds are seen in this light. These are often considered as ideally suited to children's needs. They can be performed before and after school hours and enable children to gain access to income that can be utilised to fulfil their needs and wants. Indeed, it was to protect the "British tradition of delivering newspapers" that the former conservative government in the UK secured a six-year opt-out from the EU Directive on the Protection of Young People at Work in 1994 (Lavalette, 1998). The opt-out was hailed as a victory for British school children. Paper rounds were the most common types of jobs held by children in Belfast. One in four of those who participated in term-time employment were involved in delivering newspapers. This figure is consistent with previous studies into child employment which indicate that between 16 per cent and 33 per cent of child workers are involved in traditional newspaper rounds (O'Donnell and White, 1998; Hobbs and McKechnie, 1997; Pond and Searle, 1991). However, these studies also indicate that substantial numbers of children are employed in jobs commonly held by adults. This aspect of child employment challenges stereotypical notions of child work as relatively light and harmless and limited to a few appropriate occupations ideally suited to children.

In Belfast, child employment is characterised by its heterogeneity rather than being limited to a few specific occupations. This is illustrated in Table 12.1.

The table indicates that children commonly work alongside adults in a diverse range of occupations. They are found working in shops, pubs, in hotels and catering, in offices, on building sites and in a host of other occupations. The category "other work" revealed small numbers of children working in a wide variety of different jobs including street entertainment, hairdressing, working on a race-course, working in betting establishments and selling door-to-door. While it is not my intention to provide the legislative framework surrounding child employment in Northern Ireland, it is worth stating here that many of these occupations are banned by the existing legislation. The Employment of Children Regulations (Northern Ireland) Act (1996) for example, prohibits manual labour and labels this type of work as inappropriate for school children yet, as the table indicates, this was the third most popular type of employment. The data indicates that there is a clear need to challenge the common-sense view of child employment as limited to appropriate tasks and protected by current legislation.

Table 12.1: Job Type

Type of Job	No. of Children	Percentage
Newspaper delivery	30	25
Shop work	21	18
Manual work	16	13
Hotel/Catering	15	13
Pub work	6	5
Office work/Computers	5	4
Milk deliveries	5	4
Other delivery work	4	3
Other work	18	15
Total	120	100

In the Republic of Ireland, employers may employ 15-year-olds in "light work", part-time during school term as part of an approved work experience or educational programme (Byrne, 1999). Yet a study carried out by the Association of Principals of Vocational and Community Colleges found a similar diversity in children's term-time employment experiences. Children were working in shops, restaurants, bars and as cleaners, gardeners and farmers. Eithne Fitzgerald, former Junior Minister at the Department of Enterprise, Trade and Employment, states that during her time in office her Department received many complaints about the employment of children for long hours, at low wages and often with the complicity of parents or guardians. She states that the "areas of complaint include, in particular, employment conditions in supermarkets, public houses, catering and fast food establishments, petrol service stations and the services sector generally" (1997, p. 103). Hence, the Belfast research supports a number of other empirical studies which indicate that children are a permanent feature of the adult labour market rather than being solely involved in jobs typically defined as children's work.

HOURLY WAGE LEVELS

One reason why children are employed as part of the adult labour force concerns their tendency to work for less money than adults employed in similar occupations. Child employment in Belfast was characterised by low wage rates. Just over one-quarter of the children employed earned between £1 and £2 per hour. A further quarter earned between £2 and £3 per hour. Hence, the average wage rate for the sample was within the £1 to £3 wage range. This is consistent with the wage levels found in a study carried out in the Republic of Ireland which indicated that half of the second-level students surveyed were paid £2 per hour or less (Byrne, 1999). Of course, these averages conceal highly exploitative internal variations. One 15-year-old in Belfast earned just 15p per hour. In North Tyneside, O'Donnell and White (1998) found examples of children working for just 17p per hour. Hobbs and McKechnie (1998) found that the average hourly rates of pay for their respondents ranged from £1.79 to £2.34 per hour. However, they recorded instances of children working for 10p per hour. Previous research carried out by the author in one low-income area of Belfast revealed that children were working for low rates of pay and exploitation was at its height where children were employed by members of their wider kinship network (Leonard, 1998). The children's awareness of their low wage levels is reflected in the following quotes:

> I get very low pay for many hours work.

> I think that just because we are young, we shouldn't get paid less than someone else for doing the same job. It's not fair.

> Young people are exploited and underpaid.

> I feel I am a slave labourer.

> Young people who have jobs get treated fairly but they do not give us enough wages. We should get wage slips stating hourly wage rates. . . .We are exploited.

Of course, it is problematic to compare average earnings of children working in different parts of Britain and Ireland as such a comparison often conceals the nature of the local labour market and regional differences in average adult rates of pay. Nonetheless, these studies collectively demonstrate that children's labour is often under-valued and exploited. It is also important to note that the majority of working children have no employment contract. They are often considered not as workers but as school pupils with term-time jobs. As a result, their bargaining position is weak even in relation to other flexible workers. As Lavalette points out (1996, p. 177), child labour is a particular form of marginal "poor work' in capitalist society.

HOURS WORKED

One of the primary concerns associated with child employment is its potentially negative influence on educational potential and achievement. The general consensus among researchers on child employment is that moderate levels of work, defined as under ten hours per week, have no detrimental effect on a child's education (Hobbs et al., 1993; Green, 1990; Steinberg et al., 1981). Indeed Hobbs and McKechnie (1997) found that the most academically successful group in their research were pupils who worked a low number of weekly hours. However, this advantage was overturned the more hours a pupil worked. Pupils who worked over ten hours per week in term-time did tend to perform less well than non-working pupils. It must be remembered when assessing the number of hours that children work during term-time that children on average spend around 30 hours per week in the educational system. Hence, hours worked should be added to this figure. This means that if children work over ten hours per week, they may have greater commitments than the average adult in full-time employment. Almost two-thirds of children in Belfast worked under ten hours per week. However, almost one-third worked in excess of this figure. In this respect working children differed from non-working children in that they were more likely to complain of feeling tired while at school. One in four children stated that they often felt tired during school hours because of their term-time employment. These views are reflected in the following quotes:

> I'm too tired in the mornings and this affects my school work.

> I am a bit too tired to go into school on Monday mornings.

Byrne (1999) reports that teachers in the Republic of Ireland complain that part-time work causes pupils to fall asleep during the day and this affects their learning ability. Indeed, 13 per cent of previously employed children stated that they had given up their jobs because they felt it interfered with their school work. The following quotes illustrate this view:

> Sometimes I would work until midnight and then I would be very tired in the mornings and feel very sleepy at school.

> I used to fall asleep during school.

> I was working too many hours to study properly and I fell behind with my school work.

> The late nights meant it was very hard to get up for school.

> I gave it up because I never had any time for school work. If I maybe had something to hand in I wouldn't have enough time to get it finished by the set date.

This indicates that some pupils may pay a high price for working during term-time.

GENDER DIFFERENCES IN TERM-TIME EMPLOYMENT

The survey found considerable differences in the types of jobs undertaken by males and females. Hotel and catering work and shop work were more significant for females than males. Half of the females who took part in the survey were involved in these two job types compared to less than one-quarter of males. Other occupations were dominated solely by males. These included some types of delivery work such as milk and coal, pub work and manual work. There were some variations in the numbers of hours worked with females tending to work slightly longer hours than males. This supports O'Donnell and White's (1998) findings where a substantial proportion of females worked 20 hours a week or more. As indicated earlier in the chapter, the majority of male and female pupils earned between £1 and £3 per hour. However, there were some variations between males and females at the top and bottom range of the wage levels documented. Just under 18 per cent of males earned over £4 per hour compared to under 15 per cent of females. At the lower end of the pay scale, more females earned under £1 per hour compared to males, the figures being 14.7 per cent compared to 10.5 per cent.

These aspects of the data are worrying. They indicate that school pupils tend to experience the labour market in gender-specific ways. Females were not only limited to certain types of child employment but when they did work, they tended to work longer hours and for lower rates of pay compared to males. While it is not my intention to depict child workers as victims of gender segregated work roles but as creative agents able to actively shape their work roles, nonetheless, there is a need for further research into the long-term effects of early labour market experiences on the subsequent work experiences of both males and females.

AGE AT STARTING WORK

While the survey concentrated on pupils aged 15 years of age, some attempt was made to gauge the age at which pupils started work by asking them to state their age on first experiencing employment. The legal regulations specify that a child must have reached the age of 13 before commencing employment. Yet 29 per cent of the sample of currently employed pupils had started work before the age of 13 with the most common starting age being ten years of age. Some 32 per cent of the sample were aged 13 when they commenced work while 22 per cent were 14 before they started work. These responses indicate that while the older a child is the more likely they are to enter term-time employment, nonetheless, many children have experience of such employment at a very young age. This issue can be further highlighted by examining the previous employment experiences of those pupils currently unemployed. Just under one-third of the non-working pupils had a previous term-time job. If this figure is added to those currently employed, then 47 per cent of the sample have experience of term-time employment excluding babysitting. Just under a quarter of previously employed school children started work before the age of 13. This focus on previous employment indicates that to look solely at current employment trends among school pupils provides only a partial picture of term-time employment and may lead to an under-estimation of the numbers of pupils who have work experience. McKechnie et al. (1997) suggest that children move in and out of the labour market, often with great rapidity. Hence to get a realistic picture of the numbers of children in employment, it is necessary to obtain data on the previous employment experience of children. Such an approach effectively challenges the view that not many school children have experience of the labour market.

CHILDREN'S PERCEPTIONS OF THEIR TERM-TIME EMPLOYMENT

So far, the chapter has provided a descriptive analysis of the nature and extent of child employment in Belfast. What is missing from this account is children's perceptions of the work that they do and their evaluations of the costs and benefits of term-time employment. It is only recently that sociology has paid attention to children's views of their lives. As James and Prout (1997, p. 7) point out, "the history of the study of childhood in the social sciences has been marked not by an absence of interest in children but by their silence". Essential to our understanding of modern childhood is the notion of children having rights. This view was enshrined in the UN Convention on the Rights of the Child ratified by the UK government in 1991 and by the Irish government in 1992. As Ennew (1995, p. 23-4) informs us, the importance of the Convention is not:

> Article 32 which is designed to protect children from economic exploitation, but articles such as 12 and 15 (those establishing the rights of children to freedom of expression and association) which add . . . participation to the range of

children's rights. Thus children . . . are redefined as capable
social actors rather than deficient pre-adults. . . . This opens
up the possibility for their voice to be heard.

The new sociology of childhood has responded to these
changes by a commitment to a study of children's social relationships and cultures as worthy of study in their own right. In
relation to term-time jobs, this means finding out about children's perceptions and understanding about the role that employment plays in their everyday lives. It means paying greater
attention to children's own accounts of their employment experiences.

Such a perspective suggests a need to understand children's motivations for participating in term-time employment.
A number of questions in the survey were designed to elicit
pupils' perceptions of the good and bad aspects of their employment. These questions were left deliberately open-ended
to ascertain the pupils' own reasons for working and their perceptions of the costs and benefits. These issues were explored
further during classroom discussions and tape-recorded interviews with 15 working pupils. As might be expected, the single
most frequently listed benefit from working was "earning
money". However, only 23 per cent of the overall sample listed
this as their key reason for working. Fifteen percent of the sample listed "meeting others" as the main benefit of their job, 13
per cent listed the "good atmosphere at work" while 18 per
cent suggested that term-time jobs were "quite easy to do" and
they saw this as the major positive aspect of their employment.
Hence, taken together, these attitudes indicate that the majority
of pupils listed factors related to working conditions rather than
money as benefits to be gained from working. Furnham and
Stacey (1991) argue that young people's evaluations of their
jobs are not significantly different from adults in that both tend
to cite intrinsic features in the job as more important than
wages. These positive views of working are reflected in the
following quotes:

It gives me something to do. I enjoy doing it and I get paid.

I like the people I work with and I just enjoy doing it.

> Work keeps me occupied and stops me from getting bored.

> It's also good to have some extra money at the weekend.

> I have achieved a sense of direction which I didn't have before.

> I have met new people. I have also earned my own money and have become more independent.

> I enjoy working with people and being able to have some responsibility.

Other cited benefits were related to the ability to be able to renegotiate age and its link with childhood identity. Hence working children, unlike non-working children, felt that they were able to move between the status of child and adult. Since many children were employed in jobs working alongside adults then their status as children was temporarily suspended and age became a less relevant category within the context of their employment. Similar observations were made by Solberg (1996) during her employment in a fishing community in northern Norway. In this industry, children worked alongside adults and "the status of worker seemed to make the status of child subordinate". Solberg describes the teamwork among adults and children where each depend on the output of the other and where the age of the worker becomes meaningless. This ability to move beyond being categorised as a child was important for some children in Belfast. The following quotes typify the responses received:

> I like being treated as an adult and not as a child. It's good experience.

> I have got experience of working with a real job which is meant to be for men.

> I have had a chance to be an adult by having a job and getting an income.

Of course, children were also critical of some aspects of their employment. One prevalent problem for working children was fatigue with 18 per cent of the sample complaining that they often felt tired due to their term-time employment. A number of related concerns were problems with hours/shifts, weather conditions and heavy work-loads. The majority of children who listed these as disadvantages were newspaper deliverers who complained about getting up early in the mornings, carrying heavy paper loads and delivering papers in bad weather conditions. These views are reflected in the following quotes:

> The paper bag is not well designed as it rips and the strap hurts my back. Sometimes I get a sore back for a couple of hours after I have finished work.

> I fell and another time got bitten by a dog. This happens to a paperboy regularly.

> When dogs come running at you, it can be scary and dangerous.

> When it rains I get soaked yet you still have to work on.

By focusing on various media reports on paper rounds, Lavalette (1996) questions the idealised, image of newspaper delivery as "light" work especially suitable for children. He reports on an agreement reached between the Post Office and the Union of Communication Workers which prohibits postal cadets (16 to 18-year-olds) from carrying more than 20 lbs. on foot or 26 lbs. on a suitably adapted bike. Yet some children were found to be carrying weights varying from 21.5 lbs. to 68.5 lbs. One boy was undergoing serious back surgery attributed by the medical profession to his job as a newspaper deliverer. Moreover, unlike postal cadets, children doing paper rounds are rarely provided with appropriate waterproof clothing. Hence, although many children see work as providing them with confidence and experience for future adult work, the negative features of such employment need to be addressed.

CONCLUSION

The purpose of this chapter is to highlight the invisibility of children as workers in modern Irish society. As the data in the chapter indicated, significant numbers of children in Belfast have experience of the labour market prior to leaving school. This is particularly the case, where previous employment is taken into account. The research demonstrated that, while some children are employed in occupations commonly referred to as "children's work", others are involved in jobs that are indistinguishable from those of adults. However, typically children are paid less than adults for similar work and their jobs are characterised by a greater level of insecurity. Despite these disadvantages, children tend to view their work in positive rather than negative terms. The research indicated that some children did not place emphasis on economic reward for its own sake, as might have been expected, but placed emphasis on job satisfaction and access to networks. For some children, work promoted self-reliance and responsibility. By highlighting the positive responses of children to their term-time employment, I do not wish to absolve society of the responsibility for monitoring and regulating child employment. It is clear that many abuses of child labour exist and it is important to document these and examine ways of making the experience of work less exploitative for children. However, this needs to be done in conjunction with children rather than on behalf of children. Their own perceptions of employment should be central to any future debate on the role of employment in modern childhood. The experiences of children in the workforce remind us that childhood is a social rather than a biological construction. Children can and do actively construct their own social identity sometimes in collusion with adults. Distinctions between childhood and adulthood become blurred once children enter the labour force. In the sociology of work, it is about time that children are seen and heard.

References

Aldridge, J. and Becker, S. (1993) *Children who Care: Inside the World of Young Carers,* Loughborough: Department of Social Sciences, Loughborough University.

Byrne, A. (1999) "Part-Time Study", *The Irish Times*, 23 February.

Ennew, J. (1995) "NATS (working with children and adolescents): historical emergence of a category", *NATS: Working with Children and Adolescents International Review*, Vol. 10. pp. 19-26.

Fitzgerald, E. (1997) "Legislative Action from the Irish Government" in S. McCluskey (ed.) *No Time to Play*, Belfast: One World Centre.

Furnham, A. and Stacey, B. (1991) *Young People's Understanding of Society*, London: Routledge.

Green, D.L. (1990) "High School Student Employment in Social Context: Adolescent's Perceptions of the Role of Part-time Work" *Adolescence,* Vol. 15, pp. 32-36.

Hobbs, S. and McKechnie, J. (1998) "Children and Work in the UK: The Evidence", in B. Pettitt (ed.) *Children and Work in the UK: Reassessing the Issues*, London: Child Poverty Action Group in association with Save the Children.

Hobbs, S. and McKechnie, J. (1997) *Child Employment in Britain*, London: The Stationery Office.

Hobbs, S., Lindsay, S. and McKechnie, J. (1996) "The Extent of Child Employment in Britain", *British Journal of Education and Work*, Vol. 9 No. 1, pp. 5-18.

Hobbs, S., Lindsay, S. and McKechnie, J. (1993) "Part-time Employment and Schooling" *Scottish Educational Review*, Vol. 25., pp. 53-60.

James, A. and Prout, A. (1997) *Constructing and Reconstructing Childhood*, London: Falmer Press.

Lavalette, M. (1998) "Child Labour: Historical, Legislative and Policy Context" in B. Pettitt (ed.) *Children and Work in the UK: Reassessing the Issues*, London: Child Poverty Action Group in association with Save the Children.

Lavalette, M. (1996) "Thatcher's Working Children: Contemporary Issues of Child Labour", in J. Pilcher and S. Wagg (eds.) *Thatcher's Children? Politics, Childhood and Society in the 1980s and 1990s*, London: Falmer Press.

Lavalette, M., Hobbs, S., Lindsay, S. and McKechnie, J. (1995) "Child Employment in Britain: Policy, Myth and Reality", *Youth and Society*, Winter, No.47, pp. 1-15.

Leonard, M. (1998) "Children's Contribution to Household Income: A Case Study from Northern Ireland" in B. Pettitt (ed.) *Children and Work in the UK: Reassessing the Issues*, London: Child Poverty Action Group in association with Save the Children.

Mayall, B. (1994) *Children's Childhoods: Observed and Experienced*, London: Falmer Press.

McCloskey, S. (1997) *No Time to Play*, Belfast: One World Centre.

McKechnie, J., Hobbs, S. and Lindsay, S. (1997) "Bringing Child Labour Centre Stage" in S. McCloskey (ed.) *No Time to Play*, Belfast: One World Centre.

McKechnie, J., Lindsay, S. and Hobbs, S. (1994) *Still Forgotten: Child Employment in Dumfries and Galloway*, Glasgow: Scottish Low Pay Unit.

McKechnie, J., Lindsay, S. and Hobbs, S. (1993) *Child Employment in Cumbria: A Report to Cumbria County Council*, Paisley: University of Paisley.

Morrow, V. (1994) "Responsible Children? Aspects of Children's Work and Employment outside School in Contemporary UK" in B. Mayall, (ed.) *Children's Childhoods: Observed and Experienced*, London: Falmer Press.

O'Donnell, C. and White, L. (1998) *Child Employment in North Tyneside*, London: Low Pay Unit.

Policy Planning and Research Unit (1994) *The Use and Demand for Childcare Services and Nursery Education Among the Parents of Children aged 0-7 in Northern Ireland*, Occasional Paper No.27 Belfast: PPRU.

Pond, C. and Searle, A. (1991) *A Hidden Army?* London: Low Pay Unit.

Prout, A. and James, A. (1997) "A New Paradigm for the Sociology of Childhood? Provenance, Promise and Problems" in James, A and Prout, A (eds.) *Constructing and Reconstructing Childhood: Contemporary Issues in the Sociological Study of Childhood*, London: Falmer Press.

Solberg, A. (1996) "The Challenge in Child Research: From Being to Doing" in J. Brannen and M. O'Brien (eds.) *Children in Families: Research and Policy*, London: Falmer Press.

Steinberg, L.D., Greenberger, E., Vaux, A. and Ruggerio, M. (1981) "Early Work Experience: Effects on Adolescent Occupational Socialisation", *Youth and Society*, Vol. 12., No. 4., pp. 403-422.

Thompson, E.P. (1968) *The Making of the English Working Class*, Harmondsworth: Penguin

Whitney, B. (1998) "Child Employment Legislation: Changing the Focus" in Pettitt, B. (ed.) *Children and Work in the UK: Reassessing the*

Issues, London: Child Poverty Action Group in Association with Save the Children.

This research was supported by a grant from Save the Children and I would like to acknowledge their support in funding this research and to thank Ciaran Acton for his help in computing the data.

Notes:

---

[1] The twelve schools included six secondary, five grammar and one integrated (mixed religions) school. These schools were selected to reflect the overall breakdown of schools in Belfast.

[2] The minimum school leaving age in Northern Ireland (as in the rest of the UK) is sixteen years of age. Moreover, child employment laws relate to children under the age of sixteen, hence this age category was utilised to define the term `children" in the research.